KAMAKALAVILASA

Owing to the antiquity and rarity of this book, certain pages are regrettably absent, and readability is compromised due to the blurring of the original text. If you possess any insights regarding the availability of these missing sections, kindly inform us. Your assistance is crucial in ensuring the completion of this significant work for the benefit of future generations.

KAMAKALAVILASA

ARTHUR AVALON

GYAN

Published by

Gyan Publishing House
5, Ansari Road
Daryaganj, New Delhi-110002
Phone: 011-47034999, 9811692060
E-mail: books@gyanbooks.com

Distribution Network
gyanbooks.com
India, USA, Canada, UK, Australia

ISBN: 978-93-6920-397-0 (HB)
First Published, 1953

2nd Impression 2025

Printed at: Gyan Press, Delhi.

KAMAKALAVILASA
Author: ARTHUR AVALON

KĀMAKALĀVILĀSA

बिन्दुत्रिकोणवसुकोणदशारयुग्ममन्वश्रनागदलसंयुतषोडशारम् ।
वृत्तत्रयं च धरणीसदनत्रयं च श्रीचक्रमेतदुदितं परदेवतायाः ॥

SHRI YANTRA

DESCRIPTION OF THE CAKRAS FROM THE CENTRE OUTWARD

1. Red Point—Sarvānandamaya. (vv. 22-24, 37, 38).
2. White triangle inverted—Sarvasiddhiprada. (vv. 25, 39).
3. Eight red triangles—Sarvarogahara. (vv. 29, 40).
4. Ten blue triangles—Sarvarakṣākara. (vv. 30, 41).
5. Ten red triangles—Sarvārthasādhaka. (vv. 30, 31, 42).
6. Fourteen blue triangles—Sarvasaubhāgyadāyaka. (vv. 31, 43).
7. Eight-petalled red lotus—Sarvasaṁkṣobhaṇa. (vv. 33, 41).
8. Sixteen-petalled blue lotus—Sarvāśāparipuraka. (vv. 33, 45).
9. Yellow surround—Trailokyamohana. (vv. 34, 46-49).

KĀMAKALĀVILĀSA

BY

PUṆYĀNANDANĀTHA

WITH THE COMMENTARY OF
NATANĀNANDANĀTHA

TRANSLATED WITH COMMENTARY

BY

ARTHUR AVALON

WITH

NATHA-NAVARATNAMALIKA
WITH COMMENTARY MAÑJŪṢA
BY BHĀSKARARĀYA

2nd Edition
Revised and enlarged

PUBLISHERS:
GANESH & CO., (MADRAS) LTD., MADRAS—17
1953

PUBLISHERS' NOTE

The Orientalists' system of transliteration has been followed in this work.

अ a, आ ā, इ i, ई ī, उ u, ऊ ū, ऋ ṛ, ॠ ṝ, ऌ l, ॡ l̄

ए e, ऐ ai, ओ o, औ au, ं ṃ or ṁ, : ḥ.

क् k, ख् kh, ग् g, घ् gh, ङ् ṅ,

च् c, छ् ch, ज् j, झ् jh, ञ् ñ,

ट् ṭ, ठ् ṭh, ड् ḍ, ढ् ḍh, ण् ṇ,

त् t, थ् th, द् d, ध् dh, न् n,

प् p, फ् ph, ब् b, भ् bh, म् m,

य् y, र् r, ल् l, व् v, श् s',

ष् ṣ, स् s, ह् h, ळ् ḷ.

PREFACE

THE KĀMAKALĀVILĀSA is an important work in S'rīvidyā by Puṇyānanda an adherent of the Hādimata, who is also the commentator on the Yoginīhṛdaya, a section called Uttaracatuḥs'atī of the great Vāmakes'vara Tantra. The same Catuḥs'atī as also the Pūrvacatuḥs'atī have commentaries by Bhāskararāya. The Kāmakalāvilāsa which means the spreading or emanation or evolution of the Kāmakalā that is the Supreme Triangle formed of the Bindu and Visarga, of Prakās'a and Vimars'a, of S'iva and S'akti, of the 'I' (Aham) and 'This' (Idam) or Universe is, in the supreme sense, the S'iva-Svarūpa and S'akti-Svarūpa. To put it quite shortly Kāmakalāvilāsa is the evolution of the One in its twin aspect as changeless Consciousness (Cit or Saṁvit) and changing Power (Cit-S'akti and Māyā-S'akti) into the multiple universe. This evolution is represented by the greatest of Yantras—the S'rīyantra figured on the cover and in a separate Plate showing in colours its several Cakras extending from the Point or Bindu (called Sarvānandamaya), the Supreme S'iva-S'akti in the centre, to the outermost section of the Cakras the Bhūpura which is called Trailokyamohana.

The S'rīcakra or S'rīyantra is the Yantra of Lalitā or Trīpurasundarī the Devatā of S'rīvidyā. Every Devatā has his or her Yantra. A general but by no means exhaustive list of the Yantras is given in the Tantrasāra of Kṛṣṇānanda of which there are several editions published in Bengal.

Lalitā is the Supreme S'akti aspect of the Brahman the Aniruddhasarasvatī (the all-spreading and Itself Unlimited

Power). It is claimed by great Kaulas, among whom may be mentioned the great Naiyāyika commentator Bhāskararāya, that this aspect of the Brahman is recognised in the Vedas and that among others the Mantra, Catvāra*h* Īṁ bibhrati Kṣeṁayanta*h* (Ṛg-veda V. 47. 4) has reference to Her.

The Kāmakalā is the first display of activity in the Brahman Substance after Pralaya when the Devī holds absorbed in Herself all the Thirty-six Tattvas of which the Universe in all its variety is composed. She is then Kavalīkṛta-nibs'eṣa-tattva-grāma-svarūpiṇī. She remains for some time in this state holding within Herself all the Tattvas until rest is disturbed by the desire or will (Kāma) to create. The movement or stress of this Desire manifests as the Kāmakalā. Puṇyānanda has here described the unfolding of the Kāmakalā according to the Hādimata.

All Tantras have referred to the Kāmakalā. The Gandharva-Tantra, which is a work of great authority and of philosophic thought, speaks (Ch. XXX) of the three aspects of Kāmakalā. The first which is, it says, the Sthūla or gross aspect—that in which She is meditated upon as something outside the Sādhaka (Bāhyabhāvanā). The only text of the Gandharva-Tantra available to me at the moment is unfortunately defective so far as the account of this aspect is concerned. It states that the Sun Bindu is Her face, the Moon and Fire Bindus are Her two breasts, and Her womb or Yoni is Hārdhakalā. Dr. Bhandakar in the account he gives of the Kāmakalā (Vaiṣṇavism and S'aivism, p. 145) does not seem to have understood the scheme. He appears not to be familiar with the technical terms and has not followed the commentator Lakṣmīdhara whose text he had before him and as a result he has made some errors. Thus he says that Ha is called Ardhakalā or half part, whereas the half of Ha is Kalā. Again the Devī is not in Herself "Aham" for the latter is the Sakala aspect of the Brahman.

I have referred elsewhere to his translation of the term Bindu as "Drop". Bindu is here not a "Drop" but a technical name for a particular state of S'aktī; namely, Ghanībhūta S'akti. The Symbol of the Point is well known in both East and West. Here it is a Metaphysical Point of Energy about to manifest. The term is fully explained in my "Garland of Letters."

The Sādhaka is directed to realise his identity with the Kāmakalā. This aspect is alluded to in V. 19 of the Saundaryalaharī, a beautiful poem the authorship of which has been unanimously attributed by all great commentators such as Rāghava Bhatta, Bhāskara, Lakṣmīdhara and others to the great S'aṁkarācārya, though present day Orientalists, both Indian and Western, incline to cast doubt upon the traditional account of its authorship. The Saundaryalaharī in verse 11 speaks of the S'rīcakra also. The second aspect of Kāmakalā which is spoken of as Subtle (Sūkṣma) and inward (Āntara) is that in which She is the Devī Kuṇḍalinī like a luminous flash of lightning extended from the Mūlādhāra through the six centres to the Brahmarandhra. See my "Serpent Power". She is to be meditated upon as half of Ha in the lotus of a thousand petals. This Kāmakalā is also active (Jāgarti) in all that is moving and motionless. The third aspect of Kāmakalā is called Mantratanu (Mantra body) also Trayīmayī as existing in everything. In this aspect Sāmaveda is Her face; Ṛk and Yajus are Her two breasts and the Atharvaveda is the Hārdhakalā. "The Kāmakalā (the text proceeds) is the One highest (Turīya) Brahman Itself." The Tantrāntara Tantra quoted in the Sarvollāsa speaks of one Bindu as the state of Laya; two Bindus as the state of creation (Sṛṣti); three Bindus as the state of continuance (Sthiti) and the return to One Bindu as the state of Laya (absorption) when the Devī is as the Vāmakes'vara-Tantra says, Kabalī-kṛta-niḥs'eṣa-tattva-grāma-svarūpiṇī. The S'yāmārahasya quotes from the S'rīkrama Tantra a full account of Kāmakalā.

The S'rīcakra is described in great detail in the Tantrarāja of the Kādimata the first eighteen chapters of which form Vol. VIII of this series. It also forms the subject of the Nityāṣoḍas'ikārṇava Tantra which has been published by the Ānandās'rama Press of Poona. For a general description of the Cakras the reader's attention is drawn to the Introduction to Vol. VIII.

The aim of the Sādhaka of Lalitā is to realise his identity first with the Yantra and Mantra and then with Lalitā or Tripurā, the Mahās'akti Who is the creator and director of the universe and Who ultimately withdraws creation within Herself. Some form of Union with the Ultimate Real or Sat is the aim of all the different classes of Sādhakas of the Hindus. In Chap. VII of the Gautamīya-Tantra, greatly venerated by Vaiṣṇavas, the Sādhaka is directed to realise that "he is Kṛṣṇa (Ahaṁ Kṛṣṇa*h*) and no one else (na cānyo'smi)" that "sorrow is not his portion (na s'okabhāk) and that "he is Sat Cit Ānanda". It is also there said that the bar between Kṛṣṇa and the Sādhaka can be removed by Kṛṣṇa's wish.

The S'ākta Sādhaka seeks to realise the identity of himself with the Mantra, the Yantra, the Guru and the Iṣṭadevatā for they are all Brahman. ***Sarvaṁ khalvidaṁ Brahma.*** Lalitā is the Brahman as the active principle in creation. When Her Power is fully evolved the S'ākta seeks Her alone. It is She Who, visible through Her Manifestations, counts for him. [***Tasyām pariṇatāyām tu na kas'cit para iṣyate.***]

"Pure (Vimalā) Cit S'akti of the Lord is Caitanya". Bhāskara in commenting on the text above says that the Cit S'akti, which is inherent in the Paracit (Paracinniṣṭhā), accepted by the Upaniṣads, is by reason of the multitudinousness of Her aspects called Māyā. Her evolution (Pariṇāma) is called creation (Prapañca) and this creation is

Cidrūpā, or a form of Consciousness in the Sense of Cit. That being so it is real. [See my book "Reality".] This does not conflict with Monism since S'akti and S'aktimān are incapable of separation. Further on he says that the S'ākta does Sādhanā of S'akti because without S'akti the Subtle (Sūkṣma) S'iva has neither name (Nāma) nor the power of manifestation (Dhāma). So there can be no duty to one who is nameless nor can such an one help the Sādhaka in attaining Nirvāṇa. Bhāskara follows the Kādimata. But both the Kādi and the Hādi are agreed that by the worship of S'rīcakra is meant the Sādhanā whereby the identity of the knower (Jñātā), the means of knowledge, and knowledge (Jñāna *i.e.* Yantra which is the body of both the Devī and the Sādhaka) and the object of knowledge (Jñeya *i.e.* Tripurā) is realised. The Tantrarāja (xxxv. 6) says:

> *Jñātā svātmā bhavej jñānam arghyaṁ jñeyaṁ bahiḥ-*
> *sthitam s'rīcakra-pūjanaṁ teṣāṁ ekīkaraṇaṁ īritaṁ.*

The meaning of this is that the Svātmā or self of the Jīva or Sādhaka is the Jñātā or knower. Jñāna knowledge and means of knowledge is the body of Jīvā which is the Yantra and offering (Arghya) and Jñeya or object of knowledge is what is "outside" (Bahiḥ-sthitam) by which is meant the Devī Who to the ordinary man is something other than himself. The worship of S'rīcakra is done to effect an union with, or to realise the identity of, these three. There are some slight differences between the accounts of the S'aktis as given in the Kāmakalāvilāsa and Tantrarāja Tantra. These will be pointed out in the Introduction to the second part of the Tantrarāja-Tantra now in preparation. It has been alluded to in the Introduction to the First Part.

There are some who to-day believe that the feminine aspect of the Brahman is unknown in the Vedas and the Upaniṣads. But this is quite erroneous. Thus in the

Chāndogya Upaniṣad we come across the texts 'Tadaikṣata' 'Seyaṁ Devataikṣata.' The first text by the word 'Tat' speaks of the Brahman as neuter or nirguṇa. The second speaks of the Brahman as feminine (Sā iyam). The function is the same, namely, that of Īkṣaṇa prior to creation. There are many other texts which might be cited such as the celebrated Devī-Sūkta.

In fact for man the second is the more important of the two. As already stated, in dissolution (Pralaya) the Devī is what remains—that is what the universe is in its essence (Svarūpinī)—after all the Tattvas (Tattva-grāma) have been completely (niṣeṣa) swallowed up (Kavalīkṛta) or absorbed by Her. Then the verse continues "when however She is fully evolved (Tasyām pariṇatāyāṁ) from out this state in which the universe lies absorbed as mere tendency or potentiality, then no other Supreme (Kas'cit para) that is the changeless Niṣkala S'iva is desired or thought of (Iṣyate). This, says the commentator Bhāskararāya, is the S'ākta's point of view, for the Niṣkala or Sūkṣma S'iva has neither name nor manifestation and there is neither any duty towards, nor benefit from, Him. What Divinity may be in Itself, apart from Its governance of the universe, is of no practical concern to those who form part of it. The S'aktisangama Tantra (1—3) establishes the identity of the Kāmakalā—this first creative movement with the Praṇava.

A text of this work was obtained in Kashmir but it was found to be defective; another manuscript was then secured from the valuable collection of Tantras in the Andul Rajbati which is more reliable and forms the basis of the present edition. When the present text, the publication of which has been somewhat delayed, was going through the Press, another edition in Sanskrit was published in Triplicane (Madras) which contains some valuable additional illustrative citations which are not to be found in the manuscript from which this edition has been printed. I have added some further notes and given the references to the S'ruti and other texts quoted by the commentator Natanānanda Nātha.

The Kāmakalāvilāsa is of great value in S'rīvidyā because of its clear and succinct account, from the Hādi standpoint, of the initial development of S'akti and of the great S'rīyantra, and is now translated for the first time.

Calcutta, ARTHUR AVALON
25th Nov. 1921

By the same Author

THE SERPENT POWER

The Serpent Power is a description and explanation in fuller detail of the *Serpent Power*—Kuṇḍalini S'akti—and the yoga effected through it, a subject occupying a pre-eminent place in the Tantra Shastra. It consists of a translation of two Sanskrit works "Shat Cakra Nirūpaṇa" (description of and investigation into the six bodily centres) and "Pādukā Pañcaka" (Five-fold foot-stool of the Guru). To it is appended a translation from the Sanskrit commentary by Kalicharana. To the translation of both the works is added some further explanatory notes by the author.

This edition contains also the Sanskrit Texts of the works here translated and nine half-tone plates taken from life showing some positions in Kuṇḍalini Yoga besides eight original coloured plates of the Chakras. The book is bound in full cloth and gilt.

5th Edition (1953) **Price Rs. 25/-**

INTRODUCTION

KĀMAKALĀVILĀSA is an ancient and authoritative work on S'rīvidyā by Punyānandanātha. It was first published in 1918 by the Kāshmir Government as No. 12 in its Sanskrit Publications Series with a commentary from the pen of Mahāmahōpādhyāya Mukundarāma S'āstri of the Research Department of that State. In 1921, Sir John Woodroffe published it with a fuller commentary by Sri Natanānandanātha. A second edition has been long overdue and is now brought out. It is much to be regretted that that veteran Tāntric scholar is not in our midst now to contribute to this edition the benefit of his ripe experience and deep knowledge in this field of sacred literature.

As he has well pointed out in his Preface to the first edition, " What Divinity " may be in itself, apart from its governance of the universe, is of no practical concern to those " who form part of it " and there can be " neither any duty towards nor benefit from Him " conceived of as unrelated to the world of Name and Form. Any substance, be it gold or mud, has no inherent name or inherent form of its own but when we seek to have relationship with it, it must be clothed in some name and some form. We are therefore concerned with God not in His abstractness but in His practical aspect as in relationship to the world of our experience.

God as the ultimate reality transcends all distinctions and is therefore neither a *He* nor a *She* but is best expressed by the neuter word Brahman. But conceived as the cause of the universe, it is clothed with a father-mother aspect, the static non-active principle being considered as the father and the dynamic active principle being considered as the mother. Both are aspects of the same reality but seem to split it up into two. Where a person stands before a mirror, it is true that he does not undergo any change but a duplicate person appears instantaneously in the mirror. That reflected person is essentially not different from the original person and yet is not identical with him. The former is evanescent seeming while the latter is true Being. Similarly at the beginning of creation, God the ever changeless Being "desired" to be a ever-changing seeming. The absolute Being took on the role of relative becoming. This desire and its fruition brought on the entire universe of name and form. The subject self conceived of itself as an object of its own cognition. The *I* became the *this*. This initial desire impulse responsible for the creation of the world is given the name of Kāma. The desireful supreme entity is known as Kāmēśvara and his active desire as Kāmēśvari. The entire universe is the outcome of the union of these two primary parents. Though this truth is never lost sight of, more importance is given to the mother aspect in Devi worship.

The numeral six is a reality but is an abstract mental concept essentially independent of the particular things to be counted. The concept is the same for all who can conceive of it and is not limited by any considerations of country or language. The sound that is produced when the word six is pronounced has really nothing to do with the conception of the numeral but is only a sound-symbol of that concept used for the purpose of expression in the English language. As languages and dialects vary, the sound symbols also will vary though the concept may remain the same. The concept is intangible while the sound symbols are certainly tangible. Again, the figure 6 which appears in uniting has really nothing to do with the sound produced when the word six is pronounced, much less with the abstract concept behind it. The figure 6 is but a form symbol of that concept. As in our experience we are attaching more importance to the ear and the eye than to the other faculties of sensation, we clothe every concept with a sound symbol and with a form symbol so that we can through them relate ourselves to the abstract concept which alone is real.

Similarly when we conceive of Godhead or any aspect of it, we have necessarily to give it a sound symbol and a form symbol. The conceptual reality is known as Dēvatā, the sound symbol as Mantra and the form symbol as Yantra. It is said that the Dēvatā is the life principle, the Mantra its subtle body and the Yantra the gross body. The Archā or Image ordinarily used for worship is a still grosser body.

In the Vedic and Tantra literature, symbols in sound and in form have been prescribed as can most appropriately and accurately represent the Dēvatā. The ancient seers have pointed out that, just our body of flesh and blood though seemingly inert is permeated by the life principle in us in every particle of it, so does the Dēvatā permeate the Mantra and the Yantra appropriate to that Dēvatā. Any the slightest variation therefore either in the sound of the Mantra or in the form of the Yantra will effect a corresponding change in the concept of the Dēvatā and may possibly do great harm. In this Kāmakalāvilāsa, the Dēvatā dealt with is the highest conceivable one, namely the Divine Mother Tripurasundarī; Her Mantra is the Pañcadaśākṣarī and Her Yantra is Srīchakra. The intimate relationship between the Dēvatā, the Mantra and the Yantra is brought out in this book in several ways and the devotee is asked to identify himself with them as a necessary step towards the ultimate realisation.

The commentator Natanānandanātha is a disciple of Sankarānanda and Nāthānanda and is the author of several works besides a commentary on Yōginīhridaya. He refers in his commentary itself to Saccidānanda-Vāsanā and Cidānanda Vāsanā as his works. Only extracts from the commentary are reproduced in the English translation. The commentary is simple, explanatory and very useful in understanding the text and is replete with quotations from cognate literature. All the same the treatise will remain a closed book to the lay reader. As the commentator has pointed out more than once, the details and the method of worship are really matters to be learnt only after acquiring the requisite competency and getting initiation from a knowing Guru.

In this volume is included S'rīnātha-navaratnamālikā of Mahēs'anātha with the commentary of Bhāskararāya the leading authority on Tāntric worship. Under the guise of Guru stōtra, the author has analysed our life breaths in various ways and has pointed out their correspondence with the details of the Mantra and the Yantra. This work is more cryptic and less intelligible to the uninitiate. The commentary on the first stotra mentions that the stotra consists of *ten* slōkas and the tenth sloka which gives the Phalas'ruti refers to the previous slokas as being compiled by Bhāskararāya himself. This has to be somehow reconciled with the preamble to the tenth sloka and with the colophon which attribute the authorship to Mahēs'anātha.

The publication of this book making its contents available to all and sundry does not and cannot dispense with the two indispensable conditions of competency and initiation already referred to. To those who have them not, the contents may seem to be meaningless jabber. So is a book on integral calculus to a history student. The publication however is useful in creating in the reader an interest which in course of time may ripen into earnest endeavour to appreciate and realise the eternal truths taught here.

Srirangam R. KRISHNASWAMI AIYAR
11-6-53

विषयानुक्रमः

ADDENDA AND CORREGENDA

(*Continued from page 110*)

PAGE	LINE		PAGE	LINE	
३	१०	०ज्ञातं	४३	६	पूर्वोक्त०
,,	२१	विमर्श: omitted	४५	४	०मिदमेव
५	११-१४	निर्दिश्य . . . . . . इति	,,	२६	०त्यर्थ:
		omitted	४६	१२	शुक्ल०
१४	१३	गर्भित	४७	१०	पश्यन्त्या
१५	१०	परम: शिव:	४८	४	०न्तीवपुषा
१७	३	एतद्भूतं	,,	२५	०धारात्
,,	१४	अहं ब्रह्म०	५३	१	परि०
,,	,,	तथैव	,,	६	त्रय०
१८	५	अहंतया	६४	२१	०मानन्द०
,,	१५	शब्दा: अर्था:	७६	१७	ललितो०
२८	२५	इत्यक्ष	७८	४	भावाकर्षित०
३६	२०	व्यञ्जनानि	७९	२	स्वरस्य
३८	१२	इत्यादिना	८३	१९	सप्तशतो०
,,	१९	उदाहरिष्याम:	९५	३	मुदा०

KĀMA-KALĀ-VILĀSA

BY

SʼRI PUṆYĀNANDANĀTHA

VERSE 1

MAY the great Lord, who is ever wakeful in the blissful play of the repeated acts of Creation, Maintenance and Dissolution of all the worlds which issue from Him, protect ye. He is mere illumination (*Prakāsʼa*). Merged in Him is *Vimarsʼa* (*-sʼakti*).

COMMENTARY BY SʼRĪ NATANĀNANDANĀTHA

Here the honoured Yogī Puṇyānanda wishing to instruct in the Mantra, Cakra and worship of Tripurasundarī, the presiding Devatā over all Vidyās[1], speaks in the first place of Her form as Kāma-kāmesʼvarī[2].

Who is ever wakeful . . . issue from Him (*Sakalabhuvanodaya-sthiti-laya-maya-līlāvinodanodyuktah*). *Udaya* or rising or springing up or appearance is Creation (*Sṛṣti*); *Sthiti* or continuance is Maintenance; *Laya* is absorption or Dissolution (*Nāsʼa*) of all the worlds (*Sakalabhuvana*)[3]. These three (*Sṛṣti*, *Sthiti*, *Laya*) imply *Nirodha* and *Anugraha*, as by *Trivṛtkaraṇa*, *Pañcīkaraṇa* is meant. He is wakeful in this pleasant play (*Līlā*) which consists of many of these five kinds of action which relate to the world (*Pañcavidha-kṛtyam hi jagannisṭham*), whilst the play is that of the Lord (*Līlā tu Pāramesʼvarī*).

Worlds (*Bhuvana*). That which comes from Him is *Bhuvana* (*Bhavatyasmāt iti bhuvanaṁ*). Therefore the word *Bhuvana* qualified by 'all' (*Sakala*) signifies all the *Tattvas* beginning with *S'iva* and ending with *Kṣiti*, because the *Tattvas* have their origin from, continue through and disappear in Brahman. So *S'ruti* says (*Taitt. Up.* 3·1-1):—'That from which these Bhūtas were born, by which after being so born they live, to which they go and into which they enter; know that well, for that is Brahman.'

Wakeful (*Udyukta*). By 'wakeful' is meant that He willed and inclined towards Creation (*Samkalpa-vis'iṣta-lakṣaṇa-sṛṣtimukha*). *S'ruti* says (*Chā. Up.* 6-2-1):—'Oh gentle one! At first there was merely this Being (*Sat*), which is One without a second, Brahman.' Also 'May I be many and born as many,' and thus He made Himself into the world as it exists within Himself. By this is meant that the acts of creation are for the Lord merely His play and are not necessitated (*Na prayojanam*). So it has been said—'By His mere wish He throws out and withdraws the universe in its entirety.' Also it is elsewhere said—'The Great Lord having drawn on Himself the picture of the world by the brush which is His own Will is pleased when looking thereon.' *S'ruti* also says—'As the spider throws out and takes back its thread, so Īs'vara projects and withdraws the universe.' Thus the one great Lord becomes the material cause (*Upādāna*) from out of which the world is made, as says the Text, 'May I be many.' The *Vāmakes'vara Tantra* also says—'When She is fully developed (*Pariṇatā*) there is no further need of Him for Creation'[4] (*Nityāṣodas'ikā*, IV-5). By this is meant the inseparateness of the world from the *Svarūpa* (own form) of Brahman.

That being so it may be asked what is the *Svarūpa* of the Brahman as transcending the world. The author therefore says—

Merged in Him is Vimarsa (*Antarlīna-vimars'a*). Vimars'a is experiencing 'This' (*Idam*), and 'This' (*Idam*) is the universe (*Prapañca*). By *Idam* is meant the world created by Paramātmā. In the passage in the *Taittirīya S'ruti* which begins with 'From the Ātmā originated Ākās'a,' and ends with 'This the tip of the tail is completion (*Pratiṣṭā*),' the word 'this' (*Idam*) is the world as object of experience (*Prapañca-parāmars'a*). By the word '*Idam*' is indicated the universe (*Prapañca*) as contrasted with Brahman (*Brahma-pratiyogibhūta*). So it has been said—'Dissolving (*Pralayang kurvan*) in the *Aham* (I) the *Idam* (This) which is its correlative.' *Antarlīna-vimarśa* means that within Him is dissolved *Vimarśa* or *Prapanca* which is above spoken of. The significance of all this is that the Paramātmā Who is supreme Bliss and supreme Illumination and within Whom is the experience of perfect 'I-ness' (*Paripūrnāhaṁ-bhāvabhāvanā-garbhita*) withdraws into Himself the manifold universe. *Vimarśa* may also mean the experience (*Parāmarśa*) that 'I am the uncreated cause of the Creation, Preservation and Dissolution of the universe.' So it has been said by Nāgānanda: '*Vimarśa*' is the experience that "I am the uncreated one (*Akṛtimo'haṁ*)" in the form of the universe (*Viśvākāreṇa*), in the manifestation of the universe *Viśvaprakāśena*) and in the absorption of the universe (*Viśvasaṁhārena*).'

Merged (*Antarlīna*). By *merged* is meant inward-facedness (*Antarmukhatvam*)[5]. *Antarlīna-vimarśa* thus refers to Him whose experience of full I-ness is inward-turned. The *S'vachchhanda Tantra* says: 'That inward-faced-ness (*Antarmukhatva*) which is the state of omniscience and the like ever is[6], because it is detached from[7] any object'[8].

He is mere Illumination (*Prakāśa-mātra-tanuh*)[9]. This means that Parabrahman who is the Supreme Lord and transcends all, is nothing but Illumination (*Prakāśaikasvabhāva*). Such is His nature[10].

The *Kāṇva*[11] says: 'The Devas worship that which is the deathless One (*Amṛta*)[12], which is verily Itself Life[13] and the Light of Lights.' The *Katha* says: 'There shines nor Sun, nor Moon, nor stars. There flashes no lightning. What need have we then to speak of Fire. All luminaries derive their light from It. By Its light all is illuminated.'

Āgama also says: 'The innermost Light which is Light Itself is the imperishable (*Anapāyinī*) Parā Vāk'[14].

Illumination (*Prakāśa*). By illumination is meant the experience of I-ness (*Aham-rūpa-vimarśa*) indicated in the words 'wish,' 'know' 'do' and the like in the first person singular[15]. Here it is said of Param Brahman as united with the five S'aktis of All-mightiness, All-knowingness, All-activity, All-completeness, All-pervadingness. It may be said that if the Sun and other bodies have the power of illumination, then why should the Brahman alone be called Paramātmā? To meet this the latter is called the Great Lord (*Mahes'a*). He is Great (*Mahān*) because neither space nor time limits Him; and He is Lord (*Īs'a*) because He has the power to control all. The *S'irah S'ruti*[16] says: 'The Eater (*Saṁbhakṣah*) eats all He constantly creates, maintains and dissolves. Therefore He is called the Great Lord (*Mahes'a*).' The *Mahānārāyaṇa*[17] also says: 'That *Svara*[18] which is uttered in the beginning and end of the Veda is that in which Prakṛti is merged (*Prakṛiti-līna=Prakṛtyātmaka*)[19]. He Who is beyond, is Mahes'vara.'

Protect ye. He has this power. Mantra is so called, because it protects or saves by thinking (*Manana*) on it (*Mananāt trāyate*). Puṇyānanda says: 'May Parames'vara protect ye'. Protection is one of the powers of Paramātmā. May the Great Lord who is Illumination (*Prakās'a*) protect ye. The Ācāryā[20] has also power to illuminate, Mantra also has the power of illumination. Therefore the unity of the Devatā, Guru, and Mantra is here shown.

NOTES

[1] *i.e.* either the fifteen Nityās or all Mantras.

[2] United Kāmes'vara and Kāmes'varī.

[3] *Sakalabhuvana*—the Universe with all its parts consisting of the thirty-six *Tattvas*.

[4] This is a translation of the second line of IV-5 of *Nityāṣodas'ikā* (part of *Vāmakes'vara*). The verse runs thus—

Kavalīkṛta-nis'eṣa-tattva-grāma-svarūpiṇī
Tasyām pariṇatāyāṁ tu na kas'cit Para iṣyate.

At the time of dissolution all the *Tattvas* are absorbed into Her and She remained in Her own form (*Svarūpa*). When She is fully developed there is no further need of Him for creation.

By the '*Tattvas*' according to *Puṇyānanda*, *Bhāskararāya* and others is meant the thirty-six *Tattvas*. *Lakshmīdhara* interprets it to mean the five *Tattvas*. That is, the Universe is the creation of Para (*S'iva*) and Parā (*S'akti*). Under His influence She works and when Her work is completed there is no further need of Him for that purpose.

[5] Consciousness is either looking inwards (*Antarmukha*) or outwards (*Bahirmukha*). The first indicates the supreme experience, the second world-experience. Therefore the essence of becoming as universe is the conversion of one into the other. Consciousness is given "another" direction, strictly an outer direction, because the supreme experience is beyond all relations.

[6] *that is*, is not destroyed.
[7] *or*, independent of.
[8] *that is*, is transcendent.
[9] *lit.*, His body or substance is mere Illumination.
[10] *lit.*, body.
[11] One of the recensions of the Bṛhadāraṇyaka Upaniṣad.
[12] This word is derived from *na* (not) *mrita* (death).
[13] Āyuh.
[14] The supreme 'Word'. See A. Avalon's "*Garland of Letters.*"
[15] 'I wish,' 'I know,' and so forth.
[16] The Atharva S'ira Upaniṣad.
[17] The Atharvaṇa Upaniṣad of that name.
[18] Om.
[19] The two are one, as stated in *Nityā-ṣodas'ikhā.*
[20] Guru.

VERSE 2

SHE the Primordial S'akti who excels all and who in Her own true nature is eternal, limitless Bliss, is the seed (Bīja, that is, source or cause) of all the moving and motionless things which are to be, and is the Pure Mirror in which S'iva experiences Himself.

COMMENTARY

He here says that the Source of all is also Our Supreme Lady.

She the primordial Sakti who excels all (*Sā jayati s'aktirādyā*). By this is meant that Our Supreme Lady (*Parā bhattārikā*) Mahā-tripura-sundarī is above all.

She (Sā). By this is meant the Tripurā spoken of in all the Upaniṣads, in whom are the thirty-six *Tattvas* beginning with *S'iva* and ending with *Kṣiti*; who is in the form of all the universes (*Sarva-prapañcātmikā*) and is also beyond them (*Taduttīrṇā*). This is the meaning of the name Tripurā as given by the great Yogīs, Knowers of the true tradition (*Satsampradāyavid*). She who is above (*Purā bhūtā*) the three Lights (*Tribhyas tejobhyah*), that is, "Sun", "Moon" and "Fire" (explained later) is called Tripurā. Her supremacy is proclaimed everywhere in many S'rutis and Smṛtis. It is She who is denoted by '**She whose true nature is eternal, limitless Bliss,**' (*Nija-sukhamaya-nitya-nirupamākārā*). *Nija* means natural (*Svābhāvika*). By *Sukhamaya* (Bliss) is meant in whom there is no sorrow. *Nitya* is being at all times (*Trikāla, i.e.* past, present, future). *Nirupama* is 'incomparable', as there is nothing with which She can be compared. Such is Her nature (*Ākāra*. that is, *Svarūpa*). She is the unlimited, uncreated Brahma-bliss (*Ātmānanda*). *S'ruti* says that the Brahman who is transcendent Bliss is in all and above all.

The *Chāndogya* (7-2-3 says: 'That which is the Immense (*Bhūmā*) that is Bliss (*Sukha*). There is no Bliss in the little. The Immense is Bliss itself. Every endeavour should be made to know the Immense.' Having so said it proceeds. 'There where one sees nothing else, hears nothing else, knows nothing else, that is the Immense (*Bhūmā*).' It thus describes the Brahman who is Perfect Bliss (*Aparicchinnānanda*).

The *Bṛhadāraṇyaka* says, that 'other beings enjoy (*Upajīvanti*) only a fragment (*Mātrā*) 'of this Bliss.' It thus says that all other beings are but drops (*Viprut*) in the ocean Brahma-bliss.

The seed of all . . . which are to be (*Bhāvicarā-carabījam*). *Bhāvī* is that which is about to and will come. She is the Cause of all moving and motionless things which will be and which are.

The *Katha S'ruti* says (5-2-12): 'The one Controller (*Vas'ī*) of all who is the Inner Self (*Antarātmā*) of all created beings (*Sarva-bhūta*) transforms His unity (*Ekam rūpam*)[1] into many.'

Āgama also says: 'When She the Supreme Power (*Paramā S'akti*) who is in the form of the universe (*Vis'varūpinī*) sees[2] her own impulse towards becoming (*Sphurattā*), then the Cakra[3] comes into being. As the great tree exists as potency[4] in the seed of the Bata tree[5], so does this moving and motionless world exist in the seed in the heart (*Hṛdayabījastham*) (of the Lord)'.

It may be said that as it is not possible for S'iva to create without S'akti nor for Parā S'akti without S'iva, how can She be said to be 'the seed.' To meet this it is said that **She is the pure mirror in which Siva experiences Himself** (*S'ivarūpa-vimars'a-nirmalādars'ah.*) The *Svarūpa* or nature of S'iva is 'I' or *Aham* (*S'ivasya svarūpaṁ ahaṁ ityevaṁ ākāraṁ*). The experience (*Vimars'a*) again of That (*Tasya vimars'ah*) is the experience of 'I-ness' (*Ahaṁ ityevaṁ rūpaṁ jñānaṁ*). This pure mirror makes manifest this knowledge (*Tasya prakās'ane nirmalādars'ah*).

The sense may be thus illustrated. A handsome king looking at his reflection in a mirror which is before him knows 'I am he who is thus reflected.' So Parames'vara looking at His own S'akti (*Svātmas'akti*) who is within himself (*Svādhīnabhūtā*) knows his own nature (*Svasvarūpaṁ*) as 'I am all' (*Paripūrno'ham*). If there be nothing before the mirror then there is nothing to be reflected.

Similarly if the *Parāśakti* were not united with *Paraśiva*, She could not produce the universe (*Prapañca*) which is within Herself. Therefore the world cannot be created by S'iva alone nor by S'akti alone. It is by both of them that all the *Tattvas* are produced.

Āgama says: 'Without S'iva there is no Devī. Without Devī there is no S'iva. As between moon and moonbeam there is no difference, so there is no difference between S'iva and S'akti.'

NOTES

[1] Some read *Bīja* (seed) for *Rūpa* (Form).

[2] *Paśyet*, that is, creatively produces, and, in the form produced, experiences.

[3] The first Cakra in the S'rīyantra, as to which see *Yoginīhṛdaya*, Ch. I, vv. 9, 10.

[4] S'akti.

[5] *Ficus indica*.

VERSE 3

THE Supreme S'akti is resplendent. She is both the seed (*Bīja*) and sprout (*Angkura*)[1] as the manifested union of S'iva and S'akti. She is very subtile. Her form is manifested through the union of the first letter of the Alphabet (*A*) and the *Vimars'a* letter (*Ha*).

COMMENTARY

Now some say that the experience (*Vimars'a*)[2] 'I am all' (*Paripūrṇo'ham*) is the Brahman. Then how can it be said (it is argued) that the experiencer (*Vimars'aka*, that is, He who is conscious of being the supreme 'I') is the Brahman. The verse is written to meet this difficulty.

Supreme. Here by *Supreme* (*Parā*) is meant Tripurasundarī as She is before creation (*Prakṛta*). She is so called because *S'ruti* speaks of Her as 'Consciousness, Bliss, Will, Knowledge, Action (*Chidānandecchājñānakṛyārūpā*).'

She is both the seed and sprout (*Sphuta-s'iva-s'akti-samāgama-bījāngkura-rūpiṇī*). She is the manifested (*Sphuta*=*Vyakta*) union of S'iva and S'akti and is therefore both the seed and the sprout. For it has been said: 'From the seed the sprout and from the sprout the seed.' She produces in their order all the *Tattvas* beginning with *S'iva-tattva* and ending with *Kṣiti-tattva*.

Siva. Here by the word 'S'iva' is meant *Jñāna-s'akti* because S'iva-tattva is inherent (*Adhiṣthāna*) in *Jñāna-S'akti*; and by the word 'S'akti' is meant *Kṛyā-S'akti*, for S'aktitattva is inherent in *Kṛyā-S'akti*. It must also be noted that She who is *Cidānandasvarūpā* effects the creation of the universe by *Jñāna* and *Kṛyā*.

Subtile. She is also further spoken of as very subtile (*Anuttara-rūpā*, that is, of very subtile form). *S'ruti* says, 'Verily more subtile than the subtile is eternal Beingness (*Sattva*), Thou verily art That.' *Āgama* also says, 'the Devī is smaller than the smallest (*Aṇū*) and greater than the greatest.'

Her form is manifested . . . letter (Ha) (*Anuttara-vimars'a-lipi-lakṣya-vigrahā*). By *Anuttara-lipi* is meant the letter before which there is no other, and that is the letter *A*. By *Vimars'a-lipi* is meant the last letter which is '*Ha*. By the union of *A* and *Ha* (*Aham*=I) Her Self (*Vigraha*=*Svarūpa*) becomes known (*Lakṣya*=*Visible*). The sense of these words is that the Para-s'akti is 'I-ness' (*Ahamātmikā*) within whom (*i.e.* between the letters *A* and *Ha*) are all the letters of the alphabet[1] (*Antar-garbhita-samasta-varṇa-kadaṁbaka.*) Her form is the fifty letters beginning with *A-kāra* and ending with *Ha-kāra* (*Akārādi-hakārānta-pañcās'ad-akṣara-rūpinī*). She is the Mother (*Janayitrī*) of all the universe consisting of *Varṇa*, *Pada*, *Mantra* and of *Kalā*, *Tattva*, *Bhuvana*. She is the supreme object of veneration (*Parā bhattārikā*, the innermost self of all things (*Samasta-bhūtāntarātmā*). Everywhere in the Vedānta She appears spoken of as 'I' (*Ahamahamityevākāreṇa*). This is what has been said in this verse. So it has been said in the *Kānva-s'ruti*: "This Brahman verily in the beginning was. It knew Itself (*Tadātmānam eva veda*), 'I Brahman am'." '*A* is Brahman, from That came *Aham* (*i.e.*, I).'[2] The worship of *Ātmā* is the meditation 'I am all' (*Pūrnāham-bhāva-bhāvanā*), and should be kept very secret. *S'ruti* enjoins that it should be learnt only from the mouth of the Guru.

NOTES

[1] As seed She is cause, and as sprout, effect or universe.

[2] *Paripūrṇo'ham iti vimars'am eva Brahma.* Reference is made to the experience as a state contrasted with that of which it is a state.

VERSE 4

UPON the mass of the rays of the Sun Paras'iva being reflected in the pure *Vimars'a*-mirror, the Mahābindu appears on the *Citta*-wall illumined by the reflected rays.

COMMENTARY

The author being desirous of describing the Kāmakalā in the form of all the letters, commences in this and the following three verses to speak of Her letter-hood (*Akṣara-svarūpa=Brahma-svarūpa.*[1]

Mass of the rays of the Sun Parasiva (*Paras'ivaravikarnikare*). *Paras'iva* is the adored Lord Paramas'iva who is mere *Prakās'a*· *Prakās'aika-svabhāvah.*) The mass of His rays (*Karāh=Kiraṇāh*) is the pure (*Vis'uddha=Nirmala*) *Vimars'a*-mirror (*Vimars'a-darpaṇa*). *Vimars'a* is the S'akti or movement (*Visphuraṇa-s'akti*)[2] which is limitless (*Anavadhikākārā*). So it is said in *Pratyabhijñā*: 'She is *Sphurattā.* (*Sā sphurattā*).' She is here compared to a mirror because of Her thereby manifesting Herself (*Sva-svarūpa-prakās'atvāt*)[3].

Reflected. By 'Reflection' (*Pratiphalana*) is meant seeing one's own self (*Svasvarūpāvalokana*). When the self is seen by reflection in this way, then '**Mahabindu appears on the Citta-wall**' (*Cittamaya=Jñānaika-svarūpa*) which is beautifully illumined.[4] The *Citta* is compared to a 'wall' (*Kudya*) because on it appears (the reflection of the) Mahābindu. In ordinary experience we see that if a mirror is kept facing the sun, the rays after being reflected therefrom appear on any wall nearby as a luminous spot (*Bindu*) produced by the rays of the sun. In the same way when Parames'vara who is *Prakās'a* (*Prakās'a-rūpa-parames'vara*) comes into connection with *Vimars'a* which is like a mirror (*Darpaṇāvat-svarūpa-vimars'a-sambandhe jāte*), there shines forth the Mahābindu who is Parames'vara as *Pūrṇo'ham*— 'I am all.'

S'ruti also says: 'Oh gentle one, this Being alone there was in the beginning, the one, non-dual Brahman alone.[5] That said: 'May I be many and be born.'[6] Also 'She this Devatā said':[7] 'This Brahman alone there was in the beginning, That knew Itself as 'I (*Aham*) am the Brahman'. 'He said (and thought), truly I shall create these worlds (*Lokas*).'[8] Texts in *S'rutī* like these say that the Parabrahman who is looking towards (*Abhimukha*) His own S'akti (*Svātmas'akti*) is the Cause of the universe.[9]

Āgama also says: 'When She the Paramā S'akti[10] sees Her own *Sphurattā*, there comes into being the Cakra.'

In *Pratyabhijnā* also it is said: 'She the *Sphurattā* is the great Being-ness (*Mahāsattā*) beyond time and space (*Des'a-kāla-vis'esinī*).[11] It is She who is spoken of as the essence of all (*Sāratayā coktā*) in the Heart of the Supreme Lord.

NOTES

[1] That is, Her *svarūpa* as the substance of all the letters. *Cf.*

A-kārah sarva-varṇāgryah Prakās'ah paramah S'ivah,
Ha-kāro'ntyah kalārūpo Vimars'ākhyah prakīrtitah.

[2] *Sphuraṇa* is a common term in these S'āstras. The word means impulse, vibration, throbbing, pulsation, quivering and then springing up, breaking forth, blossoming, starting into view, expanding and lastly flashing, glittering, sparkling manifestation, in short, both as impulse towards and as fact.

[3] *Sva-svarūpa-prkās'atvāt* may also mean: Because She makes manifest the *svarūpa* of Brahman (Sva=Brahman=Ātman) in Her as in a Mirror.

[4] That is, by the rays reflected back on it.

[5] Chā., 6-2-1.

[6] Chā., 6-2-3.

[7] Chā., 6-3-2.

[8] Aitareya, 1. 1.

[9] He contemplates and assumes Power.

[10] Yoginīhridaya, 1. 9.

[11] She limits, that is, is beyond both.

VERSE 5

Ahaṁkāra, which excels all and is the massing together of S'iva and S'akti and the fully manifested union of the letters *A* and *Ha*, and which holds within itself the whole universe, is *Cit.*[1]

COMMENTARY

In this verse he describes the notion of "I-ness" (*Ahaṁbhāva*) which arises from the gaze of S'iva upon His own luminous S'akti. *Ahaṁkāra* is the *Vimars'a* which is 'I-ness' (*Yo'yaṁ aham-ahamity-eva vimars'ah*). *Ahaṁkāra* is the cause (*Kāra=Kāraṇa*) of the experience of 'I-ness' (*Ahambhāva-vimars'a*) which manifests (*Vyañjaka*) on the uprising (*Udbhūta*) of the experience which is self-recollection (*Ātmasmaraṇa*). *Ahaṁkāra* such as this excels all. So it has been said, 'In the *Aham* experience (*Ahaṁbhāva Prakās'a*) rests in Itself (*Ātma-vis'rānti*).'[2]

Cit (*Chittamaya*) is mere *Jñāna* (*Jñānaika-svabhāva*).

Manifested (*Suvyaktāhārṇa-samarasākāra*) owing to the form which is produced by the combination of the letters *A* and *Ha*, each giving rise or making manifest the other (*Parasparodbhūtarūpau*).

Union (*Samarasa=Eka-lolībhūta*) or the union in the form of *Ahaṁkāra* of these two letters in which each desires to be united in an equal degree with the other.

Massing together of Siva and Sakti (*S'iva-s'akti-mithunapiṇda*). S'iva=*Prakās'a*, S'akti=*Vimars'a*. These are the two who make the divine Husband and Wife (*Divyadaṁpatīmaya*). The union of these two, in which they desire to be united in equal degree, is *S'iva-s'akti-mithunapiṇḍa*. *Ahaṁkāra* for reasons implied in what is aforementioned contains within it (*Kavalīkṛta*) the sphere (*Maṇḍala*) of the universe (*Bhuvana*). By *Bhuvana-maṇḍala* is meant all that is composed of Thirty-six Tattvas. The meaning, by the rule of *Pratyāhāra*, is that from the union of *Prakās'a* and *Vimars'a* which is *Ahaṁkāra*, within which are the many letters of the alphabet, emanates the whole universe consisting of Word (*S'abda*) and its Meaning (*Artha*). So also says *S'ruti*[3]: 'The letterless (*Avarṇa*) full of meaning (*Nihitārtha*) by union with S'akti in various ways generates many letters (*Varṇa*)'. In another Upaniṣad[4] occurs this text: 'Who art thou?' 'It is I (*Ahaṁ*) (the reply): All this is surely I (*Ahaṁ*)'. Therefore the term '*Ahaṁ*' or 'I' denotes all things (*Sarvābhidhānaṁ=Sarvavācakam*).'

NOTES

[1] *Chittamaya*. Or the verse may be translated—"Haṁkāra is *Cittamaya*. The form (*Aham*) is the manifested union of the letters *A* and *Ha* or the coupled S'iva and S'akti in massive union which even endures after the universe has been withdrawn into Itself."

[2] *Prakās'asyātma-vis'rāntir ahaṁbhāve hi kīrtitaḥ.*

[3] Svet., 14-1.

[4] Nṛsiṁha Uttara, 7.

VERSES 6 & 7

THE two Bindus, white and red, are S'iva and S'akti, Who, in their secret mutual enjoyment, are now expanding and now contracting. They are the Cause of the creation of Word (*Vāk*) and Meaning (*Artha*), now entering and now separating from one another. Bindu which is Ahaṁkāra (*Ahaṁkārātmā*) is the Sun which is the union of these two (white and red Bindus). The Sun is *Kāma*, which is so called because of its desirableness; and *Kalā* is the two Bindus which are Moon and Fire.

COMMENTARY

Having described in V. 4 in the passage 'The Mahābindu appears on the Citta-wall', the *Svarūpa* of the Bindu he now describes Kāmakalā.

The two Bindus white (Sita) and red (Sona) are Siva and Sakti playing in secret with one another, that is, in mutual enjoyment the one with the other (*Vivikta-s'iva-s'akti = Anyonya-viharaṇapare S'iva-s'akti*), now contracting or closing together [1]), now opening out as the creation of the universe (*Prasarah=Jagat-sriṣṭirūpo vikāsah).*

The Cause of the creation of Vak and Artha (*Vāgarthasrṣṭihetuh*). By *Vācah* [2] is meant all the sounds Parā, Pas'yanti and so forth; and by *Artha* is meant the thirty-six *Tattvas* beginning with S'iva and ending with *Kṣiti*. The creation of these is the creation of the world (*Jagat*) of six *Adhvās.*[3]

It has been said, 'Oh Deves'i, In Thee who art Cit (*Cidātmani*) are the six Adhvās, namely *Varṇa, Kalā, Pada, Tattva, Mantra* and *Bhuvana.*' These two Bindus which enter one another and separate (*Paras-parānupraviṣtavispaṣtam*) are the united white and red Bindus *(Sitas'oṇabinduyugalam)* which are known as Kāma-Kāmes'varī, the divine Husband and Wife. The great secret here is this. On the authority of *S'ruti*, 'He who is supreme *(Para)* is Mahes'vara'. And the supreme Lord *(Parames'vara)* who is the first letter *(A)* which generates all sounds of the Vedas and so forth attains the state of Bindu *(Bindu-bhāva)* after having entered *Vimars'a-S'akti* who is His own body *(Svāṅgabhūtā)* and in whom *(S'akti)* all the universe *(Prapañca)* is dissolved. Thereafter the *Vimars'a-S'akti* also enters into the *Prakās'amaya Bindu* which is within Herself. On that the *(Mis'ra)* Bindu becomes ready for action *(Uchchūna)*. From that Bindu issues Nādātmikā S'akti[4] within whose womb are all the Tattvas, who is all energy *(Tejomayī)* and in seed form *(Bīja-rūpā)* and subtile like the tip of a hair and assumes the form of a *S'ṛṅgātaka.*[5] In this way *Prakās'a* and *Vimars'ā* which are the *Svarūpa* of Nāda and Bindu assume body as 'I' *(Aham)*. In the same way, of the pair, one, namely *Vimars'a*, is the Red Bindu, and the other, *Prakās'a*, the White Bindu, and the union of the two is the mixed *(Mis'rarūpa)* and all powerful *(Sarvatejomaya)*, the *Svarūpa* of which is the Paramātmā *(Paramātma-svarūpa)*.

S'ruti also says: '*Avarṇa* (letterless) which is full of meanings *(Nihitārtha)* by union with S'akti in various ways generates many letters.'

He further elucidates these three Bindus by speaking of them as *Ahaṁkārātmā* and so on. The (mixed) Bindu which is (composed of) the Red and White Bindus *(Binduh sita-rakta-svarūpah)* is one with the combined first letter *A* and the last letter *Ha* *(Sphārarūpa-ha-kāra)* between which are all the other letters. The *Kāra* in *Ahaṁkāra* signifies that *A* and *Ha* are letters according to the Sūtra '*Varṇāt kārah.*' This Bindu is therefore the union of the two letters *A-kāra* and *Ha-kāra*, which signify the union of *Prakās'a* and *Vimars'a* *(Etan-mithuna-samarasākārah)*. The union of these two divine Husband and Wife *(Divyadampatirūpasya)* is their mutual helpfulness *(Samarasah=Ānukulyam)* in entering into or co-operating with one another. This mutual action is in the very nature *(Ākāra=Svarūpa)* of the Bindu. The Sun is the Mixed Bindu *(Mis'ra-bindu)*, being the union in the manner stated of the White and Red Bindus *(Sita-s'ona-bindu-samarasī-bhūtah)*.

In ordinary experience also (*Loke'pi*) the mixed character (*Mis'ra-rūpatvam*) of the Sun is spoken of, because it is said that He enters into and issues out of Fire and Moon. *S'ruti* says: 'So does Fire enter into the risen Sun. In the evening again the Sun enters into Fire.'[6]

The word *Amāvāsyā*[7] is so called because the Sun and Moon are in conjunction (*Amī*=with, *Vasatah*=are). Therefore the entrace of the Sun and the Moon into one another is well known. The Sun consequently is the mixed (*Mis'rā*) Bindu.

Kama. That He is the object of adoration (*Upāsya*) is shown by the word '*Kāma*'. *Kāma* is that which is desired (*Kāmyate*) by the great Yogīs, who know the Supreme Reality (*Paramārtha*) as being their very Self (*Svātmatvena*). The reason for their doing so is given when its desirableness (*Kamanīyatva*) is spoken of, since all beauty is desired.

The *Chāndogya Upaniṣad* (speaking of the *Puruṣa* in the Sun) says: 'Golden-bearded, golden-haired, all gold from the tip of the nails.' The *Īs'āvāsya* also says: "He the Paramātmā, radiant, bodiless (*Akāya*), imperishable one, without subtle body, without material body,[8] pure (*S'uddha*), beyond Dharma and Adharma, pervades all."

The same *Upaniṣad* says: 'That most beneficent form of Thine, that do I see by Thy grace. That *Puruṣa* (in the *Āditya-mandala* whose body is the *Vyāhṛtis*) He I am.'

By describing Kāmes'vara as beneficent the author praises his greatness (*Mahimā*).

Kala. Kalā is *Vimars'a-s'akti.*

Bindus which are Fire and Moon *Dahanendu-vigrahau bindū*). The meaning of this is that *Vimars'a-S'akti* is in the nature of Fire and Moon (*Agnī-Soma-rūpiṇī*).

Mahātripurasundarī who is in both these and inseparate from Kāmes'vara is the collectivity of the Bindus and is Kāmakalā. In all *Āgamas* it is proclaimed that She is the object of adoration. So it has been said: 'When white S'iva is in red S'akti, Parā being pierced by S'aṁbhu, then such red S'aṁbhu is in S'akti as Paratattva. When red S'iva is in white S'akti, then is the state of Para-S'aṁbhu and such red S'iva in white S'akti indicates Saccidānanda.' And again it is said, 'Oh Paras'ivā, I make obeisance to Thy supreme Kalā, whereof the upper Bindu is Thy Face, two other Bindus are Thy two breasts, and Nāda-bindu (that is, *Hārdakalā*)[9] is the place of *Ras'anā* (*Nāda-binduras'anāgunāspadam*).'[10]

'The Bindu which is above *E-kāra*[11] is the Sun and Her Face, and below are placed Fire and Moon, Her two breasts, and the *Kalā* which is half of *Hakāra* is her *Yoni*.'

The *Nityāṣodas'ikā*[12] says: 'Having made the *Bindu* the Face and below it the two breasts and below it again half of that which follows *Sa*,[13] meditate upon it[14] as downward turned.'

All this is very secret.

The gist of all this is that the excellent Yogīs, the great Māhes'varas, constantly worship the mother Mahā-tripurasundarī who is Kāmakalā, the collectivity of the three Bindus in the radiant, imperishable and all-pervading Brahman (*Bindutraya-samaṣṭi-rūpa-divyākṣararūpinī*), whose very self is the Bliss which is *Prakās'a* (*Prakās'ānandasārā*), and who is in the nature of complete I-ness (*Purṇāhamtārūpinī*), within whom is the seed (*Vīrya*) of the endless mass of letters (*Anantākṣararās'i*) and great Mantras (*Mahāmantras*).

The *Vijñānabhattāraka* also says: "By passing through the different Mandalas (of the *S'rīcakra*) where the gross letters (*Sthūla-varṇa*) are rising up to Arddhendu, Bindu, Nādānta[15] and to the S'ūnya in the *Bindurūpa-cakra*, one becomes S'iva."[16]

Notes

[1] *Saṁkuchan*=*Mukulī bhavan*, *i.e.* closing like a flower.

[2] Plural of *Vāk*.

[3] See Woodroffe's "*Garland of Letters*", Chapter on the Ṣadadhvās.

[4] *Nādātmikā S'akti*, i.e., *Shakti* as *Nāda*. *Cf.* Woodroffe's "*Garland of Letters*."

[5] A triangular pyramidal figure.

[6] In day time the Sun absorbs the light of fire and in the evening with the disappearance of the Sun other lights appear.

[7] *Tithi* of the new moon.

[8] *Asnāviram*: veinless.

[9] See next note.

[10] The place of the Waist-chain; the Yoni being there.

[11] The *Bīja* formed by the union of *A-kāra* which is *Prakāśa* and *I-kara* which is *Icchā śakti.*

[12] 1-20.

[13] *i.e., Ha.*

[14] *i.e.*, the triangle.

[15] For these terms see Woodroffe's "*Garland of Letters.*"

[16] The gross letters in *Vaikharī* form are in the outer *Mandalas* and passing through the subtler forms of *Śabda*, the *Śabdabrahman* and then *Śūnya* is attained.

VERSE 8

Now this is the *Vidyā* of Kāmakalā which deals with the sequence of the Cakras of the Devī. He by whom this is known becomes liberated and Mahātripurasundarī Herself.

COMMENTARY

Having thus explained the nature of Bindu (*Bindusvarūpam*) he says that the fruit of this knowledge and worship is *Brahmabhāva.*

Now (*Iti*). That is, after what has been described in the previous paragraphs.

Vidya of Kamakala. Kāmakalā is Mahātripurasundarī. By Her *Vidyā* is meant *Jñāna* regarding Her; and to complete the sense, it is said that this knowledge consists in knowing the sequence or the order of arrangement of the Cakras in Her S'rīcakra.

Sequence or Order (*Krama*). By this is meant the order in which the Cakras, Mantras and Devatās are placed, beginning from Sarvānandamaya till all is fully manifest.

He by whom (*Yena*). The suggestion is that the man on whom the grace of S'akti has fallen (*S'aktipāta*: descent of S'akti) is drawn into enquiry concerning the Brahman and meditates and becomes liberated after attainment of knowledge.

Known (*Vidita*). Mastered through sitting at the feet of the Guru and so forth.

Becomes liberated (*Mukto bhavati*). He, the great Yogī, enjoys (*Viharate*) and is yet able to free himself of all desire, after having conquered the whole world through his consciousness (*Bhāvanā*) 'I am always the full and whole I' (*Paripūrṇāhaṁbhāva*).

So it has been said in *Pratyabhijñā*: 'He who is fully instructed in the greatness (*Ais'varya*) of the Lord by *Vidyās* is massive Consciousness (*Cidghana*) and is verily liberated'[1].

The *Bṛhadāraṇyaka*[2] says: 'Men think that by *Brahmavidyā* we shall be all in all[3]. Now, what is that which when it is known, we become all-knowing ?'

In the end[4] he becomes Mahātripurasundarī Herself, that is, our Supreme Lady (*Parābhattārikā*).

S'ruti says: 'They enter the Supreme Light of Tripurā (*Traipuraṁ dhāma*)'; also 'the knower of the Brahman is the Brahman'. The *Chāndogya* says[5]: 'He alone who sees thus, who meditates thus, who knows thus, he verily is drawn to the Ātmā, has love-play with the Ātmā, and is united wlth Ātmā which is Bliss Itself (*Ātmarati, Ātmakrīda, Ātmamithuna, Ātmānanda*)'.

In the *Svacchanda Tantra* also occur Texts like the following—'When (the *Sādhaka*) is united in the same abode with his Devatā[6], then for him there is no more birth or death. He attains the state of true Devotion and becomes the Lord of the Universe (*Cakra*)'.

NOTES

[1] *Cidghana* is the Brahman. The sense of the text is that man becomes Brahman Itself. *Cf.* 'He who knows the Brahman is Brahman'.

[2] 1-4-9.

[3] The text begins, "Seekers after Brahman say."

[4] *Ante'pi*, that is, after death.

[5] 7-25-2.

[6] *that is*, here Tripurā.

VERSE 9

FROM the Red Bindu about to create arose sound[1] *(Ravah)* which is the Nāda-brahman sprout. From that (Sound) came Ether, Air, Fire, Water, Earth and the Letters of the alphabet.

COMMENTARY

Here the Yogī Punyānanda after having realised within himself (*Ātmatvena anubhūya*) the Primordial Sundarī[2] whose name is Kāmakalā, now speaks of the origin of the world foom the Bindu before Creation (*Prakṛta-bindu*) which is the Highest Reality (*Paramārtha*) as also of Her spreading forth (*Vilāsa*) as Devatā, Mantra and Chakra.

From the Red Bindu about to create (***Sphuritādarunād bindoh***). *Sphurita*=*Ucchūna*, that is, 'swelling', 'pregnant'[3], which has been previously described.

Sound which is the Nadabrahman sprout (*Nādabrahmāṅkuro-ravah*). *Nāda* is the sound (*Varṇa*) which is the cause of the origin of all sounds.[4] This is the Brahman which is Nādabrahman. This is the Producer (*Angkura*=*Utpādaka*). So it has been said: 'One *Avaraṇa*[5] which is *Nāda* (*Nādātmaka*) is divided into all letters. As it nevet disappears[6] it is called *Anāhata*[7]. This is S'ruti.'

Vyoma, Bindu, Nada. This is the order.[8] Sound (*Rava*) which is the sprouting Nādabrahman becomes manifest in the form *Pas'yantī* and so forth. It is proved[9] that the mass of sound is the S'aktis *Parā*, *Pas'yantī* and so forth. This sound (*S'abda*) is the origin of the five *Bhūtas*, Ether, Āir, Fire, Water, Earth, and the letters beginning with *A* and ending with *Kṣa*. From *Nāda-bindu* issues the entire world. *S'ruti* also says[10]: 'From *Akṣara*[11] originates this universe.'

NOTES

[1] That is, the creative movement which as sensed by the ear is experienced as physical sound.

[2] *Sundarī*=a beautiful woman. Here it is the Devī. All Devīs are beautiful, the Devī Tripurasundarī being the most beautiful of all. See a Dhyāna of Her in Chapter I, vv. 138-152, *Nityāṣodaśikārṇava.*

[3] The state of immediate readiness to produce.

[4] And, therefore, of everything else, for all things have a common origin.

[5] *A-kāra* is the first of all letters and is *Prakāśa* and *Paramaśiva.* But this is *lakṣaṇārtha,* that is, after the universe is produced the first letter *A* indicates the Brahman. But the *Brahmasvarūpa* is *A-varṇa* in the negative sense, that is, letterless and soundless (*niḥśabda*). *A-varṇa* here is undifferentiated Power which manifests as the particular letters and other particulars of the universe.

[6] *Lit.*, 'always is', *that is,* during the Kalpa. All creative activity is withdrawn at *Pralaya* when Power is one with the Power-holder (*Śaktimān*).

[7] *Āhata*=struck, and *anāhata śabda* is that sound which is not caused by the striking of two things together, that is, by contact of matter. It is Eternal Power.

[8] Ether originates from the self-dividing or 'bursting' *Bindu,* on which self-division there was *Nāda.* That is, *Nāda* is the productive action which manifests as the produced *Vyoma* and the rest. *Cf. Ambāstotra,* v. 3.

[9] Later, in Verse 20.

[10] *Muṇḍaka,* 1-7.

[11] *that is,* Brahman. The word means both 'letter' and 'imperishable'.

VERSE 10

THE White Bindu also is the origin of Ether, Air, Fire, Water and Earth. The Universe from the most minute to the Brahmā-spheroid consists of these five *Vikṛtis*.

COMMENTARY

Having spoken of to the all-pervadingness (*Sarvātmatva*) and all-creativeness (*Sarvasṛṣtitva*) of the Red Bindu he now speaks of the sameness of the White Bindu and Red Bindu, because of the inseparateness of the former from the latter.

White (*Vis'ada*), All-illuminating (*Sarvaprakās'a*). It is from and into this Bindu, which has been previously described, that the appearance and disappearance of the Endless Brahmā-spheroids composed of the five *Bhūtas*, Ether and the rest take place.

So *S'ruti* says[1]: 'In which all the Beings (*Bhāvas*) disappear and having disappeared become manifest again and then again and again disappear like bubbles.'

In this way it is established that from Brahman, which is the White and Red Bindus, which are *Prakās'a* and *Vimars'a*, all this (universe) originated.

Āgama also says: 'I bow to the *Mahāpītha*[2] of *Saṁvit*[3] which is S'iva and S'akti (*S'ivas'akti-padās'raya*)[4] wherefrom emanate countless world-rays[5] made manifest (*Vilasita*) or flashed forth by Creative Will (*Icchā-s'akti*).

NOTES

[1] *Chūlikā Up.*, 8.

[2] A word which here conveys the sense of a place of great sanctity.

[3] That is, *Parajñāna.*

[4] *Lit.*, the refuge which is the feet or place of S'iva and S'akti.

[5] From the Effulgent Consciousness imaged as a Mass of Light which is all Wisdom and Power, rays shoot forth which are the worlds, as, it is said elsewhere, sparks from the great central fire.

VERSE 11

As the two Bindus are indistinguishable and inseparable, so also are *Vidyā* the indicator (*Vedaka*), and Devatā, the indicated (*Vedya*).

COMMENTARY

Having spoken of the inseparateness (*Abheda*) of the two Bindus he now says that similarly there is oneness of the Mantra and the Devatā.

Two Bindus (*Bindudvitaya*)—' The two Bindus previously mentioned which are in the nature of *Prakās'a* and *Vimars'a* (*Prakās'a-vimars'ātmakam*). As these two are inseparate, the wise say that S'iva and S'akti are one *Tattva* '. The two are blended, the one with the other (*Parasparāliṣta*). In the same way there is not the slightest distinction between *Vidyā* which is the indicator (*Vedaka*= *Vācaka*) and the *Devatā* which is the indicated (*Vedya*=*Vācya*).

Vidya is the Mantra of fifteen letters (*Panchadashākshari*) and **Devata** is Mahātripurasundarī.

So it has been said in *Tantrasadbhāva*: ' All Mantras consist of letters (*Varnātmaka*). They again, O beloved, are at base S'akti. S'akti again is Mātṛkā and She again is S'ivātmikā. She the Mātṛkā who in the world appears possessed of the energy and brilliance of the Supreme (*Paratejah-samanvitā*) pervades all this universe beginning from Brahmā and ending with *Bhuvana*.'

VERSE 12

WORD (*Vāk*) and its meaning (*Artha*) are always united, They are S'iva and S'akti which are three-fold as Creation. Maintenance and Dissolution, and as the three *Bijas*.

COMMENTARY

He here wishes to say that the world arises out of the inseparate *Nāda-bindu* couple, and therefore says that that Couple of its own wish differentiated themselves.

Word and its meaning (*Vāk and Artha*). *Vāk* is in the form of *Varṇa, Pada, Mantra* (*Varṇapadamantrarūpā*), *Artha* is *Kalā, Tattva* and *Bhuvana*[1] (*Kalātattvabhuvanātmā*). Such is the form of S'iva-S'akti, because, as *S'ruti* says,' out of *S'abda* (*Vāk*) and *Artha* which are *Prakās'a* and *Vimars'a* (*Prakās'a-vimars'ātmaka*), the whole world consisting of six Adhvās (*S'adadhvātmaka*) originated. They are therefore always united (*Nityayutau*=*Nirantara-saṁsaktau*) and not casually or accidentally so, like a jar and picture which may be put together. If the union were merely accidental, then the ordered universe would not exist. These two go through the three-fold changes of ***Creation, Maintenance*** and ***Dissolution*** (*Sṛṣti-sthiti-laya-bhedau tridhā-vibhaktau*).

Creation, Maintenance and Dissolution. By Creation (*Sṛṣti*) is meant the appearance of all the *Tattvas* beginning with *S'iva* and ending with *Kṣiti*. *Sthiti* is the Maintenance thereof, and Dissolution (*Laya*) is their reunion with, or return to, that which at base they are (*Svātmasākṣātkāra*). These three (functions) are from, in and into the *Ātmā*. So it has been said by the honoured Abhinavagupta[2]; 'Creation, Maintenance and Dissolution are (all) within the Ātmā (*Svātmagāh*) in their own nature (*Svarūpatvena*)'. These two (*Vāk* and *Artha*) are mutually (*Paraspara*) united *S'iva* and *S'akti*

(*S'ivas'akti-mayau*) and forms of *Prakās'a* and *Vimars'a* (*Prakās'a-vimars'a-svarūpau*), the activity of these two being of one and the same thing (*Ubhayor eka-kṛttvāt*), just as in the case of fire and the function or S'akti of burning (*Vahnidāhakatvavat*) there is no difference (*Tattvāntara*).

As an honoured teacher also says: 'The identity (*Tādātmya*) of these two is everlasting (*Nityam*) like that of Fire (*Vahni*) and S'akti or power which burns (*Dāhika*),'

Āgama also says: 'As We two are the Self of the World (*Jagadātmatvāt*) We two are one with it. By reason of Our identity with one another We are at all times the life of the world (*Jagat-prāṇa*)'.

Threefold (*Tridhā-vibhaktau*). The united *Prakās'a* and *Vimars'a* are divided in three ways (*Vibhaktau=Prithagbhūtau*). These three ways or forms are the three *Bījas*. The three *Bījas* are *Vāgbhava*, *Kāmarāja* and *S'akti Bīja*. The meaning of this is that Mahātripurasundarī who is Brahman as *Kāmakalā* composed of the three Bindus collectively (*Bindutrayasamaṣṭībhūtā*), is the object of adoration of all.

The *Vāmakes'vara*[3] says: 'Tripurā is known by the three *Tattvas* (*Tattvatrayavinirdiṣṭā*) and is the threefold S'akti of the three letters (*Varṇa-s'akti-trayātmikā*)[4]. *Vāgīs'varī* which is *Jñāna s'akti* is in *Vāgbhavabīja* and is *Mokṣa-rūpiṇī* or Liberation itself, that is, grantor of Liberation. *Kāmakalā* is in *Kāmarāja* (*Bīja*) which is *Kriyā S'akti* (*Kriyātmikā*) and *Kāmarūpā* (as *Kāma* or Will, that is, grantor of desires). *Icchā* which is the *Parā S'akti* is in *S'akti Bīja* and is *S'iva-rūpiṇī*[5]. Such is Devī Mahātripurasundarī who is the three *Akṣaras* (*Bījas*), who loosens the bondage to this world, and is known by the tradition handed down by the line of Gurus to their disciples (*Pāramparyeṇa vijñātā*)'.

NOTES

[1] These six constitute the six Adhvās (see "*Garland of Letters*"), of which the first three are in *Vāk* and the remaining three in *Artha*.

[2] *Ācārya* of the Kāshmīra School.

[3] *Nityās'odas'ikā*, IV, 16-19.

[4] The Varnas or letters here are the three Bījas.

[5] *S'iva-rūpiṇī=Dharmapradā*, giver of *Dharma*.

KNOWER, Knowing, Known are the three *Bindus* and forms of the *Bīja*. The three Lights, the three *Pīthas* and the three *S'aktis* are that by which they (the *Bindus*) are known.[1] In these again in their order are the three *Lingas* as also the three *Mātṛkās*. She who is this threefold body is the *Vidyā* (*Devī*), who is the fourth *Pītha* (*Turīyapītha*), and the root of all differentiation (*Ādibhedinī*).

COMMENTARY

He here commences to make the *Vidyā* (*Mantra*) of fifteen letters by describing certain details immanent (*Antargata*) in the three divisions (*Khanda*), *Vāgbhava* and others.

Knower (*Mātā*) is the Lord (*Īs'vara*) who knows.

Knowing (*Mānam*) is the Vidyā whereby He knows (*Avagati-sādhana-bhūta vidyā*).

Known or Object of knowledge (*Meya*) is Mahātripurasundarī who is to be known (*Jñāyamana*).

Forms of the Bija are these three, namely Knower, Knowing and Known divided into three separate Bindus (*Bindutrayabhinna-bīja-rūpāṇi*).

The three Bindus are those already described, namely Red, White and Mixed. The *Bīja* is divided into these three Bindus. The *Bīja* is the *Nirvāṇa Bījā* which is the collectivity of all the three Bindus (*Sarvasamaṣti-bhūta-nirvāṇākhyam*). By "form" (*Rūpa*) is meant that they manifest the Bīja (*Tadrūpāṇi*=*Tatprakās'akāni*). The sense of the above is that She who is the Supreme transcendent Light (*Paraṁjyotiḥ*) which is Consciousness (*Cit*), Bliss (*Ānanda*), and the massive Ātmā (*ghanātmā*) with the experience of *Ahambhāva* or "I-ness" (*Sarvātītā-cidānandaghanātmānubhava-rūpāham-bhāva-s'ālinī*) enjoys Herself in the form of experience in which there is

Knower (*Mātṛ*), Knowing (*Māna*) and Known (*Meya*) (*Mātṛ-māna-meyabhāvam anubhūya viharati*).

The *Kāṇva*[1] says: 'This Ātmā there was alone in the beginning as Puruṣa. He saw and saw nothing outside Himself. "He I Am" (*So'haṁ asmi*): Thus first did he say. Thereupon arose '*Ahaṁ*'. Therefore even now a person on being accosted first says, 'It is I' (*Ahaṁ ayaṁ*) and then given his individual name.'

The meaning of the passage is: The *Ātmā* is the supreme Lord. '*Idaṁ*' is the visible Universe. 'In the beginning' means first. 'He was', that is, with the Universe within himself. Therefore, that *Paramātmā* having seen as Himself (*Ātmatvena*), the Universe, with Himself (*Svātmasātkṛta-prapañcam*) did not see any other; that is, He saw nothing beyond Himself, because He had withdrawn all things into Himself. At that time He showed Himself to Himself as 'I am the universal form' (*Svasādhāraṇarūpa*), that is, 'I am the experience which is continuous (*Akhaṇda*), Massive (*Ghana*), Being (*Sat*), Consciousness (*Cit*), and Bliss (*Ānanda*) (*Akhaṇdasaccidānanda-ghanātmānubhavo'haṁ*)'. In the beginning, that is, before creation He enjoyed himself, that is, he showed (*Prādarśayat*) Himself to Himself. Thereupon arose '*Ahaṁ*' (I) *Ahaṁ-nāmābhavat*). Because thus Brahman shows His own self (*Svarūpa*) to Himself as 'I' (*Ahaṁ*), this is itself the name of Brahman. Therefore even in this world if a person be accosted he answers first 'It is I' (Aham) and after thus giving his *Brahmasvarūpa*[3], he next gives his other[4] name. These distinctions of Knower and the like are seen to derive from the Brahman as we can perceive by examining ourselves.

The *Catuhśatī*[5] says, that the Supreme Energy (*Paraṁtejah*), which is transcendent (*Atītam*=which is beyond the *Bindu*) is *Svasaṁvit* (=*Svetarviṣayakaṁ jñanaṁ*=knowledge, the object of which is nothing other than Self). Its characteristic is manifestation (*Udayātmakaṁ*=(*Udayaikasvarūpam ṣadbhāva-vikārarahitaṁ*). By Its mere wish (*i.e.* by mere *Ikṣaṇa* without being dependent upon or having recourse to any other being or thing), it made the world-picture (*Viśva-mayollekhah*=*jagadātmakam chitram*). It is all prevading (*Viśva-rūpaka*=*Sarvtmaka*) Consciousness (*Caitanya*) pleasing Itself in its own blissfulness[6]. Such is *Ātmā* (*Ātmano rūpaṁ*). Its light is contracted (*Saṁkucatprabham*) in Its evolution as Knower (*Mātṛ*), Knowing (*Māna*), Known (*Meya*) and true Knowledge (*Pramā*).

Three Lights (*Dhāmatraya*). These are the three Mandalas of Moon, Sun, Fire.

Three Bijas (*Bījatraya*). These are *Vāgbhava* and others.

Three Pithas (*Pīthatraya*). These are *Kāmagiri* and others[7].

Three Saktis (*S'aktitraya*). These are *Icchā* and others[8].

They (*Bindus*) are known (*Bhāvita*) under these three aspects (*Bheda*). These are forms of the Mahābindu (*Mahābindumaya*). Therefore in these Three Lights and others there are in their order (*Krameṇa=Ānupūrvyā*) the three *Lingas, viz., Svayaṁbhu* and the others[9], the threefold *Mātṛkā* classified as *A, Ka, Tha* and the rest[10]. Tripurā who is in the form of and is the collectivity of all things (*Tat-samaṣtirūpā*) is the *Parās'akti* who appeared, and hence it is said 'She who is the threefold body' *Itthaṁ tritaya-purī yā*). Her body is threefold in manner hereinbefore described. She is therefore the highest or *Fourth Pīta* (*Turīyapīthā*) as the basis (*Bhū*) wherefrom appears and into which disappears the whole universe which is threefold (*Trividhātmaka-sarvaprapancāvirbhāva-tirobhāva-bhūh*). So the *Catuh-s'atī*[11] says: '(I bow to) *Mātṛkā* who is *Pītha-rūpinī*'.

She who in this way is the *Turīyapīthā* and is the root of all *differentiates* Herself (*Ādibhedinī*). She within whom is the endless mass of Tattvas produced by Her own will (*Svecchayā udbhāvitānanta-tattva-kadaṁbinī*) is in Herself (*Svātmany eva*) continuous impartite (*Akhaṇḍa*) *Saṁvit*.

An honoured sage (*Abhiyukta*) has said: 'Because the Devī created the three forms (*Trimūrti*), because She is before all (*Purobhava*), because She is in the form of the three (*Trayīmayī*)[12], because even after dissolution of the three worlds She recreates them again, the Mother's (*Aṁbikā*) name is appropriately Tripurā.'

In the *Catuh-s'atī*[13] She is spoken of as the Devī Tripurā who is Knowledge as Supreme experience itself (*Svasaṁvit*).

NOTES

[1] Knower, Knowing and Known are the three Bindus which are forms of the *Nirvāna Bīja* or *Mahābindu* the collectivity of all three. The three

Bindus again are the three lights, three *Pīthas*, three *S'aktis*, three *Liṅgas* and three *Mātṛkās*. That is, these are their various aspects.

[2] *Bṛhadāraṇyaka*, 1-4-1.

[3] That in which he is one with *Brahman*.

[4] Individual.

[5] *i.e.*, *Nityāṣodas'ikā*, VI-49-51.

[6] *i.e.*, its blissfulness is not the result of anything outside Itself.

[7] *Pūrṇas'aila* and *Jālandhara*. These reflect and are *Vṛtti* of *chit*.

[8] That is, *Jñāna* and *Kriyā S'aktis*.

[9] Namely *Bāṇa*, *Itara* and *Para*.

[10] The *Trikoṇa* of that name. See "Serpent Power" by A. Avalon.

[11] *Nityās'odas'ikā*, Ch. I-vi.

[12] *i.e.*, the vedas consisting of *Karma*, *Upāsanā* and *Jñāna Kāṇdas*, not, as usually stated, *Ṛk*, *Yajus*, *Sāman*.

[13] Ch. V- 41.

VERSES 15, 16 & 17

SOUND, Touch, Form, Taste, Smell these are the subtle *Bhūtas*. (Of these) each is the producer (*Vyāpaka*) of that which follows (*Vyāpya*), and thus taking them all in their order there are fifteen properties (*Guṇas*).

The *Nityā* (Tripurā) who is (the Mantra) of fifteen letters is known as She appears in the Bhūtas (*Bhautikā'bhimatā*). She is surrounded by the fifteen *Nityās*[1] who are distinguished by the different properties (*Guṇas*) of sound and so forth (*S'abdādi-guṇa-prabheda bhinnāh*).

The (fifteen) *Nityās* represent the (fifteen) lunar days (*Tithyākārāh*). The lunar days again are the union (*Samarasa*) of S'iva and S'akti. They consist of days and nights. They are the letters in the Mantra and have the double nature of *Prakās'a* and *Vimars'a*.

COMMENTARY

He has spoken of the creation of the five Bhūtas in the passage: 'From that came Ether, Air, Fire, Water and Earth.' He here commences to speak of the nature (*Svarūpa*) of each of the Devatās who are one with (each of) the letters of the great Mantra by a description of the *Guṇas* of the first created five *Bhūtas*.

Sound (*S'abda*) is the Guṇa of *Ākās'a*, Touch (*Spars'a*) of *Vāyu*, Form (*Rūpa*) of *Tejas*, Taste (*Rasa*) of *Apas*, Smell (*Gandha*) of *Pṛthvī*. These Guṇas from *Ākās'a* to *Pṛthvī* increase by one and thus fifteen Guṇas are obtained[2]. As there are fifteen different Guṇas the *S'rīvidyā* is of fifteen letters. In other words, She who is the own form (*Svarūpa*) of the Mantra appears as such. Therefore the fifteen letters are Her form (*Rūpa*).

She is known as She appears in the Bhutas (*Bhautikā'bhimatā*). She is on this account worshipped as in or in relation to Her bhautika aspects (*Bhūta-sambandhitvena iṣṭā*). As the Guṇas which emanate from Her are fifteen in number, so the letters of the *Vidyā*[3] are fifteen. The *Nityā* whose form is that (*Mantra*), who is the *Svarūpa* of that (*Mantra*), is unmoving, changeless and supreme (*Kūtasthā*); just as the ocean is that in which appear and disappear the waves, bubbles and froth, so She is That in which all the Tattvas appear and disappear. So the *Bṛhadāraṇyaka*[4] says: 'This great Being (*Bhūta*= Brahman) is endless and without limit and is massive knowledge. It evolves from Itself these *Bhūtas* as *Devas*, men, and so forth, and, withdraws them also, that is, withdraws these forms of Itself.'

In the *Muṇḍaka-Upaniṣad* also it is said: 'That in which all forms of experience (*Bhāva*) disappear.'

He next speaks of the sixteenth *Nityā* who is *Kūtasthā* as being of fifteen limbs (*Avayava*), as in the fifteen lunar days (*Tithi*) which are the fifteen *Devatās*, and as in the form of the Mantra of the fifteen letters.

The fifteen Nityas represent the (fifteen) lunar days (*Nityās-tithyākārāh*). The *Nityās* are in the form of the lunar days. These are the *Nityās* beginning with *Kāmesvari* and ending with *Citrā*. They are in the form of the lunar days (*Tithyākārāh*), that is, they are Devatās who are the Tithis (*Tithyabhimāninyah*). The *Tithis* also begin with *Pratipat* and end with *Pūrṇimā*.

The lunar days again are the union of Siva and Sakti (*Tithayas'ca S'iva-S'akti-samarasākārāh*), or in other words, they are the united form of *Prakās'a* and *Vimars'a*. They are therefore of the form of day and night. *Prakās'a* and *Vimars'a* are day and night. So it is said in *Cidvilāsa*: 'She the Night makes all the worlds sleep. He the Day is verily the waker-up of all.'

These *Tithis* again are the letters in the *Vidyā* (*Srīvarṇāh*) being in manner aforesaid fifteen in number. They have further the double forms, that is, they are likewise *Prakās'a* and *Vimars'ah*) (*Prakās'a-vimars'a-rūpāh*). This *Vidyā* of fifteen letters has been enunciated in *S'aunaka-S'ākhā* of the *Atharva-veda* by the Mantra, which runs '*Kāmo yonih kamalā*' and so forth. Some say that this *Vidyā* is also shown in the fifth *Maṇḍala* of the *Ṛgveda* in *Catvāraiṁ bibhrati kṣemayantah*' and so forth.

The sense of all this is that this Parāsakti who is both *Prakāśa* (S'iva) and *Vimarśa* (S'akti) and appear as the five Bhūtas (*Prakāśa-Vimarśa-mayī* and *Pañca-bhūtātmikā*), becomes by a progressive increase of Guṇas the *Mantra* of fifteen letters, the fifteen Tithis, and is manifest as the fifteen *Devatās* (*Devatāsvarūpiṇī*).

So *Āgama* says: 'There is some, only one Supreme Mahesvara whose name is *Prakāśa* and the name of whose S'akti is *Vimarśa*, She is called *Nityā* by the wise. She the Devī whose name is *Vimarśa* becomes fivefold as Ether (*Ākāśa*), Air (*Anila*), the Seven-flamed (*Saptārcih*) Fire, Water (*Salila*) and Earth (*Avanī*). By the increase of Guṇas, one by one, She reaches the number of the *Tithis* (fifteen). The Devī who is *Vimarśa* (*Vimarśa-rūpiṇī*) is known as the sixteenth (*Ṣodaśī*). The Paramesvarī who is Mahātripurasundarī undergoes these sixteen forms, the last of which is *Citrā*. She spreads Herself all over (the *Cakra*). The subject is only here hinted at. It should be known from One's own *Āgama*. He who worships these Devīs one after the other day by day, from *Pratipat* to *Pūrṇimā* attains, oh beloved, good fortune (*Saubhāgya*).'

NOTES

[1] Devīs, who are to be distinguished from the supreme Nityā Tripurā.

[2] That is *Ākāśa* has one *Guṇa*, namely *S'abda*; *Vāyu* has two *viz.*, *Sabda* and *Sparśa*; and so on.

[3] *Mantra.*

[4] 2-4-12.

VERSE 18

THE *Vidyā* which is composed of the three Bindus[1], the vowels and consonants collectively and separately, is both immanent in and transcends the Thirty-six *Tattvas* and is by Herself alone.[2]

COMMENTARY

Here the author wishing to strengthen what has previously been said says that the *Devatā* is immanent in and transcends the Universe, so also does the *Vidyā*.

The **vowels** (*Svara*) are the letters beginning with *A* and the **consonants** (*Vyañjana*) are the letters beginning with *Ka*.

The three Bindus (*Bindutraya*) are the three Bindus which make *Anusvāra* and *Visarga*. These taken either singly or in a group make Her body (*Vibhāvitākārā=udbhāvitasvarūpā*).

She is thus in the Thirty-six Tattvas (*Ṣattriṁs'at-tattvātmā*) that is, Her body is made up of the *Tattvas* beginning with *S'iva* and ending with *Kṣiti*, and **She also transcends them** (*Tattvātītā ca*), for She is the place and origin of all the *Tattvas* (*Tattvasamudāyasthānā*). She is therefore **alone** (*Kevalā*), because there is nothing besides Herself (*Sva-vyatiriktasya abhāvāt*).

Such is the *Vidyā* of fifteen letters (*Pañcadas'ākṣarī*).

The divisions of its parts are as follows: The honoured Punyānanda, a strong adherent of *Hādividyā*[3], speaks of this *Vidyā* as a whole, that is, as immanent in the *Tattvas* (*Tattvātmakatva*) and transcending them (*Taduttīrṇatva*) of this *Vidyā*.

In the first part *Vāgbhava* contains five vowels and seven consonants, that is, twelve letters. In the secoud *Kāmarāja* there are six vowels and eight consonants in all fourteen letters. In the third part known as *S'akti* there are four vowels and six consonants. The total of all these make 36 letters which are the limbs[4]. This *Vidyā* as an entire whole surpasses all (the thirty-six) *Tattvas* (*Sarva-tattvātikrāntā*). This is everywhere well established and known (*Prasiddhā*).

S'ruti says that *Kādi* also possesses the double quality (*Ubhayātmakatva*) that is, as immanent and transcendent and as collective and individual (*Vyaṣṭi-samaṣṭirūpatvaṁ*). The difference between the two is that in the first part of *Hādi* there are five vowels and seven consonants, whereas in the first part of *Kādi* there are seven vowels and five consonants. So that in both *Vidyās* the total in the first section is equally twelve each. Both *Vidyās* therefore possess the double character. The method relating to the worship of both the *Vidyās* should be learnt from the mouth of the Guru.

NOTES

[1] *i.e.*, *Bindu* and *Visarga*.

[2] *Kevalā*=*Ekā*=*Advitīyā* : that is one without another.

[3] There are three *matas* or forms of worship, *viz.*, *Kādi* (*Kālikula*), *Hādi* (*S'rīkula*), and *Kahādi*. See A. Avalon's Introduction to the *Kādimata* portion of *Tantra-rāja*, Vol. 8, *Tāntrika Texts*.

[4] The grand total is thus 15 vowels and 21 consonants=36 letters

VERSE 19

VEDYĀ is also like this—She is the subtle Devī Tripurasundarī. The Great Yogīs have ever taught the inseparateness of the Vidyā and the Vedyā.

COMMENTARY

He here speaks of the twofold aspect (*Ubhayātmakatva*) of Devatā and of the oneness of Mantra and Devatā.

Vedya (=she who as the subject of knowledge is sought to be known), She whose *Svarūpa* is *Cit* and *Ānanda*, She is "**Like this**" (*Tādṛgātmā*—like the Mantra She is immanent in the Tattvas (*Tattvātmikā*) and in the universe (*Vis'vātmikā*) and is beyond and transcends both (*Taduttīrṇā*).

Subtle (*Sūkṣmā*). By this is meant She who cannot be subdivided, who cannot be defined (*Paricchettuṁ as'akyā*).

She (*Sā*) is used to indicate the fact that She is recognised (*Prasiddhā*) in all Vedāntas.

Tripurasundari—She is so called because She is Tripurā and Sundarī (beautiful). She is Tripurā because She produces all things which are in a threefold state (*Tridhāvasthita-samasta-vastupūraṇāt*), and She is Sundarī because She is the adored of Yogīs (*Sarvayogībhirupāsyatvena*) and also because of Her charmfulness (*Spṛhaṇīyatvāt*). The word Tripurā has previously been defined. The *Svarūpa* of the Devī is clear Illumination (*Svacchaprakās'arūpā*). She is the Parā-vāk whose play is creation and the like of the universe (*Vis'vasya jananādi-krīdārūpā*).

The Great Yogis . . . Vidya and Vedya (*Vidyā-Vedyātmakayor atyantābhedaṁ āmananty āryāh*). All Yogīs beginning with Parames'vara (Āryāh=*Parames'vara-pramukhāh sarvayoginah*) establish or uphold (*Pratipādayanti*) the eternal (*Atyanta=Sārvakālika*) inseparateness (*Abheda=aikya=* one-ness) of Vidyā, that is, the Mantra of fifteen letters, and *Vedyā*, that is, Tripurasundarī. So it has been said in *Catuhs'atī*[1]: "Whatever S'akti is spoken of as being in any particular category (*Padārtha*), that S'akti is the Devī Sarves'varī (the S'akti of S'iva), and He who is with Her is the Great Lord (*Mahes'vara*). She the Vidyā who is *Bhūtaguṇātmikā*[2] spreads Herself out by the fifteen letters of which Her mantra is composed and which is divided into groups of five (which are of *Vāgbhava*), six (which are of *Kāmarāja*), and four (which are of *S'akti*) letters[3]. According to the number of vowels and consonants (of which her Mantra consists) She is of thirty-seven aspects (*Saptatrims'at-prabhedinī*). By these thirty-seven aspects or variations She appears as Thirty-six Tattvas. The Vidyā Itself should be thought of as the State of S'iva Himself which excels all Tattvas[4].

NOTES

[1] *Nityāṣodas'ikā*, Ch. VII, VV. 31-34.

[2] That is, She is *Bhūtas* and *Guṇas*, or rather these are in Her.

[3] *Akṣara*=imperishable entities.

[4] *Tattvātītasvabhāvā*. Sva=S'iva; Svabhāva is the State or Bhāva of S'iva and as such it excels all Tattvas. The Devī is that.

VERSE 20

SHE whose inner nature is beyond mind is the Mahes'ī as Parā. It is She again who is known in three different aspects when manifest as the three Mātṛkās, Pas'yantī and others and evolves Herself into the Cakra.

COMMENTARY

Having previously spoken of the oneness of the Vidyā and Devatā the author wishing to speak of the identity with one another of *Cakra* and *Devatā* now proceeds to speak of the mode in which the Chakra originated (*Cakrotpattiprakāra*). "**She whose inner nature is beyond mind**" (*Yā Sāntaroharūpā*; *antara=antah-karaṇa* or mind; *ūhah* (*=Vitarkah=Itthamiti-paricchedarahitah*) is that which cannot be described as this or that). The sense is that She is beyond mind and speech (*Avāṅmānasagocaratvāt*) and therefore cannot be expressed in the words of the Vedāntas[1]. The Mahes'ī is the Cause of all (*Sarvakāraṇabhūtā*) as the ground (*Bhūmi*) wherefrom all the Thirty-six Tattvas from *S'iva* to *Pṛthivī* proceed and that is why She is called *Parā* the highest or who excels all (*Sarvotkṛṣṭā*).

S'ruti[2] says:

"[He has no body nor has He any organ of sense. There is no one seen who is equal to or greater than Him.] His S'akti is Parā who is heard of (in the Vedas) as of many aspects and immanent in Him (*Svābhāvikī*) as Kriyās'akti united with Jñāna and Bala."

Also elsewhere[3]: "That from which words along with Manas being unable to reach return (baffled)."

Āgama also says: "*Parā Vāk* (Supreme Word) which is within (*i.e.* unmanifest) is verily Light-in-Itself (*Svarūpajyotireva*)[4] and perishes not (*Anapāyinī*). When Her own form is seen (*Yasyām dṛṣta-svarūpāyām*) all duty ceases"[4]

This same (*Saiva*) Parā S'akti so described (*Evaṁbhūtalakṣaṇā*) is again known in three different aspects. That is what is said in the passage **when manifest &c. &c. Pashyanti and others** (*Spaṣṭā pas'yantyāditrimātrikātmā*). By "Manifest" (*Spaṣṭā*) Her first appearance as something objective is meant. By the expression "and others" Madhyamā and Vaikharī are intended. It is She Who as Vaikharī which is power of expression (*Abhilāpasvarūpiṇi*), is the S'akti which is in the form of the mass of fifteen letters (*Pañcadasākṣararas'imayī*)[6] and in all the many different words used in the Vedas and Tantras and in ordinary life. So it has been said in *Subhagodayavāsanā*: "Parā as Pas'yantī is the creeper born in the earth[7] as Madhyamā She is the fragrance from the flower-bunch and as Vaikharī She is the letter of the alphabet (*Akṣamālā*). Thus does She excel all." In this wise, as Trimātṛikā, She becomes the Cakra that is, becomes one with the Cakra of three parts[8].

NOTES

[1] *That is,* She is beyond the scope of the highest form of human learning and can be realised by *Sādhanā* alone by the man who deserves to be called *Vidvān.*

Cf.: *Nistattvā kāryagamyā'sya s'aktir māyā'gnis'aktivat*
Nahi s'aktiṁ kvacit kas'cit budhyate kāryatah purā.
(*Vidyāranyamuni*)

Also:
Na s'ilpādijñānayukte vidvacchabdah prayujyate
Mokṣaikahetuvidyā yā sā vidyā nātra saṁs'ayah.
(*Brahmāndapurāṇa*)

[2] *S'vetās'vatara* VI. 8. The portion within brackets has not been quoted in the commentary. "Is seen" (*Dṛs'yate*) is explained by Nārāyaṇa to mean "realised by argument" (*Yuktyā upalabhyate*). "*Bala*" here says Bhāskara (under *Nityāṣoda*, VI. 9) implies *Icchā* (*Balas'abdasya icchāparatvam*).

[3] *Taittirīya* (2, 4, 1, 2. 9. 1); *Brahma* 3.

[4] *That is,* the Brahman light.

[5] *Adhikāro nivartate i.e.* the question of competency does not apply to such a man. He becomes free from all observances.

[6] The Mantra of fifteen letters is given in *Tripurāmahopaniṣad.* 8. being published in this series.

[7] *Bhūjanma*=Earth-born *i.e.* born in the Mūlādhāra.

[8] There are nine Mandalas in the S'rī-Cakra divided into three parts of three sections each. The three parts may also be *Sṛṣti, Sthiti, Laya* corresponding with *Pashyantī, Madhyamā, Vaikharī.*

VERSE 21

THE wise know no difference between the *Mahes'ī* and the *Cakra*. *Parā* Herself is the subtle form of both these (*Devatā* and *Cakra*). There is no difference between the two in the gross form also.

COMMENTARY

In this verse he emphasises what has been previously said in the statement that the wise see no difference or distinction whatsoever between the *Cakra*, consisting of the nine sections (*Āvaraṇa*) beginning with *Trailokyamohuna* and ending with *Bindu* wherein *Sundarī* abides, and *Sundarī* Herself Who is the presiding (*Adhiṣṭhātrī*) Great Lady (*Mahes'ī*) therein. This is so because the *S'rīcakra* is the form (*Rūpa*) of the *S'rī-Sundarī.*

S'ruti[1] says: 'Alone She was at first. She became nine-fold'.

The *Vāmakes'vara*[2] demonstrates this non-difference in the passage beginning: '[The five S'aktis produce and the four Fires withdraw]. From the union of the five S'aktis and the four Fires there arises the *Cakra*. [When the Supreme S'akti sees Her own becoming (*Sphurattā*) then there arises the *Cakra*],' and ending with 'The *Cakra* is the form (*Rūpa*) of the Kāmakalā in that it is the going forth (*Prasāra*) of the Supreme Reality (*Paramārtha*).'

He speaks of the oneness of these two (the *Cakra* and the *Devatā*) in their subtle form (*Sūkṣma-rūpa*) by which is meant that which cannot be defined. The *S'rīcakra* in its subtle form is the *Bindu*. Its indefinableness is clearly shown in the passage: 'In the Supreme *Ākās'a* which is the Bindu (*Baindave paramākās'e*) and so on.' The indefinableness of the *Devatā* has also been shown in the verse beginning: 'The *Vidyā* (object of knowledge) is also like this (*Tādṛgātmā*)'. In the same way there is no difference between the two in their gross form. The grossness of the *Cakra* is in its expansions beginning with the *Trikoṇa* (triangle) and ending with the *Caturasra* (square), and the grossness of the *Devatā* is in Her gradual unfolding from *Tripurāmbikā* to *Tripurāsakti*.[3] The *Cakra* and the *Devatā*, who are as above described, cannot be separated. He gives a reason for it when he says that *Parā*, whereby is meant *Ādisakti*, is the subtle form of both these.

The *Catuhsatī* says[4]: 'The Mother of the origin of the three *Lokas* is both gross and subtle'. There is thus no difference between these two (*Cakra* and *Devatā*) for the wise.

S'ruti[5] also says: 'All this verily is the *Brahman*'. Also[6]: 'All men vanquish him who thinks that all things are outside the *Brahman*'.

The author himself says (V. 36): 'When She this *Mahesī Parā* unfolds as the *Cakra*'.

Thus it is established that the **Cakra** is the **form** (*Rūpa*) of the *Devatā*.

NOTES

[1] *Tripurā-mahopaniṣad*, 3. The meaning of the Text is—She was One as in *Binducakra* and became ninefold in the nine triangles of which the *Srīcakra* consists.

[2] *Nityā-ṣodasikā*, VI·8-24. The portion within the brackets has not been quoted by the Commentator, but added by the Translator to make it more intelligible to English readers. By "own" is meant "inherent".

[3] The nine *Cakras* of which the *Srīcakra* is composed are presided over by the Devī under nine different names, indicative of Her nine different aspects. These names are—(1) *Tripurā*, (2) *Tripuresvarī*, (3) *Tripurasundarī*, (4) *Tripuravāsinī*, (5) *Tripurāsrī*, (6) *Tripuramālinī*, (7) *Tripurāsiddhi*, (8) *Tripurāmbikā*, (9) *Mahātripurasundarī*. The first of these is in the Bhūpura and the last is in the Bindu. The *Āvaraṇa-Saktis* of each of these are classed as (1) *Prakatā*, (2) *Guptā*, (3) *Guptatarā*, (4) *Sampradāyā*, (5) *Kulakaulā*, (6) *Nigarbhā*, (7) *Rahasyā*, (8) *Atirahasyā* and (9) *Parāpararahasyā*, respectively.

[4] *Nityāṣodasikā*, IV-4.

[5] *Chāndogya*, 3-14-1.

[6] *Bṛhadāraṇyaka*, 2-4-6.

VERSES 22, 23 & 24

THE Centre of Cakra is *Parā (Parāmaya)*. This is Bindu-tattva. When It becomes ready to evolve (*Ucchūna*) It transforms and manifests as a triangle. This (triangle) is the source of the three (*S'aktis*, namely) *Pas'yantī* and others and is also the three *Bījas*. *Vāmā*, *Jyeṣṭhā*, *Raudrī*, *Aṁbikā* and *Parās'akti* are one portion (of the S'rīcakra)[1], *Icchā*, *Jñāna*, *Kriyā* and *S'āntā* are the other portion[2]. (These make nine). The two letters (*A* and *Ha*) taken separately and collectively make with the foregoing nine the eleven-fold *Pas'yantī*[3].

COMMENTARY

He here desires to speak of the S'rīcakra composed of nine triangles (*Navayonyātmaka*) which is the manifestation (*Vikāsarūpa*) of the S'aktis *Parā*, *Pas'yantī* and the rest. He first speaks of the Bindu called *Sarvānandamaya* which is *Parās'akti* (*Parās'aktimaya*).

Cakra. By this is meant the Cakra of nine triangles (*Navayonyātmaka*) and by **Centre of the Cakra**, Bindutattva. Bindusvarūpa has been already explained. The word **This** (*Idam*) signifies that It is in Itself (*Svasākṣātkṛtam*) Parā or Parās'aktisvarūpa. When this Bindutattva manifests then there is the Triangle. He therefore says **When it becomes ready to evolve.** (*Ucchūnam tac ca yadā*). The meaning is that when under the influence of the *Adṛṣṭa* of creatures the Baindava Tattva is about to **evolve** It transforms Itself into a triangle which is of the shape of a *S'ṛṅgāta* (*Trikoṇarūpeṇa pariṇataṁ spaṣṭaṁ*) and the product of the union of *A* (*Anuttarānanda*) and *I* (*Icchā*). So it has been said: When *Citi* which is *Anuttarānanda* is united with *Icchā* S'akti[4] there is a triangle which has the beauty of the joy of Creation (*Visargāmodasundaram*), Its light being dimmed as *Mātṛ*, *Māna*, *Meya* and *Pramā*. Its form is that of a *S'ṛṅgāta* or Triangle '.

This triangle is the source of the three Pasyanti and others (*Pas'yantyāditritaya-nidānam*) that is, the three S'aktis *Pas'yantī*,

Madhyamā and *Vaikharī* there originate. It is the S'aktis *Icchā*, *Jñāna* and *Kriyā* which change into the three S'aktis *Pas'yantī*, *Madhyamā* and *Vaikarī*. So it has been said in Vāmakes'vara Tantra (*Nityāṣoda*, vi. 38-40)[5]:

"She is then Icchās'akti manifesting as *Pas'yantī* (*Pas'yantī-vapuṣā sthitā*). Similarly as Jñānas'akti She is Jyeṣthā and *Madhyamā*, *Vāk* in the form of a straight line (*Ṛjurekhāmayī*) and protector of the universe. This same S'akti (Parā) as Kriyā (S'akti) is Raudrī and *Vaikharī Vāk* in the form of the body of the universe (*Vis'va-vigrahā*) and as that of a luminous triangle (*S'ṛngātavapurujjvalā*). At the time of Dissolution and Her return journey (*Pratyāvṛttikrameṇa*) She re-assumes the state of Bindu (*Baindavaṁ rūpaṁ*)."

The Triangle is the Svarūpa of the three Bījas[6] Vāgbhava, Kāmarāja and S'akti which are the three sections (*Khaṇḍa*) of the whole.

S'ruti[7] also speaks of:

"The three Puras[8] (Bindus) which move the Universe (*Vis'va-carṣaṇī*) along three paths wherein are placed the letters *A*, *Ka*, *Tha*[9] wherein again abides the impenetrable transcendent greatness of the Devatās." These and other similar texts in S'ruti speak of the celestial S'ṛṅgāta-pītha wherein abide the Mātṛkā (Mantra) of three sections which is the source wherefrom arise all Mantras. The Vāmakes'vara-Tantra (*Nityā-ṣoda*, VI, 48) also says:

"All these[10] are denoted by (*Vācyarūpāṇi*) the complete Mantra of three Bījas (*Bījatritaya-yukta*) both singly and collectively[11]. The Triangle containing three Bījas, the three S'aktis, the thee Lingas is the imperishable Kāmakalā."

He next says that the Bindutattva which becomes the S'rīcakra of nine Triangles (four of which are) upward and (five, downward turned is also the adorable Parā (*Parā-bhattārikāmayam*). He mentions Vāmā, Jyeṣthā, Raudrī and Aṁbikā by name and by the particle *cha* (also) he implies Parā S'akti and says that these are the five S'aktis indicated by the five reversed triangles which are the first portion (*Anuttarāṁs'abhūtāh = Anuttaraṁsāh*), of the S'ricakra; whilst the S'aktis Icchā, Jñānā, Kriyā, S'āntā are the other portion or the four triangles with their apex upward. (*Uttarāvayavāh = Ūrddhvamukha-trikoṇacatuṣtayarūpāh*).

The meaning of this is that Vāmā, Jyeṣthā, Raudrī, Aṁbikā, Parā S'akti, as also Icchā, Jñāna, Kriyā, S'āntā are unfolding stages of Parā (*Parāvilasanarūpāh*). These nine S'aktis are the nine triangles in the S'ricakra. This has been fully dealt with in the Vāmakes'vara Tantra (*Nityāshodashikā*, Ch. vi) in the passage which begins "When the Paramā Kalā wishes to see the Sphuraṇa" and ending "Vaikharī the body of the Universe"[12].

The two letters taken separately and collectively (*Vyastāvyasta-tadarṇadvayam*). By *Vyasta* is meant individual (*Vyaṣtirūpam*) and *Avyasta* is collective (*Samaṣtirūpam*). That is the two letter (*A* and *Ha*) which are the first and the last of the alphabet hold as in a vice between them all the letters of the Alphabet which are the mother of all Mantras within which two letters again iṣ the Experience (*Bhāva*) of complete 'I-ness' (*Pūrnā'ham*) which is the union of Prakās'a and Vimars'a or Bindutattva the eternal Kāmakalā. All this is well established in the Upaniṣads.

Here Parabrahman as complete 'I-ness' is to be known as united with His consort and as the doer of all actions; so the *Bṛhadā-raṇyaka* (1. 4. 1) says:

"This Ātmā there verily was in the beginning"[13] and thereby establishes that the Parabrahmasvarūpa is complete and transcendent 'I-ness' (*Pūṛṇa-parāhamtāmaya*) and union of celestial Wife and Husband. The Text proceeds in the passage quoted below to show that It shines forth as the creator of all Tattvas:

"He verily did not enjoy. For one (who is alone) does not enjoy. He desired a second. He verily was like woman and man in close embrace. He made this Self of His into two. Thereafter arose Husband and Wife"[14] and so on.

So also in another place in the same Upaniṣad (1-4-17) occurs the following Text:

"This Ātmā verily was alone in the beginning. He desired 'May there be wife (*Jāyā*) of mine'. May I be born as many. May I have possessions (*Vitta*). May I do acts. This verily is His desire (*Kāma*)" and so on.

Texts like these show the Brahman as united with His consort.

The two letters (*A* and *Ha*) already described will, if taken together and carefully considered, be seen to have eleven aspects.

The S'aktis Parā to S'āntā are ten if considered individually and are collectively one. Therefore Bindutattva is elevenfold (*Ekādas'ātmaka*) and is the cause of Pas'yantī S'akti. *S'ruti* (*Chāndogya* 3-14-1) says:

"All this verily is Brahman, from which all comes, in which all lives into which all returns. Therefore adore It with mind free from either attachment or avarice."

In this way the inseparateness of Cause and Effect is established.

NOTES

[1] *Anuttarāṁs'a-bhūta=lit.* First part. These are the five inverted triangles or Yonis of the S'rīcakra, or S'rīyantra.

[2] *Uttarāvayavāh.* These are the triangles with their apex upwards in the same.

[3] *Ekādas'ātma pas'yantī.*

[4] That is, A+I=E. The tip of Ekāra is formed like a triangle. The *Subhagodayavāsanā* cited in the Madras Ed., p. 6 says that the three S'aktis Icchā and others indicate the creation etc. of creatures (*Pas'u*).

[5] The two lines preceding are not given in the Commentary. vv. 36-40 describe the evolution of Paramā Kalā or Parā S'akti:

"When Paramā Kalā wishes to see the Sphuraṇa (desire to create), of Paramas'iva then She assumes the form of Aṁbikā and is called *Parā Vāk*. When She is about to manifest (*Sphutīkartum*) the universe then in its seed state, She is Vāmā and is so called because She throws out (or vomits; *Vis'vasya vamanāt*). She then assumes the form of a goad (which is of crooked form)".

[6] Namely, *Aiṁ, Klīṁ, Sauh.*

[7] *Tripurāmahopaniṣad.*

[8] *i.e.* Tripurā.

[9] *That is*, the letters of the alphabet is in the *A-ka tha* triangle. This is formed by three Bindus between each of which there are 16 letters forming the sides of the triangle. At the corners of the triangle are the remaining three letters *Ha*, *La*, and *Ksha*.

[10] That is Lingas mentioned in the preceding verses namely the four Itara, Bāṇa, Svayaṁbhu and Parama.

[11] *Kula-kaulamayāni.* Kula=Mātṛ, Māna, Meya, that is Svayaṁbhu Bāṇa and Itara Lingas. Kaula is the collectivity of these three or Paramalinga.

[12] See the passage quoted *ante*, p. 38.

[13] See Verse 13 *ante* commentary.

[14] *Sa vai naiva reme, yasmād ekāki na ramate, sa dvitīyam aicchat. Sa haitāvānāsa yathā strīpumāṁsau samparishvaktau. Sa imam evātmānaṁ dvedhāpātayat. Tatah patish ca painī ca abhavatāṁ.*

VERSE 25

In this way the united Kāma and Kalā are the (three) letters whose own form (*Svarūpa*) is the three Bindus. It is She who is the Mother manifest as the three Gunas (*Triguṇa-svarūpiṇī*) and who assumed the form of the triangle.

Commentary

He next wishes to speak of the mode of creation of the Cakra wherein are the Cakras of eight triangles, ten triangles and so on, and before doing so explains the origin of the triangular Cakra which precedes them all.

In this way (*Evam*). That is in manner already described.

The united Kama and Kala (*Kāmakalātmā*). By Kāma is meant Paramas'iva who is pure Illumination (*Prakās'aikasvabhāvah*) and is the first letter which is *A* [1], and Kalā signifies Vimars'a the last of letters (*Ha*). This dual character (*Ubhayātmakatva*) indicates the possession of experience of complete 'I-ness' which is its true nature (*Svābhāvikaparipūrṇāhaṁbhāvas'ālitvam*). This has been fully explained in verse 7. The Kāmakalātmā who as previously described is "**the (three) letters whose own form (Svarupa) is the three Bindus**" (*Tribindutattvasvarūpavarṇamyī*). The three Bindus are the Red, White and Mixed Bindus previously spoken of. Bindutattva is the Bindus previously described. The three letters, by which is meant the Vāgbhava and other Bījas, are forms of the three Bindus. In the *Rahasyāmnāya* (S'iva addressing the Devī) says:

"Know this, that the beautiful S'ṛṅgāta which is Thy very self (*Svātma-s'ṛṅgāta*) is made up of three Bindus mixed, white and red. It is ancient (*Purāṇa*) and is the Pranava itself. It can be known by the three lines (which compose it). It is pure knowledge (*Saṁvin-mātra*) and is of the nature of S'iva. The red is self sustained

(*Nirādhāra*). The other (white) is its beloved and their union is the mixed Bindu. In the Union is the pure state which is Nirvāṇa". **It is she** (*Sā iyam*=she (is) this). By *Sā* (She), the author draws the attention of his reader to Her who is the supreme reality as the experience of the massive Bliss which is Cit (*Cidānanda-ghanarasa-paramārthā*) and who is the essence of all the tradition (*Sakalāṁnāyasārabhūtā*)[2] and by *Iyam* (This), he as it were points Her out as the One who is being experienced (*Anubhūyamānā*) as the Ātmā who witnesseth (*Ātmasākṣitvena*) by great Yogīs who are immersed in the feeling of their identity with the Universe (*Visvāhaṁbhāvanās'ālibhih*) and is **Manifest as the three Gunas** (*Triguṇasvarūpiṇī*). She is Icchā, Jñānā, Kriyā which appear (in the Pas'u) as the three Guṇas Sattva, Rajas and Tamas. It is through these Guṇas as instruments that She effects Creation and the like. She is therefore the **Mother** (*Mātā*) the one Creatrix of all the World. She is also the Parā S'akti who transcends all the Tattvas (*Sarvatattvātītā*) for *S'ruti* (*Aita.* 1-1.) says:

" This Ātmā alone, verily, was in the beginning ".

Assumed the form of the triangle (*Trikoṇarūpam yātā*) that is she changed into the form of a triangle as a result of the union of the supreme Bliss symbolised by the letter *A* with Icchā, Creative Will, symbolised by the letter *I*. This is the Cakra[3] of triangular form which is most secret and called *Sarvasiddhi-pradāyaka* or that which accomplishes all.

The wise know no difference between the Mahes'ī and the Cakra. Parā Herself is the subtle form of both these (Devatā and Cakra). There is no difference between the two in the gross form also.

NOTES

[1] *Anuttarākṣarātmā.*

[2] *That is*, it is She to whom all the *Āṁnāyas* point.

[3] The first triangle which contains the Bindu which is the first transformation of Bindu.

VERSES 26 & 27

SHE who is next (to *Parā*) is Pas'yantī the Creative Self (*Sṛṣṭyātmā*) out of which originated the individual mothers (*Vyaṣṭi-mātṛ*) Vāmā and others. By reason of this She became ninefold form (*Navātmā*). She the mother Madhyamā is as shown by her two names of two kinds (*Dvividhā*), namely, subtle (*Sūkṣmā*) and gross of form (*Sthūlākṛti*). As subtle She is ever existent and the nine sounds (*Navanāda-mayī*) as gross She is the nine groups (of letters) and bears the name of Bhūtalipi.

COMMENTARY

He next speaks of Pas'yantī who is a manifestation of Parā as of ninefold aspect (*Navātmaka*) in the form of the Cakra of nine triangles (*Nava-yoni-cakrātmanā*).

"**She who is next**" (*Tadanyā*). That is Pas'yantī who is the manifestation of Parā (*Parāvikās'abhūtā*) is **the Creative Self out of which originated the individual mothers Vama and others** (*Vāmādi-vyaṣṭi-mātri-sṛṣṭyātmā*) or in other words She is the nine S'aktis beginning with Vāmā and ending with S'āntā (*Vāmādi-s'āntānta-s'akti-navakamayī*). It is on this account that the mother (*Mātā*= *Jananī*) is of ninefold aspect (*Navātmā*), that is, she becomes the Cakra of nine triangles which is the Cause of the appearance of the group of S'aktis beginning with Vāmā and ending with S'āntā.

Vāmā is so called because she as producer of the universe (*Vis'vajanayatrī*) throws out the Universe of five elements (*Prapañca*) which is within the S'ṛṅgāta (*S'ṛṅgātāntah-sthitaprapañca-vamanāt*). Jyeṣthā is all-beneficent; Raudrī destroys or dispels all ailments and Aṁbikā grants all things desired.[1] So it has been said:

"Vāmā (is so called) because of (Her) throwing out the Universe, Jyeṣthā (is so called) because she is beneficent (*S'iva-mayī*) Raudrī destroys all disease and burns up[2] (the fruit of) all actions (*Dogdhrī cākhila-karmaṇām*)".

Of Aṁbikā the Pratyabhijñā says that "She the impulse to becoming (*Sphurattā*) is pure Being (*Mahāsattā*)". She is therefore Parā vāk who excels all (*Sarvātis'āyinī*) and sees Her own impulse to manifestation which is Her own and full Self. (*Paripūrṇa-svarūpa-svātmasphuraṇāvalokanacaturā*).

The Vāmakes'vara (*Nityā-ṣodas'ikā* vi. 36) also says:

"When the Paramā kalā sees the impulse to becoming (*Sphuraṇa*) of the Ātmā then she assumes the form of Aṁbikā and is called Parā vāk."

The S'aktis Icchā, Jñānā and Kriyā take the forms Pas'yantī, Madhyamā and Vaikharī (*Pas'yantī-Madhyamā-Vaikharī-rūpāh*). This has been stated in detail in the Vāmakes'vara (*Nitya-ṣodas'ikā*) in the verses quoted in commentary to verse 22 *ante*.

S'āntā is S'akti as Consciousness (*Cinmayī S'akti*) who is all pervading (*Niraṅkus'a*): For *S'ruti* speaks of "the transcendental (*Niṣkala*) actionless (*Niṣkriya*) and tranquil (*S'ānta*)"[3].

He next speaks of the ninefold character (*Navātmakatva*) of Madhyamā. Madhyamā is the state of Union (*Samarasāvasthā*) of Parā and Pas'yantī. She is visible or realisable by Yogīs whose minds are inward turned (*Antarmukha*). This S'akti is **by Her two names** (which describe Her function) **of two kinds** (according to Her functions). She is either **Sthula (gross)** or **Suksma (subtle)**. As subtle She can be apprehended by the power of Samādhi. As gross She is capable of utterance as letters of the alphabet alike by the learned and illiterate. As subtle She is ever-existent[4] (*Sthitā=Sarvadā vartamānā*) and as such She is the nine sounds or Nādas (*Navanāda-mayī*). As gross She is the nine groups of the letters of the alphabet (*Navavargātmā*).

The sense of the above is this:—

When the Great Mother Kuṇḍalinī who contains many kinds of sound does in consequence of the breath being restrained leave the place of Mitrāvaruṇa[5] and after piercing the lotuses of Svādhiṣṭhāna and others goes upward to reach the place of Paramas'iva who is on the lotus of twelve petals. She is experienced by the great Sādhakas of S'iva[6] when in Samādhi as their very own self (*Svātmatvena*).

She is the nine sounds (*Navanādamayī*). This will be understood from the following text from the *Haṁsopanishad* :—

" We shall now make clear the meaning of Haṁsa and Paramahaṁsa to the Brahmacārin who has controlled his inclination (*S'ānta*) who has controlled his senses (*Dānta*) and who is devoted to his Guru. This Haṁsa pervades all bodies like fire in wood and oil in sesamum seed. Knowing it, one reaches not death. The anus should (first) be contracted, then the air should be led upwards [7] and made to go round the Svādhiṣthāna three times, it should then be made to go through Maṇipūra and Anāhata and the airs (*Prāṇān*) should be stopped in the Viṣuddha Cakra, The Ājñā Cakra and then the Brahmarandhra should be meditated upon. Whilst so meditating (the Sādhaka) should constantly think of himself as the Trimātra (Oṁkāra). He should next meditate upon Nāda, as extending from the Mūlādhāra, which Nāda is like pure crystal (*S'uddha-sphatika-saṁkās'a*) for this is verily Brahman the Paramātmā." By this the Upaniṣad teaches that the Svarūpa of the Mūlakuṇdalinī, who pervades the body from the Mūlādhāra to the Brahmarandhra, is Nādātmaka.

The text in a later passage says :

" When Haṁsa becomes dissolved into (*Līna*) Nāda then (arises the state which is) *Turyātīta*, *Unmanana* (mindless) and *Ajapopasaṁhāra* (=cessation of breathing)."

Nāda is divided (by this Upaniṣad) as follows :

" Sound arises of ten kinds. *Ciṇi* is the first, *Ciṇiciṇi* is the second. The third is bell sound (*Ghaṇṭānāda*). Sound of conchshell (*S'aṁkhanāda*) is the fourth. The fifth is the sound from a stringed instrument (*Tantrīnāda*). The sound of of cymbals (*Tālanāda*) is the sixth. The seventh is the sound of a flute (*Venunāda*) and eighth that of a kettledrum (*Bherīnāda*). The ninth is the sound of clay-made drum (*Mṛdaṅga*) and the tenth the sound of thunder (*Meghanāda*). After the ninth has been experienced the tenth [8] should practised. The mind dissolves in that. When the mind is so dissolved when Saṁkalpa and Vikalpa [9] cease when merit and demerit [10] are burnt then there appears (*Prakās'ate*) Sadās'iva who is S'akti (*S'aktyātmā*) Omnipresent (*Sarvatrāvasthita*) Light itself (*Svayaṁjyotih*) Pure (*S'uddha*) Illumined (*Buddha*) Eternal (*Nitya*) Stainless [11] (*Nirañjana*) and Tranquil (*S'ānta*)."

"**She is the nine groups of the letters**" (*Navavargātmā*). The nine groups are A, Ka, Ca, Ṭa, Ta, Pa, Ya, S'a and La [12].

By **sthula (gross)** is meant that she is within the range of all ordinary experience (*Sarvaviṣaya-vyavahārinī*).

Bhutalipis are manifested letters (*Bhūtās' ceti lipayas'ceti*). The existingness (*Bhūtatvam*) of the letters consists in their capability of being uttered or expressed by particular efforts (*Ceṣtā*). The production of these letters again is merely mechanical (*Tac-ca kalpanāmāt-raṁ eva*) for the letters themselves are energies (*Tejorūpa*) and therefore S'akti (*S'aktyātmaka*). The Devī (*Madhyamā*) bears the name or designation (*Ākhyā*) of these.

The *Tantra-sadbhāva* also says:

"The Mātṛkā who (manifested) in this world is in inseparable relation with (*Samanvitā*) the Supreme Light (*Paratejah*), pervades all things from Brahmā to the worlds. (She) O adored of the Suras (=*Devas*) pervades the whole universe as Nāda. Beloved, (She is) like the letter *A* in all letters. I shall now speak so that Thou mayest clearly understand it. The S'akti who is Supreme (*Parā*), Subtle (*Sūkṣmā*) and Formless (*Nirākārā*) is asleep coiled round the Bindu in Mūlādhāra [13] like a serpent. There also is asleep the self-controlled (*Yamī*) Great Yogī who knows and desires nothing. With Her belly distended by the Moon, Sun, Fire, the Stars, the fourteen Worlds (*Bhuvanāni caturdas'a*) She is in a swoon as if poisoned. Awakened by the Great Sound (*Pareṇa ninādena*) and churned by the fire in Her belly), She becomes free from Her bondage (*Bandhana*) and conscious (*Jñānarūpiṇī*). The churning [14] is circular in movement and continued in the body of the S'akti till She wakes up. When the first unfolding or Division (*Bheda*) takes place Bindu attains the state of Nāda. Thus (or by this) Kuṇdalī the Subtle Time (*Kālasūks'mā*) is awakened. The Bindu which comes after (*Uttaraga*) S'akti (Nāda) is the Lord (*Prabhu*) who is the four Kalās [15] (*Catuṣ-kalāmaya*). In the middle part or second stage of churning (*Madhyamanthanayogena*) there is straightness (*Ṛjutva i.e.* a straight line) which is Jyeṣthā S'akti beautifully placed between two Bindus. The imperishable Kuṇdalī (*Amṛtakuṇdalī*) is led by Vaīkhārī to the Bindu-nāda state (*Bindunādatva*) [16]. She is (then) known as Lākinī [17] between the two Bindus. She is then Tripadā (Third step) and spoken of as Raudrī,

She is (also) called Rodhinī because she obstructs the path of Liberation (*Mokṣamārga-nirodhanāt*) [18]. Aṁbikā's form is that of a portion of the moon,—She is Ardha-candrikā, the half-moon. The Parā-S'akti who is one does in this way appear as three. From them [19] as thus distinguished (*Ābhyo viviktābhyah*) have originated the nine group of letters (*Navavargakāh*) which are associated (*Yuktāh*) with them. It is She (*Parās'akti Kuṇdalī*) who is thought of in nine ways being indicated by the nine groups (*Navavargopalakṣitā*) " [20].

NOTES

[1] Verses 26-28 are quoted by Lakṣmīdhara in his Commentary to the Saundaryalaharī, v. 34 and he reads them differently.

[2] The text is *Dogdhrī*=She who milks or brings forth, but probably is a mistake for *Dagdrī*=She who burns up.

[3] S'ānta is the state of absolute quiescence when there is no activity or motion; Samarasāvasthā is the state in which two are in a state of absolute and complete absorption the one by the other.

[4] *That is*, of course during the *Kalpa*.

[5] *That is*, Mūlādhāra.

[6] Mahāmāhes'varas—These are Sādhakas who have attained a high degree of perfection—adepts.

[7] *That is*, from the Mūlādhāra.

[8] The tenth is Param Brahma.

[9] The state of selection, and rejection, of this and that of all variety, in short ordinary finite experience.

[10] Puṇya and Pāpa.

[11] *That is*, one in whom there is no doubt, the perfect experiencer.

[12] This according to the commentator. Others divide the vowels into two groups and exclude the last.

[13] In the text the word is "*Hrid-Bindu.*" But this is possibly a mistake for *Mrid-bindu*, by which is meant the Svayaṁbhulinga in mūlādhāra which is the region of Earth=*Prithvī*=*Mrid*. Here the cosmic mūlādhāra is spoken of.

[14] *That is*, the cosmic *manthana*.

[15] *Nivṛtti, Pratiṣthā, Vidyā, S'ānti.*

[16] *That is*, the place where the first Bindu is.

[17] *Lākinī*=*Raudrī*. *Dākinī*=*Brāhmī*. *Rākinī*=*Jyeṣthā* or *Vaiṣṇavī*.

[18] As it were a barrier preventing what is above descending and what is below ascending and straying away from the true path. Or the reading may probably be *Bodhinī* and *Nibodhanāt*.

[19] The three S'aktis Vāmā etc.

[20] The text seems in part correct. Madras edition throws no light on the right reading, but quotes the passage practically in the same terms.

VERSE 28

THE first (*i.e.* subtle *Madhyamā*) is the cause (*Kāraṇa*) and the other (*i.e.* gross *Madhyamā*) is the effect (*Kārya*). Inasmuch as such is (the relation) between these two therefore the latter (*i.e.* the gross) is the (same as the) former (*i.e.* the subtle). There is verily no difference (between the two), for the identity of cause (*Hetu*) and effect (*Hetumat*) is axiomatic (*Diṣṭa*).

COMMENTARY

The subtle Madhyamā which is the cause of the Madhyamā of gross form is one with the latter and that is stated here.

"**The first**" (*Ādyā*) *i.e.* the one first spoken of (*Pūrvoktā*), whereby is meant the subtle (*Sūkṣmā*) Madhyamā already described. She is **the cause** (*Kārana*) because she precedes **the other** (*Anyā*). This latter is gross (*Sthūlā*) *i.e.* **the effect** (*Kārya*) because it emanates from the other (*Tajjanyatvāt*). As there is this relation of cause and effect between these two (*Anayoh*), namely, the subtle and gross Madhyamā, therefore, **the latter** (*Iyam*) is the **former** (*Sā*=She). There is no difference (*Bheda*) between the two. **Identity** (*Tādātmya*=that in which there is neither difference nor nondifference) is the characteristic of **Cause** and **Effect**, as we see in the case of mud and the (mud-made) pot.

S'ruti (*Chāndogya* 6. 1. 4) also says :

"O Gentle one, by one lump of clay all things made of clay are known. The variation is in names given to it when spoken of. The clay alone is real."

The same thing becomes different only as an object of speech. When anything is spoken of it becomes of two kinds[1].

NOTE

[1] *e.g.* A mud-pot becomes mud and pot.

VERSES 29 & 30

THE Cakra of eight triangles which is constituted of the letters S'a, Ṣa, Sa and the Pa-varga is an expansion (*Vistāra*) of the middle triangle. These nine triangles together with the Bindu make the ten (*Das'aka*) which are lighted by the light of Cit (*Cid-dīpa*). The two lights (*Chāyādvitayam*) of these ten are spread forth[1] as two Cakras of ten triangles each of which the inner set of ten triangles display the Ta-varga and *T*a-varga and the outer of ten triangles display the Ca-varga and Ka-varga.

COMMENTARY

He next speaks of the appearance (*Àvirbhāva*) of Vaikharī-S'akti by a description of the Cakra of eight triangles and other Cakras (all) which are the going forth (*Prasarana*) of the Light and Energy (*Tejas*) of the middle triangle (*Madhya-s'ṛṅgāta*).

The Cakra of eight triangles is called *Sarvarogahara* (All-disease-destroyer). The eight triangles of which it consists are the eight letters namely the letters S'a, Ṣa, Sa and the five letters of the Pa-varga. It **is an expansion** (*Vistāra=Vikāsa*) of the **middle triangle** (*Madhyatrikoṇa*). The **nine triangles** (*Navakoṇa*) are the middle triangle and the eight triangles (here spoken of); these **together with the Bindu** (*Madhyang ca*) make a group of ten (*Das'aka*). This group of ten is illumined (*Dīpita*) by the **light of Cit** (*Cid-dīpa*), that is, it is lustrous with the rays which surround Tripurā—the Mother seated in the Bindu-Cakra (*Binducakrādhirūdhāṁbā*) who is Light Herself (*Tejomūrti*). So it has been said *Nityāṣoda*. VI. 14):

"The Bindu is the seat of union of the Fire of final Dissolution and Citkalā"[1]. In this way the ten and their **two lights** (*Chāyā-dvitayam=Kāntidvitayam*) are spread out. By **the ten** (*Das'aka*) is meant the aforementioned three Cakras[3] which are a mass of light (*Tejorāśimaya*). *Chāya* here means *Kānti* (Lustre, light).

These two lights become **spread forth** (*Vitata*) as the **two Cakras of ten triangles (each)**. These are the inner and outer Cakras of ten triangles each which also are of boundless brilliance (*Niravadhika-Tejomaṇḍala*). **The two lights** (*Kānti-dvitaya*) relate to these two. The two Cakras are called *Sarvarakṣākara* (All-protector) and *Sarvārtha-Sādhaka* (All-accomplisher). By **Spread** (*Vitata*) is meant evolved (*Pariṇata*). So it has been said (*Nitāyṣoda*. VI, 15 : " The Cakra of ten triangles is the form of the manifested light of the nine triangles "[4]. The ten letters of the Ta-varga and *T*a-varga are the triangles in the inner Cakra of ten triangles and the ten letters of Ca-varga and Ka-varga are the triangles in the outer Cakra.

Notes

[1] *Vitatam*. Bhāskararāya who cites portions of these two verses in his commentary to VI. 16 of *Nityāṣodaśikā* reads *Dṛṣṭam* (seen). The two lights are the two Cakras of ten triangles each. There are in the whole Yantra 43 triangles.

[2] *Baindavāsana - saṁrūdha - saṁvartānala - citkalām*. *Baindava* = *Bindu*. This Bindu is the *Āsana* by which is meant that it is the source of the inclination of seeing (Īkṣaṇātmakavṛtti). On this is seated the union of *Saṁvartānala* and *Citkalā*. By *Samvartānala* is meant the Fire of *Pralaya*, the all-devourer *Kālāgnirudra* and *Citkalā* is Tripurā (Bhāskara).

[3] *Bindu*, *Trikona*, *Vasukoṇa* (eight triangle).

[4] *Navatrikoṇa-spurita-prabhārūpadashārakam*. The nine triangles taken individually and collectively with the Bindu make ten.

VERSE 31

THE light of these (the first) four Cakras is the fully evolved (second or outer) Cakra of ten triangles. (Then) appeared the Cakra of fourteen triangles wherein are the fourteen vowel letters beginning with *A*.

COMMENTARY

The lights of these (first) four Cakras (*Etach-cakra-catushka-prabā-sameta*). The four Cakras are Bindu, Trikona, eight-triangled and inner ten-triangled Cakras. The second or outer Cakra of ten trlangles is here described as the **fully evolved (second or outer) Cakra of ten triangles** (*Das'āraparināmah*). This second ten-triangled Cakra is united (*Sameta*=*Saṁyukta*) with the light of the first four Cakras, that is the light of the four Cakras spreads over this Cakra on account of its proximity to the others. So it has been said (*Nityāṣoda*. VI. 17:

"United with the light of the four Cakras is the evolved (Cakra)."

In this verse is also described the appearance of the Cakra of fourteen triangles wherein are the fourteen **vowel letters beginning with A**. This Cakra is called *Sarvasaubhāgyadāyaka* (Grantor of all-prosperity).

VERSE 32

PARĀ, Pas'yantī and Madhyamā in her form or aspect as (the unuttered) gross letters,—by these three is produced Vaikharī who is the fifty-one letters of the alphabet.

COMMENTARY

After giving a description of the Cakras beginning with the Bindu and ending with the Cakra of fourteen triangles, he here speaks of the appearance of Vaikharī S'akti. The Nature (*Lakṣaṇa*) of Parā and other S'aktis has already been described. What is said here is that Vaikharī[1] who is all-sound (*Sarva-s'abdātmikā*) is the creatrix (*Nirmātrī*) of the entire universe (*Akhilaprapañca*) which is composed of the collectivity of the letters (*Akṣara-rās'imaya*) beginning with A and ending with Kṣa. *Vaikharī* has been spoken of (*Nityāṣoda*. VI. 40) as pervading the universe or as the "world-form (*Vis'va-vigrahā*)."

NOTE

[1] *Madhyamā* as *Sūkṣmā* is *Navanāda-mayī* and as *Sthūlā, Navavargātmā*. The letters are formed as Madhyamā but unuttered. See vv. 26 and 27 *ante*. *Madhyamā* as the unuttered gross letters in the evolution of speech is the stage immediately preceding *Vaikharī*.

VERSE 33

THE eight groups of letters beginning with the Ka group which are Vaikharī S'akti are on the petals of the lotus of eight petals and it should always be borne in mind that, this, the lotus of sixteen petals has on its petals the (S'aktis which are the) vowel letters.

COMMENTARY

He here says that the two Cakras, *Sarvasaṁkṣobhaṇa* (All-moving)[1] and *Sarvās'āpāripūraka* (Fulfilling all hopes)[2] are composed of the Vaikharī letters (*Vaikharīvarṇātmaka*).

Are Vaikhari Sakti. By this is meant that these, **the eight groups of letters** (*Aṣṭa-vaikharīvargāh*) the first of which is the **Ka=group** (*Kādi*) are *Vaikharīs'akti* (*Vaikharīs'aktisvarūpāh*).

The lotus of eight petals. (*Aṣṭadalābja*). This is the *Sarva-saṁkṣobhaṇa-cakra*. **This the lotus of sixteen petals has on its petals the vowel letters** (*Svaragaṇa-samuditam etad dvyaṣṭadalāmbhoruham*). The vowel letters (*Svaragaṇa*) are the letters A and others, sixteen in number which are (*Samuditam=Samyagbhāvitam*) the petals of the sixteen-petalled lotus.

This (*Etat*). By this we are to understand that the author points to something visible (*Paridṛs'yamānam*).

Should always be borne in mind. (*Saṁcityam*) that is, should be meditated upon (*Sarvadā bhāvanīyam*).

NOTES

[1] Or it may be All-moulding.

[2] Or it may be Filling-all space.

VERSE 34

THE (three) circles[1] are the transformations (*Vikara*) of the three lights emanating from the three Bindus. These are the circles in the Bhūpura (*Bhūbimbatrayam etat*). The three mothers Pashyantī and others[2] here rest.

COMMENTARY

The (three) circles (*Tānī vrittāni*). These are the circles which surround the Cakras of fourteen triangles, the lotus of eight petals and the lotus of sixteen petals.

Three Bindus (*Bindutraya*). These are the previously spoken of red, white and mixed Bindus. **The three lights** (*Tejaṣtritaya*) are of the substance (*Tanmaya*) of the three Bindus as they proceed therefrom.

By speaking of the three circles as the three lights the Cakra is shown to be composed of the threefold division of Moon, Sun and Fire (*Somasūryānalatrikhandamaya*); so *Āgama* says:

"The *Mātṛkā Cakra* is of three divisions consisting of Moon, Sun and Fire."

By **transformations** (*Vikāra*) we have to understand the three circles of the three Bindus and their lights. In these circles abide the Shaktis[3] *Aṇimā* and others, *Brāhmī* and others and *Sarvasaṁkṣobhiṇī* and others.

The three mothers Pasyanti and others here rest (*Pas'yantyādi-tri-mātṛ-vis'rāntih*). The meaning of this is that the three S'aktis Pashyantī, Madhyamā and Vaikharī are up to this place luminous (*Vijṛṁbhamānā*), that is, they function from the Trikoṇa to the Bhūpura. This has been fully dealt with in the Vāmakes'vara (*Nityāṣoda*. Ch. VI. 36-40).

NOTES

[1] The three lines are according to some immediately outside the sixteen-petalled lotus.

[2] *i.e.* Madhyamā and Vaikharī.

[3] As to the place of these S'aktis there are divergent views.

VERSE 35

MOVEMENT is either Pada-vikṣepa[1] or Kramodaya and is therefore said to be of two kinds, namely, the S'aktis[2] who surround Her and the line of Gurus. These two are the movements of the lotus feet of the Mother (*Aṁbāpadāmbuja-parasara*).

COMMENTARY

After having fully described the S'rīcakra of Mahātripurasudarī he in fifteen verses (35-49) speaks of the group of S'aktis in the Cakra which surround Her (*Āvaraṇa-cakrāntargatas'aktinikuruṁba*) and of the Guru-maṇḍala which is near Her, as the unfolding (*Parinati*) of the body or limbs (*Avayava*) of the Devī.

Movement (*Kramaṇa*). The word literally means walking (*Padakrama*) Motion is effected by *Padavikṣepa* or by *Kramodaya.*

By **Padaviksepa** is meant the power of Sundarī to produce countless S'aktis who are the countless millions of Her rays.

S'ṛuti (*Aruṇopaniṣad*) also says:

"The rays which are Self-originated are what made bodies (*S'arīrāṇi*)." *Bhairava-yāmala*[3] also says:

"In the Bindu united with Sadās'iva is the Mahes'varī who creates, maintains and withdraws the Worlds (*Jagadut-patti-sthiti-saṁghāra-kārinī*) and is beyond the Tattvas (*Tattvātītā*). She is Light itself (*Jyotīrūpā*) and transcendent (*Parākārā*). O S'ivā! emanating from Her body are rays in thousands, two thousand, hundred thousand, ten millions, hundred millions there is no counting their great numbers. It is by and through Her that all things moving and motionless shine. O Mahes'ānī! It is by the light of this Devī that all things become manifest. There is nothing which bereft of Her light can be manifest. Without the creative thinking (*Citi*) of Her who is Cit (*Cidrūpā*) and S'ivas'akti this moving and motionless world would of a certainty be enveloped in Darkness (*Āndhyam āpadyate nūnam*).

"O Mahes'varī of the countless millions of rays which are Moon, Sun and Fire (*Soma-sūryānalātmanā*) there are three hundred and sixty which are spread throughout (*Vyas'nuvūvānāh*) the Brahmānda which is in the midst thereof.' Fire has one hundred and eight. Sun one hundred and sixteen and Moon one hundred and thirty-six rays. O S'aṁkarī, these illumine the macrocosm (*Brahmāṇda*) and the microcosm (*Piṇdāṇda*) also. The Sun (illumines) the day the Moon the night and Fire the twilights (morning and evening): thus is time divided (*Prakās'ayantah kālāṁ ste*) : therefore these three (Sun, Moon and Fire) are time (*Kālātmakās trayah*). Three hundred and sixty days make a year and S'ruti[4] says that Mahādeva who is lord of creatures (*Prajāpati*) is the year" (*Hāyanātmā*)."

By **Kramodaya** is meant going forth (*Prasaraṇa*) of the Devī as the Gurumandalas[5] of the Divya, Siddha and Mānava groups whose number is endless and whose nature is illumination (*Prakās'ātmaka*). **Saktis who surround Her.** *Āvaraṇaṁ* (=anything that surrounds or encloses or prevents the view) is used in the text to signify the countless S'aktis abiding in what are commonly called Āvaraṇa Cakras of the Devī. By **line of Gurus** (*Gurupaṅgktih*) is meant the circle or Mandala of Gurus (as above described). **These two** are the going forth (*Prasara=Prasaraṇa*) or efflorescence (*Vijriṁbhaṇa*) of the **lotus feet**, that is, feet which are (*S'rīpādayuga*) of the Mother Tripurā.

So it has been said :

"The light (*Mahah=Tejah*) of Tripurā is (it is so declared) divided in many million ways but in the midst of these shines transcendent Mahātripura-sundarī Herself."

NOTES

[1] The forms of *Kramaṇa* are explained in the commentary which follows. *Padavikṣepa* literally means "step by step" in defined direction. *Kramodaya*=gradual expansion and unfolding in all direction.

[2] *Āvaranaṁ i.e. avaraṇa shaktis.* These obstruct men from seeing the Devī like a patch of cloud which is much smaller than the sun yet prevents it being seen.

[3] Lakṣmīdhara in his commentary on *Saundaryalaharī* v. 24 points out that the passage in *Bhairavayāmala* beginning: "It is by the light of this Devi" explains the S'ruti text which says "There is no sun no moon" quoted under verse 1 of this book.

[4] See *Sāṁkhāyāna Āraṇyaka I. Taittirīya Brāhmaṇa* 1. 6. 2.

[5] Cf. *Bhāvanopaniṣad.* I. *S'rīguruh sarvakāraṇabhūtā s'aktih.* The Guru is the S'akti the Cause of all; also see *Tantrarāja* (XXXV. 2) (Kādimata "*Gururādyā bhavech chaktih*"—The Guru is the primordial Sakti.

VERSE 36

WHEN She, this all-excelling Great Queen changes into the form of the Cakra, then the limbs of Her body change into *Avaraṇadevatās.*

COMMENTARY

The author now speaks in an orderly form of the mode of Her going forth (*Prasāraprasaranī*).

She, this (*Seyam*). By this the author emphasizes that She is the mass of continuous and endless light and energy ***Aparicchinnānanta-tejorāśimayī***).

All-excelling (*Parā=Sarvotkṛṣṭā*) **Great Queen** (*Maheśī*). By this is to be understood that She is conscious of Her all-embracing imperial dominion (***Sāṁrājya***) and powers (***Saṁpad=Vibhūti***), that She is Bliss eternal, boundless and immense and that She is adored by countless millions of Yoginis.

Into the form of the Cakra (***Cakrākāreṇa***). By Cakra here is meant the S'rīcakra made up of nine Cakras the first of which is ***Bindu*** and the last ***Trailokyamohan.*** This is the Cakra which is spoken of (***Nityāṣoda.*** VI. 13) as " the Cakra of nine Cakras wherein are nine different Mantras." **Changes into** (*Pariṇameta*). That is when " She sees the Sphurattā of the Ātmā," [1] by which is meant when She sees the Ātmā who is complete Bliss and changes or assumes another form. (***Pariṇameta=Ākārāntaram āvaheta***).

Limbs of Her body change into (***Taddehāvayavānāṁ pariṇatih***). Her body (***Deha***) is a mass of light (***Tejahpunjātmaka***). The limbs (***Avayava***) of the body are the rays. 'Change' is assumption of another state or condition (***Parinatih=Āvasthāntarāpattih***).

Here the surrounding Devatās (***Āvaraṇadevatāh***) are the countless S'aktis such as the groups of ***Vaśinī*** and others, ***Aṇimā*** and others, who are part of the ocean of Conciousness-bliss (*Cidā-nanda-samud-rātmaka*). The countless millions of S'aktis appear and disappear like bubbles (*Budbuda*) on the face of the ocean.

S'ruti[2] says:

"That in which all beings (*Bhāvah*) disappear and from which those which disappeared reappear again and again disappear and grow again like bubbles."

Also *Āgama* (*Nityaṣod*

"Such is the Tejas (Cakra is composed, the S'aktis therei

[1] *Nityāṣoda* VI. 10 and

[2] This is seemingly *Cūl* is slightly different from the printed text.

VERSES 37 & 38

SHE (who is) Devī Tripura-sundarī abides in the *Bindu-maya-cakra.* (There) She is seated in the lap of Kāmes'vara, a digit of the moon is placed by Her as on adornment on Her forehead. She holds in Her hands the noose, the goad, the sugarcane bow and the five flowery arrows. She is red like the rising sun. The Moon, the Sun and the Fire are Her three eyes.

COMMENTARY

Before giving an account of the *Āvaraṇa-S'aktis*, namely, *Vas'inī* and others he here describes the nature (*Svarūpa*) of the Chief or Principal Devatā (*Mūladevatā*).

By the **Bindumaya-cakra** is meant the Supreme Ether (*Paramākās'a*). The Bindu has elsewhere been spoken of as Paramākās'a (*Baindave paramākās'e*). The Bindu is called *Sarvānandamaya-cakra* (Cakra of All-bliss).

By Cakra is meant the *Pītha* in which She may unite and enjoy with the Ātmā. (*Ātma-saṁkramaṇa-viharanārha-pītha*).

S'ruti says:

" Wherein She moved that became the Cakra "[1].

" **Abides in** " (*Āsīnā*) that is She is shining above the Bindu (*Bindupariprades'e virājamānā*). "**She (who is) Devi Tripura-sundari**" (*Sā Tripura-sundarī Devī.*) The pronoun **She** (*Sā*) is used here to impress on the mind the fact that She is the Tripura-sundarī who is not limited by space or time (*Des'akālākāraṇavācchinnā*) is the very Self of That (*Tatsvarūpiṇī*) and adorable (*Spṛhaṇīya*) as She is the Cause of all (*Sarvakāraṇatvena*).

She is seated in the lap of Kamesvara (*Kāmes'varāṅka-nilayā*). By lap (*Aṅka*) is meant the left thigh. Her abode or seat is the left thigh of Kāmes'vara who is the Lord adored by all (*S'rīnātha*). So it has been said in *Bhairava-yāmala*:

"The knowledge (*Vidyā*) of the greatness (*Kalā=Vibhūti*) of Parāśakti is in the form of the S'rīcakra (*S'rīcakrākārarūpinī*)[1]. In the middle of it is the place of the Bindu and in it is the Supreme Lady. She is united (*Samprktā*) with Sadāśiva and is beyond all Tattvas (*Sarvatattvātikā*) and ever-existent (*Satī*). O Īsvarī! The Cakra of Tripura-sundarī is the universe itself (*Brahmānandākāraṁ*)."

Devi. This word means that She enjoys Herself (*Vinodinī*) in the work (*Vyāpāra*) of Creation and the like of the universe.

A digit of the moon is placed by Her, as an adornment, on Her forehead (*Kalayā candrasya kalpitottaṁsā*). The digit (*Kalā*) is the one which is the life of the universe (*Visvajīvinī*). The word *Kalpita*, that is, placed (used) shows that the region of the Moon (*Candra-maṇdala*) is merely an accessory (*Upakaraṇa*) for enjoyment of Bhagavatī.

Noose (*Pāśa*) represents Icchāśakti (*Icchāśakti-svarūpa*) which is the bondage causing the distinction between the individual self and the Supreme Spirit *Svātmabheda-bandhana*).

Goad (*Aṅkuśa*) represents Jñānaśakti which is the means (*Upāya*) whereby the difference (*Bheda*) between Sva (Brahman) and Rūpa (Form) is destroyed. **The sugarcane bow and the five flowery arrows** (*Ikṣucāpa-prasūnaśarapañcaka*) represent Kriyāśakti which is cause (*Sādhana=lit.* instrument) of attachment (*Avarjana*) to things (*Ākāra=lit.* Forms) outside one's self (*Svabhinna*)[3]. The sense of this is that it is the S'aktis—Icchā, Jñāna and Kriyā which in obedience to Her behest assume the forms of Pāsa and the like and remain in Her service (*Tadupāsanam ācaranti*).

So the Vāmakesvara (*Nityāṣoda*. VI. 53) says:

"The resplendent one holding in her hand the noose (*Pāśa*) which is Will (*Icchā-śakti*), the goad (*Aṅkuśa*) which is Knowledge (*Jñāna-śakti*) and the arrows and the bow which is Action (*Kriyā-śakti*)."

NOTES

[1] *Yad eshā caṁkramat tach cakramabhavat.* The word "*cakra*" is derived from the root *kramu*=to move, to step out, to evolve or emanate.

[2] According to another reading of this text, the first portion of the translation would read thus:

Kalā (=*Hārdakalā*) =*Vidyā* (*i.e.* the Mantra of 15 letters)=Parāśakti who assumes the form of, or manifests as, the S'rīcakra.

[3] As to Pāśa, Aṅkusha, bow and arrows compare *Bhāvanopaniṣad* 21-24.

VERSE 39

THAT couple (Kāmes'vara and Tripura-sundari) are in the triangle which is constituted by the three Bindus (*Bindu-trayātmaka*) and by reason of change of aspect (*Guṇabhedāt*) she assumes the form of three other couples the first of which is Kāmes'ī-Mitres'a [1].

COMMENTARY

The author here speaks of the celestial couple who is the very self of the Gurumaṇḍalas (*Gurumaṇḍala-svarūpa*) of the Divya, Siddha and Mānava lines (*Ogha*) of Gurus who are seemingly different but not really so (*Avis'eṣa-bheda-bhinna*) **That couple** (*Tan-mithunaṁ*). By the word "That" it is to be understood that the couple Kāma-kāmes'varī recognised in all Upaniṣads is here meant.

✓ The meaning is that it is the Supreme Spirit (*Paramātmā*) which divides Itself into Female and Male and enjoys as the couple (*Mithuna-rūpeṇa viharati*). *S'ruti* also (*Bṛhadāraṇyaka* 1. 4. 3) by the text which begins "He verily did not enjoy because one cannot enjoy" speaks of the Brahman who within Itself enjoys as the paired male and female (*Mithunātmaviharaṇas'īla*).

Āgama (*Rahasyāgama*) also says that Paramas'iva who is the paired or united (*Mithunībhūta*) *Prakās'a* and *Vimars'a* brought down (*Samavatārayat*) all the Tantras:

"Sadās'iva Himself remaining in the positions of (both) Teacher (*Guru*) and Disciple (*S'iṣya*) by words cast in the form of questions and answers brings down Tantra (on Earth)."

The couple (*Mithuna*) who are the united Kāma and Kāmes'varī assume the forms of *Mitreshanātha-kāmes'varī, Uddīṣanātha-Bajres'varī* and *S'aṣthīs'anātha-Bhagamālinī* as the three pairs (*Mithuna*) of the Divya, Siddha and Mānava lines (of Gurus) [2].

NOTES

[1] Tripurā is in the centre Bindu. The surrounding Three Bindus make the inverted triangle. In the single Bindu at foot She is Guru of the *Tretāyuga*. In the upper right Bindu She is the Guru of the *Dvāparayuga* and in the upper left Bindu of the *Kaliyuga*.

[2] See *Tantrarāja* (Vol. VIII, Tāntrik Texts) Chap. I. 7 and Chap. II.

Under V. 52 *post* the names of the three Gurus and their S'aktis are given differently. Possibly one or other portion of the text is incorrect.

VERSE 40

THOSE that abide in the Cakra of eight triangles are Vas'inī and the others[1] who are red like the evening sun. This (Cakra of eight triangles) is the eight-fold (subtle) body, of the Devī, which is the Cakra and the Self thereof is the Supreme Experience (*Saṁvid*).

COMMENTARY

From here onwards he describes the form and nature (*Svarūpa-bhāvan*) of the surrounding Devatās (*Āvaraṇa-devatāh*) "**Those that abide in the Cakra of eight triangles**" (*Vasukoṇa-nivāsinyah*). The Cakra of eight triangles is the Cakra called *Sarvarogahara* (All-disease-destroyer). The eight S'aktis **Vasini and others** abide in this Cakra. They are powerful to grant the bliss arising from the experience of complete 'I-ness' (*Pūrṇāhaṁbhāvadāna-samarthāh*). It is because they are able to give the experience of complete 'I-ness' that this Cakra is Rogahara. For it has been said:

"The sense of imperfection is disease and the source misery." (*Apūrṇaṁ-manyatā vyādhih kārpaṇyaika-nidānabhūh*) These S'aktis shine like the evening sun and are therefore described as **red like the evening sun** (*Saṁdhyāruṇā*). The Devī is **the Supreme Experience** (*Saṁvidātmā*) by which is meant that Her own form (*Svarūpa*) is Knowledge-in-Itself. *S'ruti* (in reference to the Brahman) speaks of "Being (*Satyam*), Knowledge (*Jñānam*) and Eternity (*Anantam*)".

Āgama says that the "Devī Tripurā is Svasamvid". By **Devi** is meant that She in Her desire "to be many" is playfully moving about and active (*Viharaṇa-svabhāvā*).

The Cakra of eight triangles is the eight-fold (subtle) body of the Devi (*Cakratanoh puryaṣṭakaṁ*) in the form of the S'rīcakra (*Cakrātmikā*). By Cakra is meant the S'rīcakra. The subtle body

(*Puryaṣṭaka* = Eightfold body) is so called because of the eight which compose it. They are as the *Svacchanda Tantra* says:

"Citi, Citta, Caitanya, Cetanā, Indriya-karma, Jīva, Kalā and S'arīra[2].

[1] These S'aktis, are ca … ıāṣoda. VIII. 162) because they are subtle.

[2] Different stages of (… ıis commentary on *Nityāṣodas'ikā* VIII, 160 … tute the eightfold *Sthūla* body of the Devī. … (1) the *Jñānendriyas*, (3) *Manas* etc., (4) the … ʼat etc., (6) *Kāma*, (7) *Karma* and (8) *Tamas*.

VERSE 41

As for Her powers, they having assumed the forms of Sarvajña and others abide in the inner ten-triangled Cakra. They are beautiful like the autumnal moon.

COMMENTARY

Her powers[1] (*Viṣaya-vṛttayaḥ*) are in close proximity to the Cakra of eight triangles.

They (*Tāh*). By this is emphasized their well-known power (to assist the Sādhaka) to maintain the identity of his self and the (Supreme) Ātmā (*Svātmaikyarūpa-rakṣaṇa-dhāriṇītvena prasiddhāḥ*).[2] **Having assumed the form of Sarvajna and others** (*Sarvajñādisvarūpaṁ āpannāḥ*) these powers become the ten S'aktis *Sarvajnā* and others and abide in the Cakra of ten triangles known by the name of *Sarva-rakṣākara.* They are called *Nigarbhayoginīs*[3] and are white and clear **like the autumnal moon** (*S'aradindu-sundarākārāḥ*).

NOTES

[1] *That is*, they are the inner Cakra of ten triangles.

[2] This Cakra is so close to the Bindu. He who realises them is near to Self-realisation.

[3] The expression *Nigarbha* has been defined by Bhāskararāya under VII. 48 and VIII. 157 *Nityāṣoda.*

VERSE 42

THE Yoginīs in the series of angles outside this (last) are those the first of whom is Sarva-siddhipradā. They are the objects of the Jñānendriyas and Karmendriyas of the Devī and are adorned with white raiment and ornament.

COMMENTARY

In the series of triangles outside this (last) (*Tad-bāhya-paṅkti-koṇeṣu*). By "this" is meant *Sarvarakṣākara-cakra*, outside which is the Cakra called *Sarvārthasādhaka*. (Accomplisher of All-aims).

In the series of angles (*Paṅktioṇeṣu*). By this we are to understand that the angles of the triangles of which the *Sarvārthasādhaka-cakra* is composed are in proximity to the triangles of the *Sarva-rakṣākara-cakra*. The Yoginīs in this Cakra (*Sarvārthasādhaka*) are called *Kulakaulas*[1] and they are the ten S'aktis *Sarvasiddhipradā* and others.

They are the objects of the jnanendriyas and karmendriyas of the Devi (*Devī-dhī-karmendriyaviṣaya-mayāh*). These ten S'aktis are the objects of sense perception such as sound is of hearing and the like. They are clad in white raiment and their adornment is also white (*Vis'ada-veṣa-bhūṣādhyāh*). The sense of this is that these S'aktis are inseparate from or identical with (*Abhedarūpāh*) the Mantra, the Devatā and the Sādhaka's[2] self and are white, clad in white raiment and grant Siddhi.

NOTES

[1] Cf. *Nityāṣoda*. VIII. 151-'55.

[2] *That is*, they help the Sādhaka to realise his identity with the Mantra and the Devatā.

VERSE 43

THOSE (S'aktis) who have their places in the Cakra of fourteen triangles are the unfolding movements of the fourteen instruments (of mind and senses) of the Devī. They are clad in garments (red) like the evening sun and are the Sampradāya-yoginīs and they should be meditated upon as above.

COMMENTARY

This Cakra of fourteen triangles is called *Sarva-saubhāgya-dāyaka* (Giver of All-prosperity). The **fourteen**[1] **instruments** (*Manu-karaṇa*) of the Devī are five of Jñāna (*Pañca-jñānendriyāṇī*), the five of Karma (*Pañca-karmendriyāṇi*) and *Manas, Buddhi, Ahaṁkāra, Citta.* **Un-folding Movements** (*Vivaraṇa-sphuraṇa*). The movements (*Sphuraṇa*) of the senses are in the **Cakra of fourteen triangles** (*Bhuvanāracakra*) as the **Saktis** therein. The Devī Herself is in this Cakra as the fourteen Devatās who are Her fourteen instruments. The S'aktis or Devatās are *Sarvasaṁkṣobhiṇī* and others. They are called *Sampradāya-yoginīs* because they are forms of the Ādis'akti (*Ādis'aktimayatvena*). **They should be meditated upon as unmanifest** (*Avyakta*).

NOTE

[1] The word Manu is used for 14 and Bhuvana is used for the same number. There are 14 Manus and 14 Bhuvanas.

VERSE 44

AVYAKTA, Mahat, Ahaṁkṛiti and the (five) Tanmātras having assumed womanly forms abide resplendent in the lotus of eight petals. They are known as the Guptatara-yoginīs.

COMMENTARY

By **Avyakta** (unmanifest) is meant the *Avyakta-tattva i.e.* *Prakṛti*, by **Mahat** or *Mahattattva* is meant Buddhi and by **Ahamkriti** is meant *Ahaṁkāra-tattva.* The **Tanmatras** are the five Tanmātras of Pṛthivī and others. These make eight. These eight have in this Cakra **assumed womanly forms** (*Svīkṛtāṅganākārāh*). They are forms of the Devī (*Devyātmikā*).

They are called *Guptatara-yoginīs* because they are within[1] (*Antaranga-bhūtā*) the *Mūla-devī.* These eight S'aktis who are *Anaṅga-kusumā* and others abide in the Cakra of eight petals which is called *Sarvasaṁkṣhobhana.* **Abide resplendent** (*Jayanti*) *i.e.* they are there excelling all (*Sarvotkarṣeṇa vartante*).

NOTE

[1] *Antaraṅga*=*lit.* comprehended; inseparable.

VERSE 45

THE Bhūtas, the ten Senses and Mind (Manas) are the sixteen variations (*Vikāra*) of the Devī. As Kāmākarṣinī and others (*Kāmākarṣinyādisvarūpataḥ*) they dwell in the lotus of sixteen petals.[1]

COMMENTARY

By **the Bhutas** is meant the elements of "Earth" and others (*Prithivyādīni*). The **ten senses** are the sense of perception and action (*Jñānakarmobhayalakṣaṇa*). These fifteen and **Mind (Manas) are the sixteen variations of the Devi** which are in the Cakra of sixteen petals which is called *Sarvās'āparipūraka*, as the sixteen S'aktis *Kāmākarṣinī* and others (*Kāmākarsinyādiṣodaṣaṣaktyākāreṇa*). In the Cakra called *Sarvās'āparipūraka* (Fulfiller of All-hopes)[2] dwell the *Gupta-yoginīs*, *Kāmākarṣinī* and others who are the vowels (*Svarātmikāh*).

NOTES

[1] Cf. *Bhāvanopaniṣad*, (*Ṛk.* 13).

[2] Or, that which fills up all the points of compass, that is, all space.

VERSE 46

ALL the Mudrās including Trikhaṇḍā are Saṁvit and excel all. They are in the first (innermost) section of the Bhūpura and resemble the young sun in their lustre.

COMMENTARY

Including Trikhanda (*Trikhaṇḍayā saha*) that is, along with the Trikhaṇḍā Mudrā. **Are Samvit** (*Saṁvinmayī i.e.* inherent in Cidghana, Massive Consciousness or Brahman (*Cidghananiṣṭhāh*).

They . . . Bhupura. (*Ādimahīgṛhavāsāh = Ādimacaturas'ranilayāh* that is they abide in the first or innermost section of the square which is called *Mahī-gṛha*, (*Bhūpura* and the like).[1]

That the Mudrās are of the nature of Saṁvit is shown in the following text:

"Mudrā moves in the Ether or Cit (*Cid-vyomacāriṇī*). *Khecarī mudrā* is the state of S'iva (*S'ivāvasthā*).

The ten Mudrās *Sarvasaṁkṣobhiṇī* and the rest are great S'aktis who dispel fear and give great Bliss or happiness. So it has been said:

"Mudrās are so called because they free men from (the evil influences of) Grahas and the like and destroy the many bonds (which enslave men)[2]."

These Mudrās are the Queens (*Adhiṣṭhāna-nāyikā*) of the nine Cakras beginning with the square (*Caturasrādi*) and ending with the Bindu (*Baindavānta*). This has been dealt with in the Vāmakes'vara (*Nityāṣoda.* VI. 57-71)[3] where it is shown how *Cit S'akti*, when She makes manifest and cognises the Universe as "This" on Herself as the basis assumes the forms of the several Mudrās there mentioned.

NOTES

[1] This Bhūpura consists of three sections as the following verses show.

[2] 'To free' is in Sanskrit '*Muc*' "Dissolve", "Destroy" is *Drāvayanti* in Sanskrit and is derived from the root Dru=to dissolve, fuse. In the passage quoted from *Nityāsoda*. '*Drāvaṇa*' is used in the sense of "fusion."

[3] The commentator quotes only the beginning and end of the passage. The Mudrās require a more full treatment and that is why a brief summary is given here.

VERSE 47

HER nine Ādhāras[1] are transformed (*Pariṇata*) into nine Cakras. The S'aktis of the nine Nāthas therefore also become changed into (*Pariṇatā*) the forms of the Mudrās (*Mudrākāreṇa*).

COMMENTARY

The nine Ādhāras are *Akula*[2], *Mūlādhāra*, *Svādhiṣṭhāna*, *Maṇipūra*, *Anāhata*, *Vis'uddha*, *Lambikā*, *Ājñā* and *Bindu*. These are the Ādhāras of the Devī in the sense that She as the Upāsaka (*Upāsaka-svarūpiṇī*) possesses these. Similarly the (nine) S'aktis of the nine Nāthas become the nine Mudrās.

NOTES

[1] *That is*, The centres. Ādhāra means a "support"; Mūlādhāra=root support.

[2] The red lotus of thousand petals below the Mūlādhāra corresponding to the white *Sahasrāra* lotus. Cf. *Bhāvanopāniṣad* (Ṛk—13): '*Ādhāranavakaṁ mudrās'aktayah*' and Bhāskararāya's note thereto.

VERSE 48

HER seven Dhātus skin and the rest and Her form manifest as the forms of the eight Mothers Brāhmī and others. They dwell in the middle Bhūbiṁba.[1]

COMMENTARY

Seven Dhatus skin and the rest. (*Tvagādi-saptadhātavah*). These seven Dhātus of the Devī and Her form (*Ākāra*) assume the shape of **the eight Matrikas Brahmi, and others** and abide in the middle section of the Bhūpura (*Madhyama-bhūbimba-niketanagāh*).

NOTE

[1] *Bhūbimba*=the disc or circle of the *Bhūpura* which is the square and forms the base of the S'ricakra. These S'aktis are in the middle circle. The *Bhāvanopaniṣad* (Ṛk—12) says:—*Kāma-krodha-lobha-moha-mada-mātsarya-puṇya-pāpamayā Brāhmyādyaṣtas'aktayah.* And the *Tantra-rāja* also says:—*Urmayah puṇyapāpe ca Brāhmyādyā mātarah smṛtāh.*

VERSE 49

HER (eight) Powers, *Aṇimā* and others, assume the forms of beautiful young women[1] and are attainable by other practices (*Vidyās*). Being of secondary nature they are in the last (lowest) section of the Bhūpura.

COMMENTARY

Her (*Asyāh*) *i.e.* of the Paramesvarī **Her (eight) powers, Anima and others** (*Aṇimādibhūtayah*). These are the eight *Siddhis* or *Bhūtis* the first in enumeration of which is *Aṇimā*. These are in the form of beautiful young women (*Kamanīya-kāminī-rūpāh*).

Attainable by other Vidyas (*Vidyāntaraphalabhūtāh*) that is, these *Siddhis* or great powers are the fruits attainable by the practice of other *Vidyās* such as Hathayoga and others.

Being of secondary nature (*Guṇabhāvena*).[2] These not being of a nature as important as the Highest Aim which is *Mokṣa* are to be considered negligible and ultimately discarded (*Guṇa-bhāvena* = *Upasarjanībhāvena*). **Are in the last section ot the Bhupura,** (*Antyabhū-niketanagāh*). That is they are in the lowest (of the three) sections of the square. By worshipping Paramātmā in this manner the Sādhaka becomes the Great Lord (Paramesvara) Himself.

NOTES

[1] The *Bhāvanopaniṣad* (*Rk.* 11 says):
Niyatih sṛiṅgārādayo rasā aṇimādayah
and the *Tantrarāja* also says:
Srīcakre siddhayah prokta rasā niyatisaṁyutāh.

[2] The word *Guṇa* is here used to mean "Secondary" or "Subordinate" as opposed *Mukhya* which means "Chief" "Foremost".

VERSE 50

PARAMA S'iva who is the Lord and is one with the Bindu experiences the highest Bliss. It is He who in his Vimars'a (S'akti) aspect becomes gradually differentiated and assumes the form of Kāmes'a.

COMMENTARY

Having in manner described explained the stages of the unfolding of the Cakra (*Cakrakrama*) which is but a manifestation of Kāmakalā (*Kāmakalāvilāsanarūpa*), he now in his kindness towards his disciples commences to describe the series of Gurus beginning with Paramas'iva in four verses of which this is the first. For a true knowledge of the Cakra, the Devatā and Mantra can be gained by knowing the succession of Gurus who are Parames'vara (*Parames'varātmaka-guru-krama-jñāna-bhāvena labhyate*).

"**Experiences the highest Bliss**" (*Paramānandānu-bhāvah*). That is, He is the One who has the knowledge or experience (*Anubhāva*= *Jñāna*) which excels all other bliss (*Parama*=*Sarvotkṛṣta*). This Ānanda or Bliss consists in experience as complete 'I-ness' (*Paripūrṇāhaṁbhāvarūpa*). *S'ruti* also says "other creatures experience a fragment of this Bliss"[1].

Parama Siva who is the Lord and is one with the Bindu (*Paramaguru-nirvishesha-bindvātmā*). By Parama Guru is meant the First Guru (*Ādinātha*) who is Parama S'iva. The Bindu is one with Him. (*Nirvis'eṣa*=*Abhinna*), The Bindu is the Kāmakalā (*Kāmakalārūpa*). He whose Self (*Ātmā*=*Svarūpa*) is the Bindu is the Parama S'iva who is the First Lord or Guru (*Ādinātharūpī Paramas'ivah*).

The Upaniṣads contain various texts like the following: "Bliss is Brahman" (*Tait.* 3-6.) "Brahman is Truth (or Being), Knowledge and Eternal" (*Tait.* 2-9-1). "To the (Brahman who is) pure Cit

(*Cinmātra*), All-seeing (*Sarvadraṣṭā*), All-witnessing (*Sarva-sākṣī*), All-absorbing (*Sarva-grāsa*=All devouring) who is the Adored of all (*Sarvapremāspada*), who is in Itself Being (*Sat*), Consciousness (*Cit*) and Bliss (*Ānanda*) dependent on nothing (*mātra*) and massive Experience (*Ekarasa*) ", (*Nri. Uttara.* 5-8) ; and again " This Ātmā is pure Being (*Sanmātra*), Eternal (*Nitya*), Knowledge (*Buddha*), Pure (*S'uddha*), Truth (*Satya*), Free (*Mukta*), devoid of Māyā (*Nirañjana*) and Omnipresent (*Vibhu*), Non-dual (*Advaya*), Bliss (*Ānanda*), Supreme (*Para*) " (*Nri. Uttara* 9-9).

They lead to the conclusion that it is the very merciful Parames'vara, the supreme Truth as massive Consciousness and Bliss and as both Prakāsha and Vimarsha (*Chidānandaghanaparamārtha-prakāsha-vimarshātmā*) who divided His own Self into the Bindus making Kāmakalā and became Kāmakāmes'varī and other couples who are the Divya, the Siddha[1] and Mānava lines of Gurus. He thus becomes the whole body of the Gurus (*Gurumandalātmā*) and protects such as are truly devout. This is the sense. *S'ruti* also says :—" He is this Ātmā. The Ātmā verily is this S'akti. She is the Becoming (*Bhāva*) and non-Becoming (*Abhāva*), the Being and non-Being."

If *Paramagurunirvisheshabindvātmā* be read as two words as *Paramaguruh* and *Nirvisheshabindvātmā* then the meaning will be that the Paramaguru which is another name for Ādinātha is the transcendent (*Nirvishesha-Nishprapancha*) Bindu who is indicated by (*Lakshana*) Sat, Chit and Ānanda. So it has been said :—

" The Supreme Ether—(*Ākās'a*) which is the Bindu which is transcendent (*Niṣprapancha*), is Sat, Chit and Ānanda, One without a second (*Nirābhāsa*), in whom there is no distinction of subject and object[2] (*Nirvikalpa*) and is imperishable (*Nirāmaya*.)"

The Parames'vara who is like this did Himself become (*Abhūt*) the *Gurumandala* the first of whom is Kāmakāmes'varī. "**It is He**" (*Sah punah*). It is the Paramātmā already spoken of, who by degrees (*Kramena*) becomes differentiated (*Bhinnah*) in the manner to be later shown as the Divya and Siddha classes from His Vimarsha part (*Vimarshāngshāt*). By Vimarsha is meant His own S'akti as Kāmakalā. By part (*Angsha*) is meant half of this.

Assumes the form of Kamesha (*Kāmeshatvang yayau*=Changed into the state of Kāmesha). That is He himself became Kāmarāja. The sense of this is that it is the Paramātmā who of His own will divided His own self into Kāma and Kāmesvarī and as the Teacher (*Guru*) and the Disciple (*S'iṣya*) brings down all Tantras. *S'ruti* (*Bṛha. Ar.* 143) also says:—

"He divided this Ātmā into two; thereby arose Husband and Wife".

Notes

[1] *Etasyaivānandasyānyāni bhūtāni mātrām upajīvanti* (*Bṛhad. Āranyaka* 4-3-32).

[2] *Siddha*—These form the second class of Gurus in all Tantras. Different schools or Sampradāyas have different names for the Gurus of the three classes.

[3] Knower and object of knowledge.

VERSE 51

S'ĪVA the Guru who abides in the Uddīyāṇapitha did in the Kṛta Yuga impart the Vidyā to Her, His own S'akti the Vimars'a-rūpiṇī Kāmes'varī.

COMMENTARY

In this verse he further discusses what has been stated in the preceding verse. By '**Siva**' is meant the Paramātmā who is the author of all (*Sarvapravartaka*). **Guru** is he who instructs in Jñāna (*Jñānopadeṣtā*). So it has been said that "the Guru is means (of success)." (*Gurur upāyah*); also[1] :—

"The word 'Gu' signifies darkness and the word 'Ru' signifies that which dispels it, Guru is so called because he dispels darkness."

Who abides in the Uddiyanapitha. (*Āsinah s'rīpīthe*), By this is meant that the abode of S'iva is the Uddīyāṇa-pitha within the innermost triangle.

In the Krita Yuga (*Kṛtayugakāle*). By this we are to understand that it was in the beginning of Kṛta or Satya Age that S'iva imparted the knowledge of the Vidyā. By **Vidya** is meant the Vidyā which is fully established in all Upaniṣads and whereby a man can realise his oneness with the Atmā (*Ātmaikyapradāyinī*).

Did impart (*Dadau*). Fully instructed (*Upadides'a*). **Her, His own Sakti** (*Tasyai svas'aktyai*). The force of the pronoun "Her" is to press on the reader's attention the fact that it is She who gives boundless happiness to all creatures (*Sarva-bhūtānāṁ, niravadhikānandadāyinī*). His own S'akti. (*Svas'akti*). By this we are to understand that it is She who enables the Lord to manifest His own Being (*Svasvarūpasattāsaṁpradātrī*). So it has been said :—

"Even the Supreme if disunited from S'akti is unable to do anything. O Parames'āni! He is capable (of action) if He is united with S'akti."

Vimarsarupini. She is so called because She is the Supreme S'akti which is (*lit.* is the resting place of) the supreme manifesting Bliss. (*Anuttarānanda-vis'rānti-sthānabhūta-s'akti-para-rūpinī*). So it has been said, (*Saṁketapaddhati*) "The letter A is the first of all and is Prakās'a and the Supreme S'iva and the letter Ha is the last which is Kalā and is called Vimars'a."

Kamesvari. She is so called because She at all times and in every way grants all objects of desire (*Sarvābhiṣta-pradāyinī*) and is one with one's own Ātmā (*Svātmabhūtā*).

NOTE

[1] *Kulārnava Tantra* XVII. 7.

VERSES 52 & 53

SHE who is the Queen of the (three) places[1] and bears the appellations of the Eldest, the Middle or the Second and the Youngest and who is the object of enjoyment of Parama S'iva assumed the name of Mitradeva. It is She who having first purified the Gurus (by initiation) revealed the Vidyā to them who are the seeds of the (three) Ages (*yugas*) the first of which is Tretā and who are the Lords of the three Bījas. It is by these (three Gurus) that the three groups or classes (*Ogha*) are maintained. Now has been said the order of the Gurus (*Gurukrama*).

COMMENTARY

The tradition (*Sampradāya*) relating to the Gurus may be put thus:—

True that these two (Kāmes'vara and Kāmes'varī) are of equal high degree (*Samatattvau*) and are identical (*Samau*) and S'akti is ever young (*Ajarā*) and the Cause of the universe (*Vis'vayoni*) and the Sāṅkhāyana branch (of the Ṛgveda) has said "primeval s'akti is red (*Aruṇā*)[2] the mother of the universe (*Vis'vajanyā*)" yet Parama S'iva who was desirous of revealing His secret system (*Rahasyatantra*) containing the essence of all the Upaniṣads did so by the aid of Kāmes'varī Herself who is the Cause of all (*Sarvakāraṇa rūpiṇī*) as is shown by the expression "*Vis'va-yoni* or *Vis'vajanyā.*"

After the creation of the universe in the First (*Ādi i.e. Satya* or *Kṛta*) Age abiding as He was in the *Uddīyāṇa-pītha* which is replete with the Bliss of His own Illumination (*Prakās'ānanda-sāramaya*) He under His name S'rī-caryā-nanda-nātha instructed the adorable Lady who is one with Him in the rules relating to *S'rī-vidyā* (*S'rīvidyākrama*). He Himself says:—

"Verily do I adore the Great centre of the Cakra which is supreme Bliss and the innermost essence of Prakāśa and Vimarśa (*Anuttara-vimarśaikasāra*) and pure experience (*Saṁvinmaya*)."

She in the Tretā, Dvāpara and Kali Ages did in the forms of the Gurus mentioned below introduce the very secret system of Śiva (*Śāmbhava Tantram*). The order of the Gurus is as follows:—

To understand the gem of Śrī-vidyā (either of) two lines of (*Saṁtāna*), may be followed. They are the line of Kāmarāja and the line of Lopāmudrā. The line of Kāmarāja is to be found in every form of Vidyā (*Sakala-vidyānusaṁdhyavicchinna*) and this has been said by even the Gurus of old. They say that the line of Lopāmudrā runs in sections (*Vicchinnatayā pravartate*). There are in this seven Gurus of the Divya class four of the Siddha class and eight of the Mānava class[8]. The order of the Divya class is as follows. In the beginning of the Kṛta Age, Parama Śiva Himself who abides in the *Uddīyāṇapītha* and is one (*Vimṛiṣṭatanu*) with Mahātripurasundarī who is His own Śakti (*Svātmaśaktyākhyā*) is the first Guru under the name of Śrīcaryānandanātha. So it has been said:

"She who is the body of Kāmarāja abides in the *Uddīyāṇapītha* which is in the middle of the (first) triangular Cakra in a soundless state (*Asvarākāratām prāpya tryaśrasaṁgketam adhyagāt*)."

At the apex of the inner inverted triangle which is *Kāmarūpa-pītha* abides Śrīmad Ūrddhvadeva-nātha who is the Guru of the Tretā Age and is one with Kāmeśvarī the presiding Devatā of *Vāgbhava Bīja*. So it has been said:

"She who is at the apex of the inverted triangle is Kāmeśī abiding in *Kāmapītha*."

At the right hand corner of the inner triangle which is the *Jālaṁdharapītha* is Ṣaṣthadeva-nātha who is the Guru of the Dvāpara Age and who is in a state of inseparate union (*Militasvarūpa*) with Vajreśvarī who is (the presiding Devatā of) *Kāmarāja Bīja*.

So it has been said:

"At the right-hand corner of the triangle which is the *Jālaṁdhara-pītha* is Vajreśī".

At the left hand corner of the middle triangle which is the *Pūrṇagiri-pītha* is Mitradevanatha who is the Guru of the Kali Age and is one with Bhagamālini who is the Devatā of the *S'akti Bīja* there. So it has been said:

"Bhages'ī who abides in the *Pūrṇapītha* is in the left corner of the triangle".

Mitres'adeva did in the beginning of the Kali Age bestow his grace on the venerated Lopāmudrā and Agastya, the couple refulgent for their great devotion (*Tapas*). Particulars about the seven who compose the Divya class can only be known from the Guru.

We now follow the text.

She (*Sā*). By this the aforementioned beloved (*Prānanāyikā*) of Parama S'iva is meant. She assumed [4] the name of Mitradevanātha. Here the mention of Mitradeva implies the Gurus of the Tretā and Dvāpara Ages. She in turn becomes the Gurus of the Tretā and other Yugas and continues the tradition.

Lady or Queen of the three places (*Sthānes'ā*). That is She is the presiding Devatā (*Īs'ā=Adhiṣthātrī*) of the apex, the right and left corners of the middle triangle where She abides as Kāmes'varī, Vajres'varī and Bhagamālinī respectively.

Bears the appellations of the the Eldest the Second and the Youngest. (*Jyeṣtha-madhya-bālākhyā*). *Jyeṣtha* means Eldest or most excellent. By this expression S'rīmad Ūrddhvadeva-nātha is meant. By Middle (*Madhya*) or Second S'rī Ṣaṣthadevanātha is meant and by Youngest (*Bāla*, which means a boy) is meant S'rī Mitradevanātha. The Devī bears these names.

The object of enjoyment of Parama Siva (*Citprāṇa-viṣaya-bhūtā*). By *Cit-prāṇa* is meant Parama S'iva because, He is the Svarūpa of Cit and is Prāṇa itself (*Prāṇarūpa*).

The *Mānduka S'ruti* (1, 7) says:

"The wise think of the non-dual S'iva who is quiescent (*S'āntam*) and in whom the universe is absorbed (*Prapañcopas'amam*). He is not inner or subjective cognition (*Antahprajñam*) nor is He outer or objective cognition (*Bahihprajñam i.e.* enjoyer of the gross world) and He is not between these two states (*Nobhayatahprajñam*) [5]. He is not massive knowingness (*Prajñāna-ghanam*). He knows not nor is any thing unknown to Him. He is unseen. He is not the subject of (pragmatic) knowledge (*Avyavahāryam*). He is beyond the scope of the senses of action (*Agrāhyam*). He has no attributes

(*Alakṣaṇam*) and is incomprehensible and cannot be described (*Avyapades'yam*), but is the essential experience of one Self (*Ekātma-pratyaya-sāram*). He is deemed to be the highest (*Caturthaṁ=lit.* Fourth). He is the Ātmā. He should be known." S'iva is thus *Cinmaya* according to *S'ruti.*

In the same way *S'ruti* speaks of Him as *Prāṇamaya* also. The *Chāndogya* (7-15-1) says:

" As the spokes (of a wheel) are fixed to the hub so is every thing fixed on to this Prāṇa. Prāṇa moves by Prāṇa (*i.e.* by its own S'akti). Prāṇa gives Prāṇa for the propagation of Prāṇa (*Prāṇāya*). Prāṇa verily is father, Prāṇa is mother, Prāṇa is brother, Prāṇa is sister, Prāṇa is preceptor (*Ācārya*) ".

The Devī is the object of enjoyment (*Viṣayabhūtā=Bhogyabhūtā*) of Parama S'iva who is as above described. So it has been said: " This Deva ever wishes to have the pleasure of playing with this Devī."

The Supreme Lady of adoration (*Parābhattārikā*) who is as above described, revealed (*Prakās'ayāmāṣa*)* the Vidyā to the three Gurus who are the seeds of the three ages beginning with Tretā as has already been described.

The words *Sthānes'ā*, *Jyeṣtha-madhya-bālākhyā* and *Cit-prāṇa-viṣayabhūtā* may be read in the plural accusative to qualify *Trigurūn.* The interpretation will in that case also be as given above.

The Lords of the three Bijas (*Bīja-trītayādhipatīn*) The three Bījas are Vāgbhava and others. They are the Lords (*Adhipati*) in the sense that these Bījas indicate them. These three kinds of Gurus (*Trividhades'ikān*) the Devī first purifies (*Parīkṣya=S'odhayitvā*). By Vidyā is meant the Adividyā which issued from the lotus mouth of Parama S'iva and is the Cause of all causes. The Devī **revealed the Vidya.** By this we are to understand that She instructed (*Upadides'a*) the Gurus in the Vidyā.

Here by the statement, **Revealed the Vidya having purified them.** (*Parīkṣya vidyāṁ prakās'ayāmāsa*), we are to understand that the most excellent Guru who is Sadās'iva (*S'rī-Sadās'ivātmā*) instructs in this path which is in accordance with immutable tradition (*Sat-saṁpradāya-siddham*), the disciple who has for a long time done Ātmopāsana, has controlled his inclination (*S'ānta*), has conquered his senses (*Dānta*) and seeks initiation (*Upāsana*). So it has been said:

"O Great Queen, it is after initiation that the Guru should give instruction relating to Sādhana of the Vidyā".

Initiation (*Dīkṣā*)[7] is of three kinds namely *Āṇavī*, *S'ākteyī* and *S'āṁbhavī*. It grants union (*Sāyujya*) with S'iva. In *Āṇavī Dīkṣā* the special articles of worship are necessary. There is also needed intense devotion to, and Tarpaṇa and Dhyāna of, the Para-Devatā. S'ākta initiation is for the attainment of Siddhi by the Sādhanā of that particular S'akti for the worship of which a disciple is qualified. So it has been said:

"When the Guru perceives that the disciple is ready for Sādhanā of (any form of) S'akti he should then initiate in that (S'akti) alone without hesitation. This is called *S'ākteyī Dīkṣā*".

S'āmbhavī Dīkṣā has been thus described:

"*S'āṁbhavī Dīkṣā* is that which by the mere grace of the Guru makes manifest the S'iva state (*S'ivatā-vyaktikāriṇī*)[8] and produces the Bliss of S'iva. The preceptor and the disciple should be selfless and without worldly desires or motives."

In the absence of any such initiation there can be no competency for Sādhanā. Initiation to be fruitful should be the outcome of mere grace of the preceptor unmixed by any motive. The preceptor is bound to initiate even at his own expense if the disciple though qualified for initiation is unable to incur it. If the Guru himself is also unable to procure the necessary articles then he should do it in a concise form. So it has been said:

"The Guru should himself with his own money initiate the poor. He should liberate the disciple by Dīkṣā and use Dūrbā grass and water if nothing more can be had."

The conclusion we thus arrive at is this—that it is only he who is fully initiated who is competent for Brahma-vidyā. It has already been said that initiation becomes effective by propitiation (*Saṁtarpaṇa*) of the Para-Devatā. Saṁtarpaṇa or propitiation can be done by the offering of oblations of particular kinds of liquid substance used in particular Ages. For it has been said:— "(Oblation) of Devatās however is by nectar." The liquid substance is wine which is like excellent nectar. With this alone can offering be made to Para-Devatā, like *Soma* in Agnīṣṭoma sacrifice.

Now if it be said that there is prohibition in texts like this: "The Brāhmaṇa should not drink wine nor should he eat flesh," we reply that we do not say that oblation to the Para-Devatā should be made by transgressing prohibitions applicable to particular cases and prompted merely by one's own desire. In what we have said we are convinced that this S'āṁbhava Dars'ana is based upon the teachings of the Upaniṣads. Now it may be said "what about the prohibition?" The answer is that this prohibition applies to the man who is uninitiated. For the initiated the best way of offering oblation to Devatā is to make it with wine. In the Sāṁkhyāyana S'ākhā which is extracted from the ocean-like Ṛgveda, it is stated that divine dignity and dominion can be attained by the worship of the Ādisundarī thus[9]:—

"Those, who after having fully realised Her offer oblations (to Her) in the S'rīcakra which is inseparate from their body, with wine which has been converted by purification into nectar,[10] become delirious in the excess of their joy, dwell in the high region where there is neither pain nor sorrow and enter the Supreme Light of Tripurā."

Notes

[1] The three angles of the triangle (Kāmakalā).

[2] The colour of the Rajas Guṇa of Kṛyā S'akti. The text quoted above is from the *Tripurāmahopaniṣat* but greatly mutilated though the sense is not. It is the second half of the 14th *Ṛk* of that Upaniṣad and runs thus:—*Samapradhānau samasattvau samojare tayoh S'aktirajarā vis'vayonih.* As quoted in the text it is not quite correct.

[3] The *Lalitārcana-mañjarī* gives the names of the Gurus as follows. The seven of the Divya class are (1) Paraprakās'anandanātha, (2) Paras'ivānandanātha, (3) Paras'aktidevyambā, (4) Kaules'varānandanātha, (5) S'uklādevyambā, (6) Kules'varānandanātha, (7) Kāmes'varyambā. The four Gurus of the Siddha class are (1) Bhogānandanātha, (2) Klinnānandanātha, (3) Samayānandanātha, (4) Sahajānandanātha; the eight of the Mānava class are (1) Gaganānandanātha, (2) Vis'vānandanātha, (3) Vimalānandanātha, (4) Madanānandanātha, (5) Bhuvanāndanātha, (6) Nilānandanātha, (7) Ātmānandanātha, (8) Priyānandanātha. Those of the first mentioned class should be worshipped behind and the other two on Her left and right respectively.

[4] *Cf. Tantrarāja* xxxv:

Gurur ādyā bhavec chaktih sā vimarsamyī matā.

also *Bhāvanopaniṣad* I:

S'rīguruḥ sarvakāraṇabhūtā s'aktiḥ.

[5] *That is,* He is not the state between Jāgrat and Svapna.

[6] *Cf. Tantrarāja* (Tantrik Text vol. VIII) ch. 1. v. 8:

Tayā tair bhuvane tantraṁ kalpe kalpe vijriṁbhate.

(She, the Devī, age after age reveals Tantra through them (the Gurus).

[7] The *Gandharvatantra* speaks of *Māntrī, S'āktī* and *S'āṁbhavī.*

[8] According to another reading "*S'ivatādātmyadāyinī*" which means that which brings about a sense of inseparateness with S'iva.

[9] *Tripurāmahopaniṣad. Ṛk.* 7.

[10] The text has '*Surayā*' but Bhāskara reads '*Sudhaya*' and the latter reading has been adopted in the translation.

VERSE 54

THIS is the end of the description by Puṇyānanda of the playful movements of the beautiful woman Kāmakalā which ever attract the desire of the amorous Para S'iva.

COMMENTARY

This is the end (*Iti*), The particle "*Iti*" indicates the end of the book composed by Puṇyānanda (*Uditah puṇyānandāt*). The literal meaning of the expression is "as arisen from Puṇyānanda" the author. **Playful movements of the beautiful woman Kamakala** (*Kāmakalānanā-vilāsah*). By Kāmakalā is meant Vimars'as'akti who is inseparable (*Avinābhūtā*) from Kāmes'vara. She is the beautiful woman (*Aṅganā*) whose Vilāsa or amorous movements appear as the form of the Cakra, the Āvaraṇa-Devatās and the like. These amorous movements which have been caused by seeing Her beloved (*i.e.* Para-S'iva) always (*Nityam*) attract the mind or heart (*Citta*) of the amorous (*Bhujaṅga=Rasika*) Para-S'iva whose nature is pure Illumination (*Prakās'aikasvabhāva*) by producing in Him an excess of desire (*Bhāva=Rāga*).

If "*Bhāvākarṣṇaharṣāya*" be read for "*Bhāvākarṣitacittāya*" then the meaning will be that the sight of the playful movements produce in the amorous Para-S'iva that gladness which accompanies the experience of the emotion of love. In ordinary life (*Loke'pi*) the sight of the amorous movements of the beloved produces in the mind of the gay lover a sense of gladness which is accompanied by the sentiment of love (*S'ṛṅgāra-bhāva*). In the same way the play (*Vilāsa*) of Kāmakalā who is Cit-S'akti which express itself in the way She walks (*Padavikṣepa*) and in other movements (of Her body) produces infinite gladness in Para-S'iva who is facing towards and looking at Her who is His own S'akti.

The name of this book is **Kamakalavilasa**. It is written by and therefore has emanated from (*Uditah*) Puṇyānanda. This book always gladdens Para-S'iva.

VERSE 55

OBEISANCE to the venerated Lord the boatman (*S'rīnātha-nāvika*) by whose grace I have crossed this Ocean of Wandering, the waters of which are desire (*Tṛṣṇāsalila*) and the surface whereof is restless with the waves of anxiety (*Cintātaraṅgacapala*).

This is the end of Kamakalavilasa *written by S'rī Puṇyānanda Yogī.*

COMMENTARY

"**Ocean of wandering**" (*Prapañcavārās'i*). By *Prapañca* is meant *Saṁsāra* or Wandering which is ocean-like (*Vārās'ih=Vāridhih*).

May good be (*S'ubhaṁ astu*).

This is the end of Cidvalli *composed by S'rī Naṭanānandanātha.*

Books By

SIR JOHN WOODROFFE

(ARTHUR AVALON)

On Yoga Philosophy, Tantra Shastra, and Mantra Shastra

"Excellent volumes. Sir John writes with power, knowledge and lucidity three rare qualities in authorship". —*The Occult Review*

"His books brilliantly inaugurate the study of the Tantras, the literature of which occupies a front rank in the religious life of Modern India". —*Prof. Sylvain Levi in La Revue Critique*

"One cannot do enough homage to the magnificent series of publications which an English savant under the pseudonym of Arthur Avalon has brought into being". —*Revue Philosophique, Paris*

Sir John Woodroffe's works are absolutely indispensable for all students of this very mixed but widespread and important phase of non-Vedic Hinduism. —*G. R. S. Mead*

These books, dealing with the secret mysticism and magic of India, are the most interesting which have been published in recent years. —*Neue Metaphysische Rundschau*

In Mr. Avalon these mystic writings have found an enthusiastic exponent and a daring investigator who is determined to disentangle the lofty conceptions of earlier and purer beliefs from much of the misconceptions and misunderstandings which have grown round them by the debasing and sensual rites practised in the name of Tantra.

—*Madras Mail*

" Mr. Avalon in his publications insists on the greatness of the Tantra and seeks to clear away by a dispassionate statement of the real facts the cloud of misconceptions which have obscured our view of this profound and powerful system." —*Sri Aurobindo in* Arya

There is no doubt that the author has done good service to the Tantra Agama and students of philosophy in general by his scholarly contribution which has filled his heart and is a labour of love.

—*Quarterly Journal of the Mythic Society*

Permit me to seize this opportunity to congratulate you on the excellent get-up of your books of which I have "SERPENT POWER", "VARNAMALA" and "SHAKTI AND SHAKTA" all of which have been most enlightening. —*A reader from Egypt*

Publishers : GANESH & CO., (MADRAS) LTD., MADRAS—17

ॐ

श्रीगणेशशारदागुरुभ्यो नमः

श्रीपुण्यानन्दविरचितः

कामकलाविलासः

श्रीनटनानन्दविरचितया

चिद्वल्ल्या संवलितः

वन्दे तन्मिथुनं दिव्यमाद्यमानन्दचिद्घनम् ।
अनुत्तरं परं ज्योतिरिति यद्भाव्यते बुधैः ॥ १ ॥
श्रीमते नटनानन्दयोगिने परमात्मने ।
रक्तशुक्लप्रभामिश्रतेजसे गुरवे नमः ॥ २ ॥
प्रणमत नाथानन्दं परया भक्त्या चिदैक्यबोधानन्दम् ।
उपनिषदर्थनिगूढं सकलजनानन्दभद्रपीठारूढम् ॥ ३ ॥
नमः शिवाय नाथाय चिद्रूपानन्दरूपिणे ।
श्रीमते चटुलापाङ्गपाटितातङ्कशङ्कवे ॥ ४ ॥
पुण्यानन्दमुनीन्द्रात्कामकला नाम विश्रुता जाता ।
आख्यां कांचिदमुष्या नटनानन्दः करोति सव्याख्याम् ॥ ५ ॥

इह हि शक्तिपातसमुन्मिषत्सकलवेदवेदान्ततात्पर्यनिर्णयविशारदाः सर्वागमार्थावधारितात्मयाथार्थ्यविदः सच्चिदानन्दसिन्धुविहरणपटीयांसः, अत्रभवन्तः पुण्यानन्दाः स्वयं परमात्मानं प्रकाशयन्तः परमेश्वरमात्मत्वेन समाविशन्तः परेषामपि भक्तिभाजां पुरुषाणामुज्जिहीर्षुतया परमात्मैकत्वलक्षणं रक्षणमाशासते—

सकलभुवनोदयस्थितिलयमयलीलाविनोदनोद्युक्तः ।
अन्तर्लीनविमर्शः पातु महेशः प्रकाशमात्रतनुः ॥ १ ॥

इति। अत्र पुण्यानन्दयोगिनः पुण्यवशात् स्वाभाविकभक्तिपरितोषितपरमगुरुवरकरुणाकटाक्षनिर्धूतनिखिलपाशस्तोमाः सत्संप्रदायनिष्णाताः सकलनिगमागमावधारिततत्त्वयाथार्थ्यविदः सकलविद्याधिदेवताभूतमहात्रिपुरसुन्दरीमन्त्रचक्रपूजाक्रमव्याचिकीर्षतया तदधिष्ठानभूतकामकामेश्वरीरूपमादावाचक्षते—**सकलेत्यादि** । सकलानां भुवनानां उदयः उत्पत्तिः, स्थितिः रक्षा, लयः नाशः, एतत्त्रितयं तिरोधानानुग्रहयोरुपलक्षणम् । यथा त्रिवृत्करणं पञ्चीकरणस्य, एतत्पञ्चविधकृत्यप्रचुरा या लीला तया विनोदनं क्रीडनम्, तस्मिन् उद्युक्तः जागरूकः । मयडत्र प्राचुर्यर्थे विहितः । "अन्नमयो यज्ञः" इतिवत् । न तादृशे चिन्मय इतिवत् । कुतः? पञ्चविधकृत्यं हि कार्यं जगन्निष्ठम् । लीला तु परमेश्वरनिष्ठा । तस्मादत्र सकलशब्दविशेषितभुवनपदेन भवत्यस्मादिति शिवादिधरण्यन्तं तत्त्वजातमुच्यते । एतेषां तत्त्वानां ब्रह्मणः सकाशादुत्पन्नत्वात्तस्मिन् स्थितत्वात्तस्मिन्नेव लयात् । तथा च **तैत्तिरीयश्रुतिः**—"यतो वा इमानि भूतानि जायन्ते, येन जातानि जीवन्ति, यत्प्रयन्त्यभिसंविशन्ति । तद्विजिज्ञासस्व, तद्ब्रह्मेति" इति । उद्युक्त इत्यनेन "सदेव सोम्येदमग्र आसीत् । एकमेवाद्वितीयम्" इति । ब्रह्मेति स्वान्तःस्थितं प्रपञ्चम्; "बहु स्यां प्रजायेयेति", "तदात्मनं स्वयमकुरुत" इति संकल्पविशिष्टलक्षणसृष्ट्युन्मुखोऽभूदित्युक्तं भवति । तथा **रहस्यगुरवः**—

"चिदात्मैव हि देवोऽन्तः स्थितिमिच्छावशाद्बहिः ।
योगीव निरुपादानमर्थजातं प्रकाशयेत् ॥"

इति । अत एवेश्वरस्य जगत्सृष्ट्यादिकं लीलामात्रम्; न प्रयोजनमस्ति । तथा च **हृदयसूत्रम्**—"स्वेच्छया स्वभित्तौ विश्वमुन्मीलयति" इति, तथा वचनमपि—"स्वेच्छयैव जगत्सर्वं निगिरत्युद्गिरत्यपि ।" इति । श्रुतिरपि—"यथोर्णनाभिः सृजते गृह्णते च" इति । वचनान्तरमपि—

"जगच्चित्रं समालिख्य स्वेच्छा तूलिकयात्मनि ।
स्वयमेव समालोक्य प्रीणाति परमेश्वरः ॥"

इति। एवं च महेश्वर एक एव जगदुत्पादननिमित्तोपादानतामयते; "बहु स्याम्" इति बहुभवनश्रुतेः। "एकमेवाद्वितीयम्" इत्यधिष्ठानान्तरनिषेधाच्च। **प्रत्यभिज्ञासूत्रेऽपि**—"चितिरेव चेतनपदादवरूढा चित्तसंकोचिनीचित्तम्" इत्यनेन परमात्मैव जीवस्वरूपमगमदित्युक्तम्। श्रुतिरपि—"अनेन जीवेनात्मनानुप्रविश्य नामरूपे व्याकरवाणि" इत्यब्रवीत्। तथा **ललितोपाख्यानेऽपि**—

"हृदयस्थापि लोकानामदृश्या मोहनात्मिका।
नामरूपविभागं च या करोति स्वलीलया॥"

इति। **चतुःशत्यां** च—"अस्यां परिणतायां तु न किंचित्परिदृश्यते।" इत्यादिस्मृतिजालमुदाहर्तव्यम्। तथा **छान्दोग्ये**—"स्तब्धोऽस्युत तमादेशमप्राक्ष्यो येनाश्रुतं श्रुतं भवत्यमतं मतमविज्ञतं विज्ञातम्" इत्येकविज्ञानेन सर्वविज्ञानं प्रतिज्ञाय, दृष्टान्तमाह—"वाचारम्भणं विकारो नामधेयं मृत्तिकेत्येव सत्यम्" इत्यादिवचनात्, ब्रह्मैव तत्तदाकारेण परिणम्य विहरतीति सिद्धम्।

ननु एतावता प्रकरणेन जगतो ब्रह्मस्वरूपाव्यतिरिक्तत्वमुक्तम्। एवं च सति जगद्व्यतिरिक्तलक्षणं ब्रह्मस्वरूपं कीदृशमित्याकाङ्क्षायामाह—**अन्तर्लीनविमर्श** इत्यादिना। विमृश्यते परामृश्यते इदमिति विमर्शः प्रपञ्चः। इदमित्येव हि परमात्मना सृष्टस्य जगतः प्रसिद्धः परामर्शः। तथा च श्रुतिः—"आत्मन आकाशः संभूतः" इत्यारभ्य, "स वा एष पुरुषोऽन्नरसमयः" इति शरीरसृष्टिमुक्त्वा, "तस्येदमेव शिरः, अयं दक्षिणः पक्षः, अयमुत्तरः पक्षः, अयमात्मा, इदं पुच्छं प्रतिष्ठा" इत्यादिवाक्येन इदमिदमित्येव हि प्रपञ्चपरामर्शो दृश्यते। **परापञ्चाशिकायामपि**—"अहमि प्रलयं कुर्वन्निदमः प्रतियोगिनः।" इति ब्रह्मप्रतियोगिभूतस्य प्रपञ्चस्य इदमानिर्देशः कृतः। एवंभूतो विमर्शः प्रपञ्चः अन्तर्लीनोऽन्तर्गतो विमर्शः यस्य स **अन्तर्लीनविमर्शः**। तदयमर्थः—स्वात्मसात्कृताखिलप्रपञ्चः परिपूर्णाहंभावभावनागर्भितः परमानन्दपरज्योतिःस्वरूपः परमात्मेति। एतच्च उत्तरत्र अहमर्थनिर्णयप्रकरणे प्रपञ्चयिष्यते। इहापि प्रसङ्गात् किञ्चिदुच्यते। ब्रह्म चाहमिति परमानन्दी भवति। तथा **चोपनिषत्**—"तस्माद्वा एतस्माद्विज्ञानमयात्। अन्योऽन्तर आत्मानन्दमयः" इति परमात्मानं निर्दिश्य; "तस्य प्रियमेव शिरः। मोदो दक्षिणः पक्षः। प्रमोद

उत्तरः पक्षः । आनन्द आत्मा । ब्रह्मपुच्छं प्रतिष्ठा ।" इति पूर्णाहंताविशिष्टं परं ब्रह्म ब्रवीति । ननु, "आनन्द आत्मा" इति आनन्दरूपत्वमात्मनः प्रतिपाद्यते, न तु पूर्णाहंताविशिष्टत्वम्; तत्कथमुच्यते? पूर्णाहंताविशिष्टत्वं परं ब्रह्मेति । आनन्दो नाम विश्वात्मभावना । तथा सुबालोपनिषदि—"अन्नमयो भूतात्मा, प्राणमय इन्द्रियात्मा, मनोमयः संकल्पात्मा, विज्ञानमयः कालात्मा, आनन्दमयो लयात्मा" इति । अत्र लयः पूर्णाहंभावना । वचनमपि—"ध्यानकोटिसमो लयः" इति, "चिदानन्दघनं महत्" इत्यत्र अमृतानन्दयोगिभिः, "चिच्चैतन्यकला, आनन्दो विश्वाहंतापरिणामः ताभ्यां घनं बहिरन्तर्निरन्तरान्निबिडम्, यथा लवणं घनम्, महत् देशकालाकारैरनाकलितं, चिन्मयत्वात् ।" इत्युक्तत्वात् एवं व्याख्यातम् । अथवा जगदुत्पत्तिस्थितिलयहेतुभूताकृत्रिमाहंभावपरामर्शो विमर्शः । तथा नागानन्दाः—"विमर्शो नाम विश्वाकारेण वा, विश्वप्रकाशेन वा विश्वोपसंहारेण वा अकृत्रिमोऽहमिति स्फुरणम् । तस्य अन्तर्लीनत्वं नाम अन्तर्मुखत्वम्" इति; तथा चायमर्थः—अन्तर्लीनोऽन्तर्मुखो विमर्शः पूर्णाहंभावो यस्येति । तथा श्रीस्वच्छन्दशास्त्रे—

"स तु योऽन्तर्मुखो भावः सर्वज्ञादिगुणास्पदः ।
तस्य लोपः कदाचित्स्यादन्यस्यानुपलम्भनात् ॥"

इति । विरूपाक्षपञ्चाशिकायामपि—

"स्वपरावभासनक्षम आत्मा विश्वस्य यः प्रकाशोऽसौ ।
अहमिति स एक उक्तोऽहंता स्थितिरीदृशी तस्य ॥"

इति । शिवानन्दस्वामिनोऽपि—"अहमित्यक्रमाक्रान्तसमस्तभुवनत्रयम्" इति । तत्तादृशपरब्रह्मणः परमेश्वरस्य प्रकाशैकस्वभावत्वं सर्वस्मात्परत्वं चाह—प्रकाशमात्रतनुर्महेश इति । प्रकाशमात्रा प्रकाशानतिरिक्ता तनुर्यस्य । तथा च छान्दोग्ये—"यदतः परो दिवो ज्योतिर्दीप्यते," "तं देवा ज्योतिरायुर्होपासतेऽमृतम्" इति । "स एष संप्रसादोऽस्माच्छरीरात्समुत्थाय परं ज्योतिरुपसंपद्य स्वेन रूपेणाभिनिष्पद्यते" इति,

"न तत्र सूर्यो भाति न चन्द्रतारकं नेमा विद्युतो भान्ति कुतोऽयमग्निः ।

तमेव भान्तमनुभाति सर्वं तस्य भासा सर्वमिदं विभाति ॥"

इत्यादि च। तथा **रहस्यागमश्च**—"स्वरूपज्योतिरेवान्तः परावागनपायिनी" "वन्दे ज्योतिरनुत्तरम्" इति च। **परापञ्चाशिकायामपि**—"य एकोऽन्तरिदं ज्योतिः स तेजांसि तमांसि च" इति। **सौभाग्यहृदयेऽपि**—"तन्महः परमं नौमि" इत्यादि। अत्र प्रकाशत्वं नाम 'इच्छामि' 'जानामि' 'करोमि' इत्युत्तमपुरुषान्तर्गतस्फुरणरूपाहंपरामर्श एव। ततश्च सर्वज्ञत्वसर्वेश्वरत्वसर्वकर्तृत्वपूर्णत्वव्यापकत्वरूपपञ्चशक्तिसंवलितं परं ब्रह्मेत्युक्तं भवति। ननु सूर्यादीनामपि प्रकाशकत्वं दृष्टम्। तत्कथमस्यैव परप्रकाशरूपत्वमित्यत आह—**महेश** इति। महांश्चासावीशश्चेति महेशः। महत्वं च देशकालाकारैरनवच्छिन्नस्वरूपत्वम्। ईशत्वं च सर्वनियन्तृत्वम्। तथा च यजुःश्रुतिः—"यतो वाचो निवर्तन्ते" इति सर्वप्रकारेणापरिच्छिन्नं ब्रह्मेति निर्दिश्य,

"तस्यैवेषा परा देवी स्वभावामर्शनोत्सुका।
पूर्णत्वं सर्वभावानां यस्या नाल्पं न वाधिकम् ॥"

इति ब्रवीति। तथा **अथर्वणवेदोपनिषदि**—"अथ कस्मादुच्यते महेश्वरः, सर्वान् लोकान् संभक्षः संभक्षयत्यजस्रं, सृजति विसृजति वासयति। तस्मादुच्यते महेश्वरः" इति। **उपनिषदन्तरेऽपि**—

"यो वेदादौ स्वरः प्रोक्तो वेदान्ते च प्रतिष्ठितः।
तस्य प्रकृतिलीनस्य यः परस्स महेश्वरः ॥"

"भीषास्माद्वातः पवते" इत्यादि। "एतस्य वा अक्षरस्य प्रशासने गार्गि सूर्याचन्द्रमसौ विधृतौ तिष्ठतः" इत्यादि च। तथा **प्रत्यक्षोपनिषत्**—"यत्परं ब्रह्म स एको रुद्रः स ईशानः स भगवान् महेश्वरः स महादेवः" इति। **परापञ्चाशिकायामपि**—

"स एव सर्वभूतानां स्वभावः परमेश्वरः।
. . . . .
स एव भैरवो देवो जगद्भरणलक्षणः ॥"

इति परमेश्वरं निर्दिश्य—

"तस्यैवैषा परा देवी स्वभावामर्शनोत्सुका ।
पूर्णत्वं सर्वभावानां यस्या नाल्पं न वाधिकम् ॥"

इति संपूर्णरूपत्वपराशक्तियोगं परमात्मनो विधाय,

"एव देवोऽनया देव्या नित्यं क्रीडारसोत्सुकः ।
विचित्रान् सृष्टिसंहारान्विधत्ते युगपत्प्रभुः ॥
अतिदुर्घटकारित्वमस्यानुत्तरमेव तत् ।
एतदेव स्वतन्त्रत्वमैश्वर्यं परबोधितम्[1] ॥"

इति ब्रह्मस्वरूपं सम्यक्प्रकल्प्य प्रपञ्चितम् । एवं पराभट्टारिकासहितः श्रीपरमेश्वरः, "एष सर्वेश्वरः, एष भूताधिपतिः, एष भूतपाल एष सेतुर्विधरण एषां लोकानामसंभेदाय" इति बृहदारण्यकोक्तरीत्या सर्वप्रकारेण सर्वरक्षकः परमेश्वरः परमात्मा युष्मान् पात्विति निरवधिकदयाशालिनः पुण्यानन्दाः पुण्यपुरुषानाशासते । पालनं चात्र परमात्मैकत्वरूपमेव । तथा चिद्विलासे—"भेदलक्षणविपक्षसंकटात् तारणं परमिहात्मरक्षणम् ।" इत्यभेदेन चिन्तनमभिप्रेतम् । इदं चात्र पुण्यानन्दानामाकूतम्; सर्वभूतसुहृत्परमात्मैवात्र लोके सद्गुरुरूपमास्थाय कतिचन भक्तिभाजः संरक्षतीति । अत्र यजुःश्रुतिः—"स चाचार्यवंशो ज्ञेयो भवत्याचार्याणामसावसावित्या भगवत्तः ।"

"आचार्यवान् पुरुषो वेद आचार्यस्तु ते गतिं वक्ता ।
त्वं हि नः पिता योऽस्माकमविद्यायाः परं पारं तारयति ॥
परीक्ष्य लोकान् कर्मचितान् ब्राह्मणो निर्वेदमायान्नास्त्यकृतः कृतेन ।
तद्विज्ञानार्थं स गुरुमेवाभिगच्छेत् समित्पाणिः श्रोत्रियं ब्रह्मनिष्ठम् ॥"

इत्यादिश्रुतिजालं श्रीगुरूपसदनद्वारा ब्रह्मप्राप्तिमभिधत्ते । यथा चागमश्च—

"शिवशक्तिसमायोगाज्जन्मान्तरकृताच्छुभात् ।
शिवपूजानुचिन्ता स्यात्कर्मे साम्यं यदा भवेत् ॥
शिव एव तदा साक्षादास्थाय गुरुविग्रहम् ।
दीक्षां करोति विश्वात्मा शंभुशक्त्यनुवेधतः ॥" इति ।

[1] परबोधिता.

गीता च—

> "तद्विद्धि प्रणिपातेन परिप्रश्नेन सेवया ।
> उपदेक्ष्यन्ति ते ज्ञानं ज्ञानिनस्तत्त्वदर्शिनः ॥"

इति । अभियुक्तोक्तिश्च—"कल्याणि देशिककटाक्षसमाश्रयेण कारुण्यतो भवसि शांभववेधदीक्षा ।" "परमशिवादिपदद्वयपारंपर्यक्रमागतं भाव्यम्" इति च ।

अत्र किंचित्प्रसङ्गादुच्यते—'पातु महेशः प्रकाशमात्रतनुः' इत्यनेन गुरुदेवतामन्त्राणामैक्यं प्रतिपादितम् । कथम्? आचार्यस्य प्रकाशकत्वम् अस्त्येव । तथा **सूत्रम्**—"गुरुरुपायः" इति । तथा तद्वृत्तिकारोऽपि—

> "गृणातीति गुरुस्तत्त्वं स्तोत्रव्याप्तिप्रदर्शकः ।
> मन्त्रवीर्यस्य तेनासावुपाय इति कीर्तितः ॥"

इति । रक्षकत्वं मन्त्रस्याप्यस्ति । मननात् त्रायत इति मन्त्रशब्दार्थः । **यथागमश्च**—"मननात्त्राणधर्माणो मन्त्राः स्युः परिकीर्तिताः ।" इति । **शिवसूत्रमपि**—"चित्तं मन्त्रः" इति चैतन्यरक्षकत्वं मन्त्रस्य प्रतिपाद्यते । अयमर्थः **चतुःशत्यामपि** अर्थषट्कनिरूपणप्रकरणे निगर्भाभिधेययोः प्रतिपाद्यते—

> "निगर्भार्थो महादेवि शिवगुर्वात्मगोचरः ।
> तत्प्रकारं च देवेशि दिङ्मात्रेण वदामि ते ॥
> निष्कलत्वं शिवे बुद्ध्वा तद्रूपत्वं गुरोरपि ।
> तन्निरीक्षणसामर्थ्यादात्मनश्च शिवात्मता ॥"

इति । एतदभिप्रायेणास्मदाचार्यवर्यैः **श्रीशंकरानन्दगुरुभिरपि** सम्यक् निरणायि;

> "नमः शिवाय नाथाय चिद्रूपानन्दरूपिणे ।
> श्रीमते चटुलापाङ्गपाटितातङ्कशङ्कवे ॥"

इत्यादि । तथा **श्वेताश्वतरोपनिषदि**—

> "यस्य देवे परा भक्तिर्यथा देवे तथा गुरौ ।
> तस्यैते कथिता ह्यर्थाः प्रकाशन्ते महात्मनः ॥"

इति। एवं च सत्संप्रदायिभिरेव माहेश्वरैः आत्मा कामेश्वरः प्राप्यते। न तु अन्यैरित्यलं प्रसक्तानुप्रसक्त्या। प्रकृतमनुसरामः ॥ १ ॥

ननु कथमयमात्मा परमशिवभट्टारक एव सर्वकर्तेत्युच्यते, तस्य सर्वकर्तृत्व-निषेधश्रवणात्। श्रूयते हि—

"न तस्य कार्यं करणं च विद्यते न तत्समश्चाभ्यधिकश्च विद्यते।
परास्य शक्तिर्विविधैव श्रूयते .... ॥"

इति पराभट्टारिकासंबन्धादेव सर्वकर्तृत्वाभ्यधिकत्वप्रतिपादनपुरःसरं पराभट्टारिकाया एव सर्वजगदुत्पत्तिश्रवणात्। किंच—"आनीदवातꣳ स्वधया तदेकम्।" इति। "श्रद्धया देवो देवत्वमश्नुते।" इत्यादि। "सा साक्षिणो विजयते तव मूर्तिरेका।" इत्यभियुक्तस्मृतिश्च। पराभट्टारिकासंनिधानादेव अस्य महेश्वरस्य सत्ताश्रवणाच्च। केवलमीश्वरस्य सर्वकर्तृत्वादिकं न संघटत इति, सत्यम्। न हि वयं परमेश्वरः परमशिवः पराभट्टारिकारहितः केवलकर्तेति वदामः। किं तु शिवशक्तिरूपकमेव तत्त्वमिति निश्चित्य तस्य कारणत्वमवोचाम। तथा प्रामाणिक-वचनम्—"शिवशक्तिरिति ह्येकं तत्त्वमाहुर्मनीषिणः" इति। श्रीस्वच्छन्देऽपि—

"तत्त्वारूढः स भगवान् शिवः परमकारणम्।
शिवःसर्वस्य कर्तेयं शक्तिः कारणमुच्यते" ॥

इत्युभयोरपि कर्तृत्वमुच्यते। तत्रैव ;

"शिवाभिन्ना परा शक्तिः सर्वकर्मशरीरिणी।
वामादीच्छादिभेदेन मिथुनत्रयतां गता ॥"

इति स्मरणात् एकमेव जगत्कारणम्। अन्यथा श्रुतिविरोधः प्रसज्येत, "सदेव सोम्येदमग्र आसीत् एकमेवाद्वितीयं ब्रह्म" इत्येकत्वावधारणात्। तस्माच्छिवस्य कारणत्ववचनं शक्तेरपि समानम्। अत एव शक्तेरपि कर्तृत्वमुच्यमानं शिवस्यापि तुल्यम्। यदाहुः,

"न शिवेन विना देवी न देव्या च विना शिवः।
नानयोरन्तरं किञ्चिच्चन्द्रचन्द्रिकयोरिव ॥"

इत्यागमसिद्धान्तरीत्या पराभट्टारिकाया अपि सर्वकारणत्वमाह—

सा जयति शक्तिराद्या निजसुखमयनिरुपमाकारा।
भाविचराचरबीजं शिवरूपविमर्शनिर्मलादर्शः॥ २॥

सेति। सा आद्या शक्तिः; अनवच्छिन्ना पराभट्टारिका महात्रिपुरसुन्दरी, **जयति;** सर्वोत्कर्षेण वर्तते। सैव शिवादिक्षित्यन्तषट्त्रिंशत्तत्त्वमयसर्वप्रपञ्चात्मिका तदुत्तीर्णा चेति सर्वोपनिषत्प्रसिद्धा त्रिपुरा अभिधीयते। एवं हि सत्संप्रदायविद्भिः महायोगिभिः पुरुषैः त्रिपुराशब्दनिर्वचनं क्रियते। कथं? त्रिभ्यस्तेजोऽबन्नादिभ्यः पुरा भूता त्रिपुरेति। तेजोऽबन्नादिभ्यः पूर्वसत्त्वमेव हि सर्वतत्त्वातिक्रान्तत्वं ब्रह्मणः, तद्द्वारा सर्वतत्त्वात्मकत्वं च; उपनिषदप्येवमेवाह, यथा छान्दोग्ये षष्ठप्रपाठके— "श्वेतकेतुर्हारुणेय आस तं ह पितोवाच श्वेतकेतो वस ब्रह्मचर्यम्" इति पुत्रस्य वेदाध्ययनादिरूपब्रह्मचर्यं विधाय; "स ह द्वादशवर्ष उपेत्य चतुर्विंशतिवर्षः सर्वान्वेदानधीत्य महामना अनूचानमानी स्तब्ध एयाय, तं ह पितोवाच, श्वेतकेतो यन्नु सोम्येदं महामना अनूचानमानी स्तब्धोऽस्युत तमादेशमप्राक्ष्यो येनाश्रुतं श्रुतं भवत्यमतं मतमविज्ञातं विज्ञातम्।" इत्यादिना शिष्ययोग्यतां निश्चित्य आचार्यो ब्रह्मविद्यामुपादिशत्। तत्र एकविज्ञानेन सर्वविज्ञानद्वारा सर्वतत्त्वानां तन्मयत्वमुक्तम्। तत्र दृष्टान्तमाकाङ्क्षमाणः शिष्यः पृच्छति, "कथं नु भगवः स आदेशो भवति" इति "यथा सोम्यैकेन मृत्पिण्डेन सर्वं मृन्मयं विज्ञातं स्याद् वाचारम्भणं विकारो नामधेयं मृत्तिकेत्येव सत्यम्" इत्यादि-दृष्टान्तपरंपरया परब्रह्मणो विश्वात्मकत्वं तदुत्तीर्णत्वं चाभ्युत्थाय, अनन्तरं च; "सदेव सोम्येदमग्र आसीत्, एकमेवाद्वितीयम्" इत्यादिना विश्वातीतं वस्त्वभिधाय, पुनश्च विश्वात्मकमभिधत्ते—"तदैक्षत बहु स्यां प्रजायेयेति" इति संकल्प्य, "तत्तेजोऽसृजत" इति तेजोऽबन्नानि सृष्ट्वा, "सेयं देवतैक्षत हन्ताहमिमास्तिस्रो देवता अनेन जीवेनात्मनानुप्रविश्य नामरूपे व्याकरवाणीति। तासां त्रिवृतं त्रिवृतमेकैकां करवाणीति सेयं देवतेमास्तिस्रो देवता अनेनैव जीवेनात्मनानुप्रविश्य नामरूपे व्याकरोत्। तासां त्रिवृतं त्रिवृतमेकैकामकरोत्" इत्यादिना तेजोऽबन्नानामहं-भावेन ब्रह्मणः सर्वपूर्ववर्तित्वं सर्ववस्तुपूरकत्वं च स्वस्वरूपकमित्युक्त्वा तेजोऽबन्नात्मक-

मेव देवादिस्थावरान्तं तत्त्वजालमाचष्टे । यथा वा "अपागादग्नेरग्नित्वं वाचारम्भणं विकारो नामधेयं त्रीणि रूपाणीत्येव सत्यम्" इत्यादिना "अन्नमशितं त्रेधा विधीयते तस्य यः स्थविष्ठो धातुस्तत्पुरीषं भवति यो मध्यमस्तन्मांसं योऽणिष्ठस्तन्मनः" इत्यादिना त्रिवृत्कृतप्रपञ्चपूरणात् त्रिपुरैव परं ब्रह्मेत्यभिधीयते । इममेवार्थमुत्तरत्र ग्रन्थकारो वक्ति—'षट्त्रिंशत्तत्वात्मा तत्त्वातीता च केवला विद्या ।' इति, **स्मृतिरपि**—"विश्वात्मिकां तदुत्तीर्णां हृदयं परमेशितुः ।" इति । **श्रीवामकेश्वरतन्त्रेऽपि**—

"त्रिपुरा परमा शक्तिराद्या जाता महेश्वरी ।
स्थूलसूक्ष्मविभेदेन त्रैलोक्योत्पत्तिमातृका ।
कवलीकृतनिःशेषतत्त्वग्रामस्वरूपिणी ॥"

इति । **श्रीस्वच्छन्देऽपि**—

"नात्र कालः कलाभावो नैकता न च देवता ।
सुनिर्वाणं परं तत्त्वं रुद्रवक्त्रं तदुच्यते ॥
शिवशक्तिरिति ख्यातं निर्विकल्पं निरञ्जनम् ।
पश्यातीतं वरारोहे वाङ्मनोऽतीतमद्भुतम् ॥
अनिष्कलं च सकलं नीरूपं निर्विकल्पकम् ।
निर्द्वन्द्वं परमं तत्त्वं शिवाख्यं परमं पदम् ॥"

इति । अस्मदुक्त**सच्चिदानन्दवासनायां** च—

"विश्वात्मिकां तदुत्तीर्णां प्रकाशामर्शरूपिणीम् ।
परापरमयीं देवीमात्मत्वेन विशाम्यहम् ॥"

इत्यादिबहुश्रुतिस्मृत्यादिषु सर्वोत्कृष्टत्वं त्रिपुरायास्तत्र तत्र चोद्घोष्यते । एतदेव विवृणोति—**निजसुखमयनित्यनिरुपमाकारेत्यनेन** । निजः स्वाभाविकः, सुखमयः दुःखासंभिन्नानन्दरूपः, नित्यः सार्वकालिकः, निरुपमः निःसमाभ्यधिकः, आकारः स्वरूपं यस्याः सा । तदयमर्थः—निरवधिकाकृत्रिमात्मानन्दरूपिणीति । **तथैवोपनिषत्**—"तस्येयं पृथिवी सर्वा वित्तस्य पूर्णा स्यात् । स एको मानुष आनन्दः," इत्युपक्रम्य "स एकः प्रजापतेरानन्दः" इत्यन्तमुत्तरोत्तरशत-

गुणितक्रमेण मनुष्यादिचतुर्मुखपर्यन्तं पुरुषाणामानन्दपरंपरामुपन्यस्य, "स एको ब्रह्मण आनन्दः। स यश्चायं पुरुषे। यश्चासावादित्ये। स एकः" इति सर्वोत्कृष्टानन्दवद्ब्रह्मणः सर्वात्मकत्वं सर्वोत्तीर्णत्वं वक्ति। उपनिषदन्तरेऽपि "भूमैव सुखं भूमा त्वेव विजिज्ञासितव्यः" इत्युक्त्वा, "यत्र नान्यत्पश्यति नान्यच्छृणोति नान्यद्विजानाति स भूमा" इत्यपरिच्छिन्नानन्दमयमेव ब्रह्म श्रूयते। तथा च "एतस्यैवानन्दस्यान्यानि भूतानि मात्रामुपजीवन्ति", इति, इतरेषां ब्रह्मानन्दसमुद्रविप्रुट्त्वमुच्यते। **वामकेश्वरतन्त्रे**—

"प्रणमामि महादेवीं परमानन्दरूपिणीम्।
अद्यापि यस्या जानन्ति न मनागपि देवताः॥
नित्यानन्दघनं परम् . . . . ।"

इति। "नित्यानन्दे निरुपमपदे निर्मले निर्विकल्पे" इति, "निष्यन्दमानसुखबोधसुधास्वरूपे" इति, "परमानन्दसंदोहप्रमोदभरनिर्भरे" इति "परमानन्दसंपूर्णपदसौभाग्यदायकम्" इत्याद्यभियुक्ततमोक्त्या च सच्चिदानन्दस्वरूपिणी त्रिपुरेति निश्चीयते। **भाविचराचरबीजमिति**; भाविनोः संपत्स्यमानयोः चराचरयोः स्थावरजङ्गमयोः बीजं योनिः कारणमित्यर्थः। अत्र **यजुःश्रुतिः**—

"यो देवानां प्रथमं पुरस्ताद्विश्वाधिको रुद्रो महर्षिः।
हिरण्यगर्भं पश्यत जायमानं स नो देवः शुभया स्मृत्या संयुनक्तु॥
स विश्वकृद्विश्वविदात्मयोनिर्ज्ञः कालकालो गुणी सर्वविद्यः।
यो ब्रह्माणं विदधाति पूर्वं यो वै वेदांश्च प्रहिणोति तस्मै॥
य ईशोऽस्य जगतो नित्यमेव नान्यो हेतुर्विद्यत ईशनाय।
एको वशी सर्वभूतान्तरात्मा एकं बीजं बहुधा यः करोति॥"

इत्यादिर्द्रष्टव्यः। **आगमश्च**—

"यदा सा परमा शक्तिः स्वेच्छया विश्वरूपिणी।
स्फुरत्तामात्मनः पश्येत्तदा चक्रस्य संभवः॥
यथा न्यग्रोधबीजस्थशक्तिरूपो महाद्रुमः।
तथा हृदयबीजस्थं जगदेतच्चराचरम्॥"

इति । **ललितोपाख्याने** च—“या ससर्ज विधातारं सर्गादौ वारिपूरितम्” इति । **परावासनायामपि**—

“ जगच्चित्रं समालिख्य स्वयमेवात्मविग्रहम् ।
स्वयमेव समालोक्य संतुष्टां परमाद्भुतम् ।
प्रकाशजीवसंलीनविमर्शात्मस्वरूपिणीम् ॥ ” इति ।

ननु शिवस्य जगन्निर्मातृत्वं शक्त्या विना कारणत्वं न बोभवीति, तथा पराशक्तेरपि परमशिवेन विना कारणत्वं न भवेदिति, तत्कथमुच्यते? भाविचराचरबीजमिति, अत आह—**शिवरूपविमर्शनिर्मलादर्श** इति। शिवस्य स्वरूपम् अहमित्येवमाकारं तस्य विमर्शः परामर्शनम् अहमित्येवंरूपं ज्ञानम् तस्य प्रकाशने निर्मलादर्शः सम्यक् प्रकाशनचतुर इत्यर्थः। अयमर्थः— यथा सिंहासनारूढः कश्चिद्राजा अतिसुन्दरः स्वात्माभिमुखावस्थितस्वच्छदर्पणतले स्वात्मप्रतिबिम्बं सम्यक् प्रसमीक्ष्य तत्प्रतिबिम्बमयमहमिति जानाति । एवं परमेश्वरोऽपि स्वाधीनभूतां स्वात्मशक्तिं सम्यगवलोक्य स्वस्वरूपमवगच्छति परिपूर्णोऽहमिति । एवं च दर्पणस्य स्वसंनिहितवस्तुसंबन्धाभावे स्वान्तर्गतप्रतिबिम्बावभासनमनुपपन्नं भवति । तद्वत् पराशक्तिरपि परमशिवसंबन्धाभावे स्वान्तस्थितप्रपञ्चनिगरणं न संघटत इत्यर्थात् लभ्यमेवैतत् । तस्मान्न केवलेन शिवेन वा, केवलया शक्त्या वा जगन्निर्मीयते । किंतु उभाभ्यामेव कामकामेश्वराभ्याम् अखिलं तत्त्वजातमातन्यते । यथा **श्वेताश्वतरोपनिषदि**—

“ य एको जालवानीश ईशनीभिः सर्वान् लोकानीशत ईशनीभिः ।
य एवैक उद्भवे संभवे च य एतद्विदुरमृतास्ते भवन्ति ॥
य एको वर्णो बहुधा शक्तियोगाद्वर्णाननेकान्निहितार्थो दधाति ।
वि चैति चान्ते विश्वमादौ स देवः स नो बुद्ध्या शुभया संयुनक्तु ॥ ”

इति । यथोक्तमभियुक्तैश्च ;

“ स्वेच्छाविभावितानन्दजगद्रश्मिविलासवत् ।
नौमि संविन्महापीठं शिवशक्तिपदाश्रयम् ॥
अखण्डितस्वभावोऽपि विचित्रां मातृकल्पनाम् ।
स्वहृन्मण्डलचक्रे यः प्रथयेत्तं नुमः शिवम् ॥ ”

इति । सशक्तिकमहमित्येवं रूपं परं ब्रह्मेति निर्णीतम् । अत्र यद्वक्तव्यं तदुत्तरत्र सम्यक् प्रपञ्च्य निरूप्यत इत्यलम् ॥ २ ॥

ननु निर्विमर्शमेव ब्रह्म वदन्ति केचन । तत्कथमुच्यते सविमर्शकं ब्रह्मेत्यत आह—

स्फुटशिवशक्तिसमागमबीजाङ्कुररूपिणी पराशक्तिः ।
अणुतररूपानुत्तरविमर्शलिपिलक्ष्यविग्रहा भाति ॥ ३ ॥

स्फुटेति । अस्यार्थः—अत्र पराशक्तिशब्देन प्रकृता ख्याता महात्रिपुरसुन्दरी अभिधीयते । "चिदानन्देच्छाज्ञानक्रियारूपा" इति या श्रुतिः जगत्प्रसिद्धा, सा त्वेव-मुच्यते—**स्फुटशिवशक्तिसमागमबीजाङ्कुररूपिणीति** । शिवश्च शक्तिश्च शिवशक्ती, तयोः समागमः संयोगः, स्फुटः व्यक्तः शिवशक्तिसमागमो योऽयं तेन ; बीजाङ्कुर-रूपिणीति 'बीजादङ्कुरम् अङ्कुराद्बीजमितिवत्' शिवतत्त्वादिक्षितितत्त्वपर्यन्तं तत्त्व-जालमुत्तरोत्तरमुद्भावयेदित्यर्थः । अत्र शिवशब्देन ज्ञानशक्तिरभिधीयते, ज्ञानशक्त्य-धिष्ठितत्वाच्छिवतत्त्वस्य ; शक्तिशब्देनापि क्रियाशक्तिरभिधीयते, क्रियाशक्त्यधिष्ठि-तत्वाच्छक्तितत्त्वस्य ; चिदानन्दस्वरूपिण्याः सर्वत्र ज्ञानक्रियाभ्यामेव प्रपञ्चनिर्माणौ-चित्यदर्शनात् । तथा च श्रुतिः—"यदिदं ते दृश्यते तदानन्दयोनिः तेन जीवति, तदेषाभ्युक्ता परो वा एष आनन्दः स भागयोनिः, कामरूपावेतौ स आनन्दयोनिः आनन्दो ब्रह्म ब्रह्मैवैषा देवी एकानेकप्रपञ्चा स्यात् चतुर्थपौरुषार्थे आनन्दरूपा" इति । **यथागमश्च**—

"यदा सा परमा शक्तिः स्वेच्छया विश्वरूपिणी ।
स्फुरत्तामात्मनः पश्येत्तदा चक्रस्य संभवः ॥"

इति । **प्रत्यभिज्ञासूत्रेऽपि**—"चितिः स्वतन्त्रा विश्वसिद्धिहेतुः" इति । **अभि-युक्तोक्तिश्च**—"सा योनिः सर्वदेवानां शक्तीनां च . . . ." इत्यादि । एवं चार्थो वर्णयितव्यः, सैव पराशक्तिः स्वयमेव शिवशक्तीभूय विश्वं सृजतीति । तथा च श्रुतिः—"या लिङ्गमया निर्विततान हेतुर्याभ्यामिदं विश्वमादौ बभूव" इत्यादि-र्द्रष्टव्या । तथा **चिद्विलासे**—

" मेदिनीप्रमुखमाशिवं मतं तत्त्वचक्रमिह चक्रमुत्तमम् ।
स्वस्वभावसमयावभासिनी देवता भवति सांविदी कला ॥ "

इति ।

" विसर्गशक्तीर्विश्वस्य कारणं च निरूपिता ।
ऐतरेयाख्यवेदान्ते परामर्शेन विस्तरात् "

इत्यभियुक्तोक्तिः । पुनस्तामेव विशिनष्टि—**अणुतररूपानुत्तरविमर्शलिपिलक्ष्यविग्रहा भातीति** । अणुतरम्, अत्यन्तसूक्ष्मं रूपम् अस्या इति अणुतररूपा । अत्र यजुःश्रुतिः—" सूक्ष्मात्सूक्ष्मतरं नित्यं तत्त्वमेव त्वमेव तत् । ", " यत्तदद्रेश्यमग्राह्यम् " " एष आत्मान्तर्हृदयेऽणीयान् व्रीहिरूपाद्वा सर्षपाद्वा " इत्यादि, । तथा वचनमपि ; " अणोरणुतरा देवी महतोऽपि महीयसी । " इति ।

अत्रेदमतिरहस्यम्—अनुत्तरलिपिरकारः ; विमर्शलिपिर्हकारः ; ताभ्यां लक्ष्य विग्रहं स्वरूपं यस्याः सा तथोक्ता । अत्र, ' अनुत्तरविमर्शलिपिलक्ष्यविग्रहा ' इत्यनेनाहमात्मिकान्तर्गर्भितसमस्तवर्णकदम्बकापरा शक्तिः अकारादिहकारान्तं पञ्चाशदक्षररूपिणी वर्णपदमन्त्रकलातत्त्वभुवनात्मकसमस्तप्रपञ्चजनयित्री पराभट्टारिका समस्तभूतान्तरात्मा सर्वत्र वेदान्ते अहमहमित्येवमाकारेण प्रतीयमाना दृश्यत इत्युक्तं भवति । तथा **बृहदारण्यके**—" ब्रह्म वा इदमग्र आसीत्तदात्मानमेवावेत् । अहं ब्रह्मास्मीति " इति । **ऐतरेयेऽपि**—" अ इति ब्रह्म तत्रागतमहम् " इति । **तापिनीयेऽपि**—" कस्त्वमित्यहमिति होवाच । एवमेवेदं सर्वम् । तस्मादहमिति सर्वाभिधानम् । तस्यादिरयमकारः । स एव भवति । सर्वं ह्ययमात्मा । अयं हि सर्वान्तरात्मा । न हीदं सर्वम् । निरात्मकमात्मैवेदं सर्वम् । तस्मात्सर्वात्मकेनाकारेण सर्वात्मकमात्मानमन्विच्छेद्ब्रह्मैवेदं सच्चिदानन्दरूपम् " इति । तत्रैवान्यत्र—" तद्वा एतद्ब्रह्म अद्वयं बृहत्त्वात् । नित्यं शुद्धं बुद्धं मुक्तं सत्यं सूक्ष्मं परिपूर्णम् अद्वयं सच्चिदानन्दं चिन्मात्रमेव " इति परमात्मानमभिधाय, तदुपासनाप्रकारमप्याह—" सुविभान्तं सकृद्विभान्तं पुरतोऽस्मात्सर्वस्मादविभान्तमद्वयं पश्यतो हंसः सोऽहमिति ब्रह्म भवति । य एवं वेद । " इति, पूर्णाहंभावभावनारूपमात्मोपासनमत्यन्तगोपनीयं रहस्यमिति

तद् गुरुमुखादेवावगन्तव्यमिति श्रुतिरेवाह, यथा छान्दोग्ये षष्ठप्रपाठके—"तदैक्षत", "सेयं देवतैक्षत" इत्यादिना तेजोबन्नात्मकरूपत्रयां सर्वजगन्निर्मात्रीं त्रिपुराममिधाय, "यो वै भूमा तत्सुखम्। यत्र नान्यत्पश्यति नान्यच्छृणोति नान्यद्विजानाति स भूमा" इति निरतिशयानन्दरूपिणीं तामेव निर्दिश्य, "स एवाधस्तात्" इत्युपक्रम्याहमात्मानं निर्दिशति; "अहमेवाधस्तादहमुपरिष्टादहं पश्चादहं पुरस्तादहं दक्षिणतोऽहमुत्तरतोऽहमेवेदं सर्वमिति" इति। तथा बृहदारण्यके—"त्वं वा अहमस्मि भगवो देवतैतासां वै त्वमसि भगवो देवता" इत्यादि। स्मृतिरपि;

"हृद्यकारं द्वादशान्ते हकारं स्थविरा विदुः।
अहमात्मैकमद्वैतं यत्प्रकाशात्मविश्रमः॥
अकारः सर्ववर्णाग्र्यः प्रकाशः परमशिवः।
हकारोऽन्त्यः कलारूपो विमर्शाख्यः प्रकीर्तितः॥
उभयोः सामरस्यं यत्परस्मिन्नहमि स्फुटम्।"

इति। श्रीविरुपाक्षपञ्चशिकायामपि—

"स्वपरावभासनक्षम आत्मा विश्वस्य यः प्रकाशोऽसौ।
अहमिति स एक उक्तोऽहंता स्थितिरीदृशी तस्य॥"

इत्यादिवचनसहस्रमनुसंधेयमित्यलमतिविस्तरेण॥ ३॥

इतः परं प्रबन्धेन प्रधानप्रतिपाद्यां कामकलाक्षररूपिणीमेव विवेक्तुकामस्तदक्षरस्वरूपां वक्तुमुपक्रमते—

परशिवरविकरनिकरे प्रतिफलति विमर्शदर्पणे विशदे।
प्रतिरुचिरुचिरे कुड्ये चित्तमये निविशते महाबिन्दुः॥ ४॥

परशिवरविकर इत्यादि **'कला च दहनेन्दुविग्रहौ बिन्दू'**, इत्यन्तम्। **परशिवः** प्रकाशैकस्वभावः परमशिवभट्टारक एव; **रविर्दिनकरः**, तस्य **कराः** किरणाः; तेषां **निकरः** पुञ्जः तस्मिन् **विशदे**; निर्मले; **विमर्शदर्पणे**; विमर्शो नाम अनवधिरेका विस्फुरणशक्तिः। तथा च **प्रत्यभिज्ञायाम्**—"सा स्फुरत्ता" इत्यादि। सैव दर्पणत्वेन निरूप्यते स्वस्वरूपप्रकाशत्वात्। **प्रतिफलतीति**। तत्र प्रतिफलनं नाम

स्वरूपावलोकनम्। तादृशप्रतिफलनस्वरूपावलोकने सति, **चित्तमये**; ज्ञानैकस्वरूपे, **प्रतिरुचिरुचिरे**; प्रतिप्रकाशमनोहरे, **कुडये**। **महाबिन्दुः** निविशते प्रविष्टो भवति। चित्तस्य कुडयत्वनिरूपणं महाबिन्द्वाविर्भावकारणत्वात्। लोकेऽपि सूर्याभिमुखस्थित-दर्पणतले सूर्यकिरणप्रतिफलनानन्तरं निकटगतकुडये सूर्यकिरणप्रतिहततेजोबिन्दुः प्रत्यक्षं प्रपद्यते। तद्वत्प्रकाशरूपपरमेश्वरस्य दर्पणवत् स्वस्वरूपविमर्शसंबन्धे जाते तदानीं तत्र महाबिन्दुः पूर्णोऽहमित्येवंरूपः परमेश्वरोऽवभासत इत्यर्थः। तथा च **छान्दोग्ये**—"सदेव सोम्येदमग्र आसीत्। एकमेवाद्वितीयं ब्रह्म" "तदैक्षत" "सेयं देवतैक्षत" इति च, "ब्रह्म वा इदमग्र आसीत्, तदात्मानमेव वेद, अहं ब्रह्मास्मीति" "स ईक्षत लोकान्नु सृजा इति।" इत्यादिश्रुतिषु स्वात्मशक्तिनिरीक्ष-णाभिमुखं परं ब्रह्म जगत्कारणमित्युच्यते। **आगमश्च**—"स्फुरत्तामात्मनः पश्येत्तदा चक्रस्य संभवः" इति। **प्रत्यभिज्ञायामपि**—

"सा स्फुरत्ता महासत्ता देशकालविशेषिणी।
सैषा सारतया चोक्ता हृदयं परमेष्ठिनः॥"

इति। **परमानन्दयोगिनोऽपि**—

"ईदृगियत्तादिवचो दूरतरं स्वानुभूतिसंवेद्यम्।
तत्तादृशस्फुरत्ताशेषं संवित्कथं नु सा वाच्या॥"

इत्यादि। अन्यत्सर्वं शिवरूपविमर्शनिर्मलादर्श इत्यत्र प्रपञ्चितम्; तत्रैवावलोकित-व्यमित्यलम्॥ ४॥

तादृगुज्ज्वलात्मकशक्त्यवलोकनोद्भूताहंभावमेव विशिनष्टि—

चित्तमयोऽहंकारः सुव्यक्ताहार्णसमरसाकारः।
शिवशक्तिमिथुनपिण्डः कवलीकृतभुवनमण्डलो जयति॥ ५॥

चित्तमय इति। अस्यार्थः—**अहंकारः**; अहमित्युद्भूतात्मस्मरणानुभावाभि-व्यञ्जको योऽयम् अहमहमित्येवं विमर्शः, तस्य कारः कारणमहंकारः। एवंभूतोऽहंकारः **जयति** सर्वोत्कर्षेण वर्तते। यथोक्तम्—"प्रकाशस्यात्मविश्रान्तिरहंभावो हि कीर्तितः।" इति। **चित्तमयः**; ज्ञानैकस्वभावः। **सुव्यक्ताहार्णसमरसाकारः**; अश्च हश्च अहौ,

सुतरां व्यक्तौ स्पष्टौ, परस्परोद्भूतरूपौ सुव्यक्ताहौ, तयोः समरसः एकलोलीभूतः आकारः निजरूपं यस्य । **शिवशक्तिमिथुनपिण्डः**; शिवः प्रकाशः, शक्तिर्विमर्शश्च, एतद्रूपं मिथुनं दिव्यदंपतिमयम्, पिण्डीभवति एकलोलीभवति यत्र स शिवशक्तिमिथुनपिण्डः । अत एव **कबलीकृतभुवनमण्डलः**; कबलीकृतम् अन्तःस्थापितं भुवनमण्डलं षट्त्रिंशत्तत्त्वसंघातमयं येन सः । अयमर्थः—प्रत्याहारन्यायेन अन्तर्गर्भितसमस्तवर्णकदम्बकाहंकाररूपप्रकाशविमर्शसंपटादेव शब्दार्थात्मकसर्वप्रपञ्चविकासो भवति । तथा च श्रुतिः—"य एको वर्णो बहुधा शक्तियोगाद्वर्णाननेकान्निहितार्थो दधाति ।" **तापिनीयेऽपि**—"कस्त्वमित्यहमिति होवाच । अहमेवेदं सर्वम् । तस्मादेवाहमिति सर्वाभिधानमिति" इति । **कैवल्योपनिषदि**—

"उमासहायं परमेश्वरं विभुं त्रिलोचनं नीलकण्ठं प्रशान्तम् ।
ध्यात्वा मुनिर्गच्छति भूतयोनिं समस्तसाक्षिं तमसः परस्तात् ॥"

इति, "स ब्रह्म स शिवः स हरिः सेन्द्रः सोऽक्षरः परमः स्वराट्" इत्युक्त्वा, "तद्ब्रह्माहमिति ज्ञात्वा सर्वबन्धैः प्रमुच्यते" इति कामकामेश्वरीरूपं ब्रह्म निर्दिश्य, तदुपासनमप्यहं ब्रह्मात्मकमेव विदधाति । तत्रैवान्यत्र "वेदैश्च सर्वैरहमेव वेद्यो वेदान्तकृद्वेदविदेव चाहम् ।" इति अहमात्मकमेव ब्रह्मेति निर्दिश्यते । **बृहदारण्यकेऽपि**—"तद्धैतत्पश्यन् स ऋषिर्वामदेवः प्रतिपेदे अहं मनुरभवं सूर्यश्च" इत्यहंरूपमुपासनमभिधाय, विपरीते बाधकमाह, "अथ योऽन्यां देवतामुपास्ते अन्योऽसावन्योऽहमस्मीति न स वेद यथा पशुः" इति, तत्रैवान्यत्र, "यत्र देव इव राजेवाहमेवेदं सर्वोऽस्मीति मन्यते सोऽस्य परमो लोकः" इति, "त्वं वा अहमस्मीति भगवो देवते अहं वै त्वमसि" इत्यादि । तथा **गीताभाष्ये**—

"उत्सृज्य स्वयमात्मानं ये ध्यायन्त्यन्यदेवताम् ।
भिक्षित्वा भूरि वित्तास्ते भिक्षित्वापि बुभुक्षिताः ॥"

इति । **विरूपाक्षपञ्चाशिकायामपि**—

"यस्य विमर्शस्य कणः पदमन्त्रार्णात्मकस्त्रिधा शब्दः ।[1]
भुवनकलातत्त्वार्थो धर्मिण इत्थं प्रकाशस्य ॥

[1] पदतत्त्वकलात्मार्थो . . . इति मुद्रितकोशपाठः ।

. . . . . .

अहमेकोऽनस्तमितप्रकाशरूपोऽस्मि तेजसां तमसाम् ॥ ”

इति ; तथा,

. . . . . .

“ अहमिति स एक उक्तोऽहंतास्थितिरीदृशी तस्य ॥ ”

इति । **रहस्यागमेऽपि**—

“ पूर्णाहंतात्मभावेन कृत्रिमाहं तया विना ।

आत्मानमात्मना साक्षाद्यः पश्यति स पश्यति ॥ ”

इति ॥ ५ ॥

इतः परं द्वाभ्यां, ‘ चित्तमये निविशते महाबिन्दुः,’ इति यदुक्तं तत्र बिन्दुस्वरूपनिरूपणद्वारा कामकलामुपदिशति—

सितशोणबिन्दुयुगलं विविक्तशिवशक्तिसंकुचत्प्रसरम् ।

वागर्थसृष्टिहेतुः परस्परानुप्रविष्टविस्पष्टम् ॥ ६ ॥

सितेति । सितशोणबिन्दुयुगलम् ; सितः शुभ्रः, शोणो रक्तः, तद्रूपौ बिन्दू तयोर्युगलम् । अत एव **विविक्तशिवशक्ति** ; अन्योन्यविहरणशीले शिवशक्ती यस्मिन् कर्मणि तत् । अत एव **संकुचत्प्रसरम्** ; संकुचन्मुकुलीभवन् प्रसरः जगत्सृष्टिरूपो विकासो यस्मिन् तत् । **वागर्थसृष्टिहेतुः** ; वाचः परापश्यन्त्यादिरूपसमस्तशब्दार्थाः शिवादिक्षित्यन्तषट्त्रिंशत्तत्त्वरूपाः ; तेषां सृष्टिः षडध्वात्मकजगन्निर्मितिः, तत्र हेतुः कारणम् । तथा **सौभाग्यहृदये**—

“ वर्णः कला पदं तत्त्वं मन्त्रो भुवनमेव च ।

इत्यध्वषट्कं देवेशि भाति त्वयि चिदात्मनि ॥ ”

इति । **परस्परानुप्रविष्टविस्पष्टम्** ; परस्परम् अन्योन्यम् अनुप्रविष्टम् अन्तर्गतम्, विस्पष्टं पृथग्भूतं च तत् । एवंभूतं सितशोणबिन्दुयुगलं कामकामेश्वरीरूपं दिव्यमिथुनं विभावयेदिति पूर्वेण संबन्धः ।

अत्रेदमतिरहस्यम्—"यः परः स महेश्वरः" इति श्रुत्युक्तरीत्या निखिलवेदादिशब्दोत्पादकोऽनुत्तराक्षराभिधेयः परमेश्वरः स्वात्मभूताखिलप्रपञ्चनिलयात्मकविमर्शशक्तिमनुप्रविश्य बिन्दुभावमयते। ततः सा विमर्शशक्तिरपि स्वान्तर्गतप्रकाशमयबिन्दुमनुप्रविशति। ततश्च बिन्दुरुच्छूनो भवति। तस्माद्बिन्दोर्नादात्मिका समस्ततत्त्वगर्भिणी तेजोमयी नीवाराग्रसूक्ष्मरूपिणी निर्गत्य शृङ्गाटरूपतामुद्वहते। एवं च बिन्दुनादस्वरूपयोः तयोः प्रकाशविमर्शयोरहमिति शरीरं भवति। एवं द्विरूपयोस्तयोर्मध्ये एको विमर्शो रक्तबिन्दुरूपं भजते; अपरः प्रकाशः शुक्लबिन्दुभावमेति; उभयोर्मेलने मिश्ररूपं सर्वतेजोमयं परमात्मस्वरूपं भवति। तथा **रहस्याम्नाये** प्रकाशविमर्शसंवादचन्द्रचन्द्रिकाख्यप्रकरणे अयमर्थः सम्यक् निरणायि—

"प्रसीद भगवन् शंभो ममात्मोपासनं प्रति।
यो यो भवति संदेहस्तं भवान्वक्तुमर्हसि॥
आत्मानुसंधयात्मानं परात्मीकृतरूपिणः।
भगवन् यः परानन्दः स कथं वद मे प्रभो॥"

इति पृष्टवतीं देवीं प्रत्याह परमेश्वरः—

"सकलाधारभूतो यः समस्तस्योपरि स्थितः।
तस्मिन्नात्मनि संधाय स्वात्मानं परमं व्रजेत्॥
आवयोर्जगदात्मत्वात्तादात्म्यादावयोरपि।
आत्मोपासनमानन्दं सर्वेषां विद्धि जानताम्॥
तादात्म्यादावयोर्नित्यं जगत्प्राणावुभौ हि नौ।
ज्ञात्वैतान्सकलान्सम्यग्जानीयात्संविदं पराम्॥"

इति। विमर्शः—

"आवयोरपि तादात्म्यं कथं योगोऽपि संभवेत्।
कर्मसाम्यं कथं केन निराचारावधूतकौ॥"

इत्यादिप्रश्नपञ्चकस्योत्तरमाह शिवः—

"शिवकामात्परं तत्त्वं वर्ण्यते इति चेच्छृणु।

स चोदयः प्रिये वक्तुं नालं वाग्विषयातिगम् ॥
परार्णाख्यशिवेच्छायां सत्यां सा विमर्शा तदा ।
अजायत परार्णाख्या बीजादङ्कुरवत्प्रिये ॥
अनुप्रविश्य तां शक्तिं वामाद्यैः पिण्डितो भवेत् ।
समस्तबीजगर्भाढ्या सूक्ष्मबिन्दुत्वमेति सः ॥
तत्प्रविश्याम्बिका भूत्वा सानन्दाकारतां गता ।
तद्व्याप्त्या जृम्भितात्तस्माद्बिन्दुरुच्छूनतां गतः ॥
तथा सा बिन्दुमुद्भिद्य नीवाराग्रवदुत्थिता ॥
तुल्यकालोदिता नित्यरश्मिकोटिविडम्बिनी ।
षट्त्रिंशत्तत्त्वगर्भाढ्या परमाद्यर्णगर्भिणी ॥
सा पुंभावपरं बिन्दुं प्रविश्य ध्वनितां गता ।
सोऽपि नादात्मिकां शक्तियोनिमेति स्वशक्तिताम् ॥
तयोर्विभेदयोरेको रक्तोऽन्यः शुक्लतां गतः ।
मध्यबिन्दुविमिश्रं तत्सुषुम्नाकन्दखात्मकम् ॥"

इत्यादिना बिन्दुत्रयनिरूपणं कृतम् । तदिह प्रसङ्गात् किंचिदुक्तम् । अन्यत्सर्वं गुरुमुखादेवावगन्तव्यम् । श्रुतिरपि—"य एको वर्णो बहुधा शक्तियोगात्" इत्यादि ॥ ६ ॥

एतदेव बिन्दुत्रयनिरूपणं विवृणोति—

बिन्दुरहंकारात्मा रविरेतन्मिथुनसमरसाकारः ।
कामः कमनीयतया कला च दहनेन्दुविग्रहौ बिन्दू ॥ ७ ॥

बिन्दुरहंकारात्मेति । **बिन्दुः**; सितरक्तस्वरूपः । **अहंकारः**; अन्तर्गर्भितसमस्तवर्णराशिः, अनुत्तरास्फाररूपाहंकार आत्मा स्वरूपं यस्य सः । "वर्णात्कारः" इति सूत्रेण अहंशब्दात् कारप्रत्ययः । ऐकार इतिवत् । अत एव **एतन्मिथुनसमरसाकारः**; एतयोः, अकारहकारवाच्ययोः प्रकाशविमर्शयोः, मिथुनं द्वन्द्वम्, तस्य दिव्यदंपतीरूपस्य मिथुनस्य समरसः परस्परानुप्रवेशरूपमानुकूल्यं तदेव आकारः

स्वरूपं यस्य सः । एवंभूतो रविः ; सितशोणविन्दुसमरसीभूतः, मिश्रबिन्दुरित्यर्थः । लोकेऽपि सूर्यस्य मिश्ररूपत्वं अग्नीषोमयोः प्रवेशनिर्गमश्रवणादेवं वर्णयति । तथा "उद्यन्तं वा वादित्यमग्निरनु समारोहति । अग्निं वा वादित्यः सायं प्रविशति" इति श्रुतेः । अमा सह सूर्याचन्द्रमसावस्यां तिथौ तिष्ठत इत्यमाशब्दव्युत्पत्त्या चन्द्र-सूर्ययोः प्रवेशनिर्गमने प्रसिद्धे । तस्माद्रविर्मिश्रबिन्दुरेव । अत एव तस्योपास्यत्व-माह—काम इति । काम्यते अभिलष्यते स्वात्मत्वेन परमार्थविद्भिः महद्भिः योगिभिरिति कामः । तत्र हेतुः—कमनीयतयेति । कमनीयत्वम् स्पृहणीयत्वम् । तथा चोपनिषदि—"हिरण्यश्मश्रुर्हिरण्यकेश आ प्रणखात्सर्व एव सुवर्णः" इति । ईशावास्येऽपि—"सपर्यगाच्छुक्रमकायमव्रणमस्नाविरं शुद्धमपापविद्धम्" इति । तथा तत्रैव—"यत्ते रूपं कल्याणतमं तत्ते पश्यामि योऽसावसौ पुरुषः सोऽहमस्मि" इति कमनीयं कामेश्वरमभिधाय तादृशमहिमानं परामृशति । तथा रहस्याम्नाये—

"निरुत्तरं निराधारं सच्चिदानन्दसागरम् ।
यदेतच्छांभवं मिश्रं निर्वाणाधारतां गतम् ॥"

इत्यादि । कला ; विमर्शशक्तिः । दहनो वह्निः, इन्दुः चन्द्रः ; तावेव विग्रहौ आकारौ ययोः बिन्द्वोः तौ दहनेन्दुविग्रहौ बिन्दू । अयमर्थः—अग्नीषोमरूपिणी विमर्शशक्तिः । तदुभयभूतकामेश्वराविनाभूता महात्रिपुरसुन्दरी बिन्दुसमष्टिरूपा कामकलेत्युच्यते । सैवोपास्यतया सर्वागमेषु चोद्घोष्यते ॥

तथा हि—

"शुक्लः शिवो रक्तशक्त्यां पराशांभववेधतः ।
रक्तशांभवरूपेण परातत्त्वेन शक्तितः ॥
रक्तः शिवः शुक्लशक्त्यां परशंभ्वैक्यभावतः ।
रक्तः शिवः शुक्लशक्त्यां सच्चिदानन्दलक्षणः ॥"

इति । अन्यत्रापि—

"अग्रबिन्दुपरिकल्पिताननामन्यबिन्दुरचितस्तनद्वयीम् ।
नादबिन्दुरशनागुणास्पदां नौमि ते परशिवे परां कलाम् ॥"

"मिहिरबिन्दुमुखीं तदधोल्लसच्छशिहुताशनबिन्दुयुगस्तनीम् ।
हसपरार्धकलारशनास्पदां भजति नित्यमिमां परदेवताम् ॥"

"एकारोर्ध्वगतो बिन्दुर्मुखं भानुरधोगतौ ।
स्तनौ दहनशीतांशू योनिर्हार्धकला भवेत् ॥"

इत्यादिरहस्यम् ॥

अयमत्र निष्कर्षः—स्वान्तर्गतानन्ताक्षरराशिमहामन्त्रवीर्यपूर्णाहंतारूपिणी प्रकाशानन्दसारा बिन्दुत्रयसमष्टिभूतदिव्याक्षररूपिणी कामकला नाम महात्रिपुरसुन्दरी मातृका परमयोगिभिर्महामाहेश्वरैरनिशमनुस्मर्तव्येति । एवंभूतमाहात्म्यं ब्रह्मोपनिषदि च प्रतिपाद्यते । यथा—"अथास्य पुरुषस्य चत्वारि स्थानानि भवन्ति । नाभिर्हृदयं कण्ठं मूर्धा च । तत्र चतुष्पादं ब्रह्म विभाति । जागरितं स्वप्नं सुषुप्तं तुरीयमिति । जागरिते ब्रह्मा स्वप्ने विष्णुः सुषुप्तौ रुद्रः तुरीयमक्षरम् । स आदित्यः, विष्णुश्चेश्वरश्च । .....स्वयममनस्कमश्रोत्रमपाणिपादं ज्योतिर्विदितम् ।" इति । अस्यार्थः—"अस्य देवस्य ससंप्रसारोऽन्तर्यामी खगः" इत्यादिपूर्वतनवाक्यजालैर्निर्णीतार्थकस्य पुरुषस्य चत्वारि स्थानानि मूलाधारहृदयकण्ठदेशोत्तमाङ्गरूपाणि भवन्ति । तेषु चतुर्षु स्थानेषु चतुष्पादं ब्रह्म सर्वव्यापनशीलं शुभ्रं स्वच्छप्रकाशम् अक्षरं न क्षरतीति व्युत्पत्त्या जगदुत्पत्तिकारणत्वान्मूलकारणभूतं विभाति । "तमेव भान्तमनुभाति सर्वं तस्य भासा सर्वमिदं विभाति ।" इति निरवधिकतेजोमयं सत् विद्योतत इत्यर्थः । एवंभूताक्षरस्य स्थानदेशेषु उपदेशद्वारा अवयवस्वरूपमुक्त्वा तुरीयं समुदायरूपं परमाक्षरबिन्दुद्वादशान्ते कामकलात्मकं परं ज्योतिर्मयमिति व्याचष्टे—तुरीयमक्षरमिति । स आदित्य इत्यारभ्य स ईश्वरश्च इत्यन्तम् । आदित्यः प्रकाशरूपः, विष्णुः व्यापनशीलः, प्राणो जीवः सर्वजीवनदायकः, पुरुषः सर्वजीववर्तिजीवः प्राणादिरूपोऽग्निः अग्रनेता । एवंभूतः स ईश्वरः विमर्शाख्यकामेश्वरीयुक्तः परमशिव इत्यर्थः । तथा चोक्तमथर्वशिरसि—"अथ कस्मादुच्यते ईशानः" इत्युक्त्वा स्वयमेव व्याचष्टे, "यः सर्वान् भावान् ईशत ईशनीभिः परमशक्तिभिः" इति । तथान्यत्र—"परास्य शक्तिर्विविधैव श्रूयते स्वाभाविकी ज्ञानबलक्रिया च ।" इति । एवंभूतः तुर्याक्षररूपः कामेश्वरः जागर्ति जाग्रतीत्यर्थः । "व्यत्ययो बहुलम्"

इति सूत्रेण सुप्तिङ्व्यत्ययविधानात् । अत्र जागरणं नाम परापश्यन्तीमध्यमा-वैखरीमयमातृकाचक्रात्मिकश्रीचक्रप्रथममध्यभूतसर्वानन्दमयाख्ये निरवधिकतेजोमण्डल-भवने,

> "बैन्दवानलसंरूढं संवर्तानलचिद्घनम् ।
> कामेश्वराङ्कपर्यङ्कनिविष्टमतिसुन्दरम् ॥"

इत्युक्तरीत्या प्रकाशानन्दनाथरूपत्वम् । एतदभिप्रायेण 'लीलाविनोदनोद्युक्तः' इत्यनेन जागरूक इति व्याख्यातम् । तत्तादृगक्षरं ज्योतिर्मयं निष्कलमित्याचष्टे । तेषां मध्ये इत्यादिना तेषां आधारहृदयकण्ठप्रदेशोत्तमाङ्गरूपस्थानविशेषोपासनावल्तृप्तावय-वाक्षराणां मध्ये यत्परं तुरीयभूतमक्षरं निर्वाणाख्यं ब्रह्म विभाति विद्योतते । एवंभूतस्य निष्कलस्य स्वरूपमह—अमनस्कमश्रोत्रमित्यादिना । परमप्रकृतमक्षरं निरूपयति—ज्योर्विदितमिति । "वन्दे ज्योतिरनुत्तरम्" इत्यादिना प्रकाशात्मकत्वादेव ज्योतिर्मयत्वं विदितं सर्ववेदान्तैर्वेदितमित्यर्थः । पुनरपि ज्योतिर्मयमक्षरं ब्रह्म सर्वात्मकं सर्वेश्वरं निर्वाणरूपमिति स्वयमेव श्रुतिः स्पष्टमाचष्टे । यथा—"यत्र लोका न लोका देवा न देवा वेदा न वेदा यज्ञा न यज्ञा माता न माता पिता न पिता स्नुषा न स्नुषा चण्डालो न चण्डालः पुल्कसो न पुल्कसः श्रमणो न श्रमणः तापसो न तापसः, एकमेवैतत्परं ब्रह्म विभाति ।', इति सर्वात्मकं ब्रह्म निर्दिश्य, "हृद्याकाशे तद्विज्ञानम्" इत्यारभ्य, "स विभुः प्रजासु ध्यानेन यो वेद" इत्युपासनास्वरूप-मुक्त्वा पुनरप्याह—"तत्परं ब्रह्म विभाति निर्वाणम् । न तत्र देवा ऋषयः पितर ईशते प्रतिबुद्धः सर्वविद्येति" इति । अन्यत्र च—"दृश्यते त्वग्र्यया बुद्ध्या सूक्ष्मया सूक्ष्मदर्शिभिः" । इत्यादिश्रुत्या परमार्थविद्भिस्तादृशमक्षरं सम्यगवगम्यते । तथा चतुःशत्यां द्वादशश्लोक्याम्—

> "यदक्षरमहासूत्रप्रोतमेतज्जगत्त्रयम् ।
> . . . . . .
> ब्रह्माण्डादिकटाहान्तं जगदद्यापि दृश्यते ।
> यदक्षरशशिज्योत्स्नामण्डितं भुवनत्रयम् ।
> रविताक्ष्येन्दुकन्दर्पशंकरानलविष्णुभिः ।
> यदक्षरैकमात्रेण संसिद्ध्यै स्पर्धते नरः ।

. . . . .

वन्दे तामहमक्षय्यां मातृकाक्षररूपिणीम् ।"

इति । प्रत्यभिज्ञायां च—

"सर्वदा त्वन्तरानन्दः सर्वतत्त्वौघनिर्भरः ।
शिवश्चिदानन्दघनः परमाक्षरविग्रहः ॥"

इति । तथा—

"स्वात्मैव सर्वजन्तूनामेक एव महेश्वरः ।
चित्स्वरूपोऽहमहमित्यखण्डामर्शबृंहितः ॥"

इति । यथा स्वच्छन्दे—

"............तदूर्ध्वे चोन्मना स्मृता

इत्युपक्रम्य,

नात्र कालः कलाभावो नैकता न च देवता ।
सुनिर्वाणं परं शुद्धं रुद्रवक्त्रं तदुच्यते ॥
शिवशक्तिरिति ख्यातं निर्विकल्पं निरञ्जनम् ।
पश्यातीतं वरारोहे वाङ्मनोऽतीतमद्भुतम् ॥
अनिष्कलं च सकलं नीरूपं निर्विकल्पकम् ।
निर्द्वन्द्वं परमं तत्त्वं शिवाख्यं परमं पदम् ॥"

इति । विज्ञानभैरवभट्टारकेऽपि—

"बिन्दुरूपस्य चक्रस्य स्थूलवर्णक्रमेण तु ।
अर्धेन्दुबिन्दुनादान्तशून्योच्चाराद्भवेच्छिवः ॥"

इत्यादि । अमृतानन्दयोगिनश्च—

"बैन्दवे परमाकाशे सच्चिदानन्दलक्षणे ।
निष्प्रपञ्चे निराभासे निर्विकल्पे निरामये ॥

अनुत्तरचमत्कारपरामर्शैपवित्रिते ।
निरुत्तरमहाशून्ये शून्यशून्यान्तवर्जिते ॥
स्त्रीपुंनपुंसकाख्याभिः कल्पनाभिरकल्पिते ।
आदिमध्यान्तनिर्मुक्ते भावपञ्चकभासिते ।
सर्वोपमानरहिते प्रकाशानुभवात्मिके ॥"

इति । **शिवानन्दस्वामिनोऽपि**—

"सकलाद्या स्थिते हृद्ये कामराजकलात्मिके ।
बिन्दुनादकलाकारे नमस्त्रिपुरसुन्दरि ॥"

इति । वयमपि **चिदानन्दवासनायाम्**—

"चतुरण्डमहारत्नमण्डितं विश्वविग्रहम् ।
क्षित्यादिशिवपर्यन्तं व्याप्यावस्थाचतुष्टयम् ॥
पिण्डं विभाव्य तन्मध्ये सर्वातीतघनां पराम् ।
तुर्यातीतां चिदानन्दरससारामनुत्तराम् ॥
तत्रापि स्वेच्छयोपात्तजागरादिदशां पराम् ।
अशेषसंविदामन्तर्मुखविश्रान्तिरूपिणीम् ॥
अनन्तकोटिचन्द्रार्कसंनिभां षोडशाधिकाम् ।
स्वान्तर्गतैकतापन्नषट्त्रिंशत्तत्त्वसंचयाम् ॥
सर्वोत्तीर्णां महाबिन्दुरूपामाराधयाम्यहम् ।"

इत्येवमादिकं श्रुतिस्मृतिजालमनुसंधेयम् ॥ ७ ॥

एवं बिन्दुस्वरूपमुपदिश्य तद्ज्ञानोपासनयोः फलं परं ब्रह्मभाव एवेत्याह—

इति कामकला विद्या देवीचक्रक्रमात्मिका सेयम् ।
विदिता येन स मुक्तो भवति महात्रिपुरसुन्दरीरूपः ॥ ८ ॥

इतीति । इति पूर्वोक्तमहाप्रबन्धेन व्याख्याता कामकला महात्रिपुरसुन्दरी । तस्याः विद्या ज्ञानम् । सा कीदृशीत्याकाङ्क्षायामाह—**देवीचक्रक्रमात्मिकेति** ।

देव्याः त्रिपुरसुन्दर्याः चक्रं श्रीचक्रम्; तस्य क्रमः चक्रमन्त्रदेवतात्मना सर्वानन्दमयादिसमस्तप्रकटपर्यन्तरूपः, तदात्मिका तद्विषयिणी। येन; शक्तिपातात्समुन्मिषद्ब्रह्मजिज्ञासुना भाग्यवता विद्यावता पुरुषेण, विदिता; गुरूपसदनादिना अवगता। सः; पुरुषो मुक्तो भवति। इहापि "विद्याभिर्ज्ञापितैश्वर्यश्चिद्घनो मुक्त एव सः।" इति प्रत्यभिज्ञास्थित्या संसारवासनानिरसनपटीयान् अनवरतपरिपूर्णाहंभावभावनाकबलीकृतसर्वप्रपञ्चः परमयोगी विहरते। तथा बृहदारण्यके—"तदाहुः यद्ब्रह्मविद्यया सर्वं भविष्यन्तो मनुष्या मन्यन्ते। किमु तद् ब्रह्मावेद्यस्मात्तत्सर्वमभवदिति" इति अन्तेऽपि महात्रिपुरसुन्दरीरूपः पराभट्टारिकारूपो भवति। तथा च श्रुतिः—"परं धाम त्रैपुरं चाविशन्ति।" इति। "ब्रह्मविद्ब्रह्मैव भवति। स एवं पश्यन्नेवं मन्वान एवं जानन्नात्मरतिरात्मक्रीड आत्ममिथुन आत्मानन्दः स एव भवति" इति। तथा प्रत्यभिज्ञासूत्रे च—"तदा प्रकाशानन्दसारमहामन्त्रवीर्यात्मकपूर्णाहंतावेशात् सदा सर्वसंहाराधिकारिनिजसंविद्देवताचक्रेश्वरताप्राप्तिर्भवतीति शिवम्" इति। अभिनवगुप्तपादाश्च—

"यस्यैषां प्रतिभात्येतत्परार्थक्रमरूपिता।
अक्रमानन्दचिद्रूपः प्रमोदात्स महेश्वरः॥
स्वतन्त्रश्चितिचक्राणां चक्रवर्ती महेश्वरः।
संवित्तिदेवताचक्रजुष्टः कोऽपि जयत्यसौ॥"

इति। तथा स्वच्छन्दशास्त्रे—

"यदा त्वेकत्र संरूढस्तदा तस्य लयोदयौ।
नियच्छन् भोक्तृतामेति ततश्चक्रेश्वरो भवेत्॥"

इत्यादिवचनशतं द्रष्टव्यम्। एवं च, 'विदिता येन स मुक्तः' इत्यादिना ज्ञानपूर्वानुष्ठानमेव ब्रह्म प्रापकमित्युक्तम्। तथा बृहदारण्यके—"यो वा एतदक्षरं गार्ग्यविदित्वास्मिन् लोके जुहोति यजते तपस्तप्यते बहूनि वर्षसहस्राण्यन्तवदेवास्य तद्भवति" इति। तथान्यत्र वामकेश्वरतन्त्रे—

"यावदेतं न जानाति संकेतत्रयमुत्तमम्।
न तावत् त्रिपुरा चक्रे परमाज्ञाधरो भवेत्॥"

इति । तस्माज्ज्ञानपूर्वानुष्ठानेनैव परमशिवो भवति । तथा चोक्तं तत्रैव—
"एतद्ज्ञात्वा वरारोहे सद्यः खेचरतां व्रजेत् ।" इत्यलं प्रसक्तानुप्रसक्त्या ॥ ८ ॥

पुण्यानन्दमुखेन्दोरुदितामानन्ददायिनीमेताम् ।
कामकलामहमनिशं मूर्ध्ना वाचा वहामि चित्तेन ॥
इति कामकला व्याख्या नटनानन्देन देशिकप्रीत्यै ।
रचिता रसिकजनानां पुंसामालोकनाय चिद्वल्ली ॥
नाथानन्दगुरूणां शिष्यास्तत्त्वार्थचिन्तकाः सन्ति ।
तेषामन्यतमोऽयं टीकामेनां चकार तत्प्रीत्यै ॥
अस्याः कामकलाया व्याख्या पूर्वैरुदाहृतानेका ।
अस्मिन् तथापि स भक्त्या नटनानन्दोऽपि भावयामास ॥

पुण्यानन्दमहात्मा कामकलारूपबिन्दुमुक्त्वैवम् ।
बिन्दोर्विकसनरूपं श्रीचक्रं नाम वक्तुमुद्युङ्क्ते ।
तत्क्रमविवरणरूपं श्रीकामकलाविलासमप्येषः ।
आरभते विवरीतुं गुरुपदकृपयैव सुन्दरीभक्तः ॥

इह महामाहेश्वराः पुण्यानन्दाः कामकलाख्यामादिसुन्दरीमात्मत्वेनानुभूय पुनरपि मन्त्रचक्रदेवतात्मकतद्विलासानुभवपराः सन्तः परमार्थभूतप्रकृतमहाबिन्दोरेव सकाशात् जगदुत्पत्त्यादिकं वक्तुमारमते—

[1]स्फुटितादरुणाद्बिन्दोर्नादब्रह्माङ्कुरो रवो व्यक्तः ।
तस्माद्गगनसमीरणदहनोदकभूमिवर्णसंभूतिः ॥ ९ ॥

स्फुटितादरुणाद्बिन्दोरिति । **स्फुटितात्**; उच्छूनात् । **बिन्दोः**; पूर्वोक्तलक्षणात्, **नादब्रह्माङ्कुरः**; नादः सर्वशब्दोत्पत्तिहेतुर्वर्णः, स एव ब्रह्म नादब्रह्म अङ्कुर उत्पादकं यस्य सः । तथा **चोक्तम्**—

[1] स्फुरितात्

"एको नादात्मको वर्णः सर्वनादविभागवान् ।
सोऽनस्तमितरूपत्वादनाहव इतीरितः ॥"

इति । **उपनिषदपि**—"ध्याता रुद्रः प्राणं मनसि सह करणैर्नादान्ते परमात्मनि संप्रतिष्ठाप्य ध्यायीतेशानम्" इति । व्योमेति बिन्दुरिति नाद इत्येवंभूतो नाद-ब्रह्माङ्कुरः । **रवः**; शब्दः, पश्यन्त्यादिरूपः । **व्यक्तः**; आविर्भूतः । उत्तरत्र 'या सान्तरोहरूपा' इत्यादिशब्दराशेः परापश्यन्त्यादिशक्तित्वेन प्रतिपादनात् । **तस्मात्**; शब्दात् । **गगनसमीरणदहनोदकभूमिवर्णसंभूतिः**; गगनसमीरणदहनोदकभूमीनां पञ्चभूतानां, वर्णानाम् आदिक्षान्ताक्षराणां च **संभूतिः**; उत्पत्तिः आम्नाता । अयमर्थः—स नादबिन्दोरेव सर्वप्रपञ्चनिष्पत्तिराम्नायते । तस्माच्छब्दात्मकं परं ब्रह्मेति ।

ननु, "आत्मन आकाशः संभूतः" इत्यादिना आत्मन एव साकाशाज्जग-दुत्पत्तिः श्रूयते । तत्कथं बिन्दुनादात्मकशब्दब्रह्मण एवेति । उच्यते—सर्वत्र वेदान्तेषु बिन्दुनादात्मकविद्याक्षरादेव परापश्यन्त्यादिशब्दात्मकसर्वप्रपञ्चाविर्भावदर्शनात् । तथा च **श्रुतिः**—"अक्षरात्संभवतीह विश्वम्" इति । **उपनिषदन्तरेऽपि**—"दिव्ये ब्रह्मपुरे विरजं निष्कलं शुभ्रमक्षरं विभाति" इत्यादि च कामराजबीजान्तर्गत-ककारलकाररहितबिन्दुत्रयसमष्टिभूतकामकलाक्षरस्वरूपं तत्परं ब्रह्म विभातीति परमप्रकृताक्षरब्रह्मणः ज्योतिर्मयत्वमुक्त्वा उपदिश्य तत्स्वरूपं निगमयति । मिश्र-बिन्दोर्निर्वाणबिन्दोर्विश्रमादक्षरात्मकमेव ब्रह्मोपनिषदादावाचष्टे । इममेवार्थमभिप्रेत्य **लघुभट्टारका** अपि—"यन्नित्ये तव कामराजमपरं मन्त्राक्षरं निष्कलम्" इति श्लोके कामकलाक्षरस्य सर्ववेदमूलत्वेन सर्वप्रकारेण सर्वपुरुषोपास्यत्वं मोक्षप्रदत्वं चाब्रुवन् । तद्व्याख्यातृभिरपि **श्रीराघवानन्दवर्यैः**—"यदीँ शृणोत्यलकं शृणोति । न हि प्र वेद सुकृतस्य पन्थाम्" इत्यादिश्रुतिजालमुपन्यस्य श्रीकामकलाक्षरस्वरूपवैभवमेवो-पन्यस्तम् । प्राञ्चोऽपि **कवयः**—

"अनादिनिधनं ब्रह्म शब्दमक्षरसंज्ञितम् ।
विवर्ततेऽर्थभावेन प्रक्रिया जगतो यतः ॥"

त्यक्षरब्रह्मण एव सकाशाज्जगदुत्पत्तिं ब्रुवन्ति । तथा, "शब्दानां जननी त्वमत्र

भुवने वाग्वादिनीत्युच्यते" इत्यमृतरूपी। स्मृतिरपि "शब्दब्रह्ममयी स्वच्छा देवी त्रिपुरसुन्दरी" इति। एवं हि शब्दस्य निष्पत्तिः, शब्दव्याप्तं चराचरमित्यादि। तथा च "आत्मन आकाशः" इत्यात्मशब्दस्य अक्षरात्मपरत्वमित्यविवादः ॥ ९ ॥

एवं शोणबिन्दोः सर्वात्मकत्वं सर्वस्रष्टृत्वं चोक्त्वा एतदभेदाच्छुभ्रबिन्दोरपि तत्स्वरूपमतिदिशति—

अथ विशदादपि बिन्दोर्गगनानिलवह्निवारिभूमिजनिः।
एतत्पञ्चकविकृतिर्जगदिदमण्वाद्यजाण्डपर्यन्तम् ॥ १० ॥

अथ विशदादिति। विशदात्; सर्वप्रकाशात्। **बिन्दोः**; पूर्वव्याख्यातात् गगनादिपञ्चभूतात्मकानन्तब्रह्माण्डाविर्भावतिरोभावौ भवत इत्यर्थः। तथा च **श्रुतिः**—

"यस्मिन्भावाः प्रलीयन्ते लीनाश्च व्यक्ततां ययुः।
पुनश्चाव्यक्ततां भूयो जायन्ते बुद्बुदा इव ॥"

इति।

"एतस्माज्जायते प्राणो मनः सर्वेन्द्रियाणि च।
खं वायुर्ज्योतिरापः पृथिवी विश्वस्य धारिणी ॥"

इति च। एवं रक्तशुक्लबिन्दुमयप्रकाशविमर्शात्मकब्रह्मणः सर्वं जातमिति सिद्धम्। **आगमश्च**;

स्वेच्छाविलासितानन्तजगद्रश्मिवितानवत्।
नौमि संविन्महापीठं शिवशक्तिपदाश्रयम् ॥

इति ॥ १० ॥

एवं बिन्दुद्वयाभेदमुक्त्वा तद्दृष्टान्ततया मन्त्रदेवतयोरप्यैक्यमाह—

बिन्दुद्वितयं यद्वद्भेदविहीनं परस्परं तद्वत्।
विद्यादेवतयोरपि न भेदलेशोऽस्ति वेद्यवेदकयोः ॥ ११ ॥

बिन्दुद्वितयमिति । **बिन्दुद्वितयम्** ; पूर्वोक्तप्रकाशविमर्शात्मकम् । **यद्वत्** ; येन प्रकारेण । **भेदविहीनम्** ; "शिवशक्तिरिति ह्येकं तत्त्वमाहुर्मनीषिणः" इत्युक्तरीत्या परस्पराश्लिष्टम । **तद्वत्** ; तेनैव प्रकारेण । **विद्यादेवतयोः** ; विद्या पञ्चदशाक्षरी, देवता महात्रिपुरसुन्दरी, तयोर्वेद्यवेदकयोः वाच्यवाचकयोः । **भेदलेशोऽपि** ; ईषद्वैलक्षण्यमपि नास्ति । तथापि ऋग्वेदशाखान्तर्गतसांख्यायनशाखायाम्—

"कामो योनिः कमला वज्रपाणिः गुहा हसा मातरिश्वाभ्रमिन्द्रः ।
पुनर्गुहा सकला मायया च पुरूच्येषा विश्वमातादिविद्या ।
षष्ठं सप्तममथ वह्निसारथिमस्या मूलत्रिकमादेशयन्तः ॥"

इत्यादिना कादिहादिविद्याद्वयमुद्धृत्य तस्य देवतैक्यमाह—विश्वमातादिविद्येति । **बृहदारण्यकेऽपि**—'योऽयं दक्षिणेऽक्षन् पुरुषस्तस्य भूरिति शिर एकं शिर एकमेतदक्षरं भुव इति बाहू द्वौ बाहू द्वे एते अक्षरे स्वरिति प्रतिष्ठा द्वे प्रतिष्ठे द्वे एते अक्षरे तस्योपनिषदहमिति हन्ति पाप्मानं जहाति च य एवं वेद ।" इत्यक्षिस्थाननिष्ठस्य पुरुषस्य भूराद्यवयवं निर्दिश्य तस्याक्षरस्य अहमात्मकब्रह्मभावमादिश्य सकलपापनिवृत्तिपुरःसरं साम्राज्यं ब्रूते । ततश्च सकलविद्यानां सकलवेदादिशब्दाद्याविर्भावकारणाहंभावरूपादिमातृकात्मकत्वात् उभयोरभेद इत्यत्र न विवादः । तथा **श्रीतन्त्रसद्भावे**—

"सर्वे वर्णात्मका मन्त्रा ते च शक्त्यात्मकाः प्रिये ।
शक्तिस्तु मातृका ज्ञेया सा च ज्ञेया शिवात्मिका ।
या सा तु मातृकालोके परतेजःसमन्विता ।
तया व्याप्तमिदं सर्वमाब्रह्मभुवनात्मकम् ॥"

इति । **आगमश्च**—

"संविदितं विदितं संविन्मयमेव भवति संवेद्यम् ।
अग्नावाहुतमाहुतमग्निमयं किं न जायते काष्ठम् ॥"

इति । **क्रोधभट्टारकोऽपि**—"पञ्चाशन्निजदेहजाक्षरमयैः" इत्याद्युक्त्वा "विश्वं व्याप्य निजात्मनाहमहमित्युज्जृम्भसे मातृके" इति मन्त्रदेवतयोरैक्यमुक्तवान् । श्लोकार्थः संपूर्णः ॥ ११ ॥

एवमभिन्ननादबिन्दुमिथुनादखिलं जगदाविर्भवतीति वक्तुं तदेव मिथुनमात्मेच्छयैव स्वभेदमकरोदित्याह—

वागर्थौ नित्ययुतौ परस्परं शिवशक्तिमयावेतौ ।
सृष्टिस्थितिलयभेदौ त्रिधा विभक्तौ त्रिबीजरूपेण ॥ १२ ॥

वागर्थाविति । अस्यार्थः—**वागर्थौ**; वाक्, वर्णपदमन्त्ररूपा, अर्थः, कलातत्त्वभुवनात्मा । अत एव तद्रूपौ, कुतः ? प्रकाशविमर्शात्मकशब्दार्थाभ्यामेव षडध्वात्मकसर्वप्रपञ्चोत्पत्तिश्रवणात् । तथा **श्रीविरूपाक्षपञ्चाशिकायाम्**—

"यस्य विमर्शस्य कणः पदमन्त्रार्णात्मकस्त्रिधा शब्दः ।
भुवनकलातत्त्वार्थो धर्मिण इत्थं प्रकाशस्य ।"

इति । अत एव **नित्ययुतौ**; निरन्तरसंसक्तौ । न हि घटपटयोरिव कादाचित्कः संबन्धः । तथा सति सर्वानुपपत्तिप्रसङ्गात् । **सृष्टिस्थितिलयभेदौ**; सृष्टिः शिवादिक्षित्यन्ततत्त्वजालाविर्भावः, स्थितिः तत्परिपालनम्, लयः तेषां स्वात्मसाक्षात्कारः, एवंभूतो भेदो ययोस्तौ । स्वात्मोत्पन्नत्वात् तेषां त्रयाणां भेदात् । तथा च **अभिनवगुप्ताः**—"स्वात्मगाः सृष्टिसंहाराः स्वरूपत्वेन संस्थिताः ।" इति । **परस्परम्**; शिवशक्तिमयौ प्रकाशविमर्शस्वरूपौ । उभयोरेककर्तृत्वात् वह्निदाहकवत् । तत्त्वान्तरं न भवतीत्यर्थः । **तथागमश्च**—

"आवयोर्जगदात्मत्वात् तादात्म्यं चावयोरपि ।
तादात्म्यादावयोर्नित्यं जगत्प्राणावुभौ हि नौ ॥"

इत्यादि । **अभियुक्तोक्तिश्च**—"तादात्म्यमनयोर्नित्यं वह्निदाहकयोरिव ।" इति । एतौ पूर्वोक्तौ प्रकाशविमर्शौ त्रिधा त्रिप्रकारेण विभक्तौ पृथग्भूतौ । केनेत्यत आह—**त्रिबीजरूपेणेति** । वाग्भवकामराजशक्तिबीजात्मनेत्यर्थः । अयमर्थः—बिन्दुत्रयसमष्टिभूतकामकलाक्षररूपिणी वाग्भवादिबीजात्मिका महात्रिपुरसुन्दरी सर्वोपास्येति । तथाचोक्तं **वामकेश्वरतन्त्रे**—

"तत्त्वत्रयविनिर्दिष्टवर्णशक्तित्रयात्मिका ।
वागीश्वरी ज्ञानशक्तिर्वाग्भवा मोक्षरूपिणी ॥
कामराजे कामकला कामरूपक्रियात्मिका ।
शक्तिबीजे पराशक्तिरिच्छैव ज्ञानरूपिणी ॥
एवं देवी त्र्यक्षरात्मा महात्रिपुरसुन्दरी ।
पारंपर्येण विज्ञाता भवबन्धविमोचिनी ॥"

इति ॥ १२ ॥

इतः परं वाग्भवादिखण्डत्रयान्तर्गतवस्तुविशेषवर्णनद्वारा श्रीपञ्चदशाक्षरीविद्यामुद्धर्तुमुपक्रमते—

माता मानं मेयं बिन्दुत्रयभिन्नबीजरूपाणि ।
धामत्रयपीठत्रयशक्तित्रयभेदभावितान्यपि च ॥ १३ ॥
तेषु क्रमेण लिङ्गत्रितयं तद्वच्च मातृकात्रितयम् ।
इत्थं त्रितयपुरी या तुरीयपीठादिभेदिनी विद्या ॥ १४ ॥

मातेति । माता; अवगन्ता महेश्वरः । मानम्; तदवगतिसाधनभूता विद्या । **मेयम्**; ज्ञायमाना महात्रिपुरसुन्दरी । एतानि ज्ञातृज्ञानज्ञेयरूपाणि । **बिन्दुत्रयभिन्नबीजरूपाणीति** । बिन्दूनां पूर्वोक्तानां त्रितयं बिन्दुत्रितयं रक्तशुक्लमिश्ररूपं तदात्मना भिन्नं पृथग्भूतं । यद्बीजं सर्वसमष्टिभूतनिर्वाणाख्यम्, तद्रूपाणि तत्प्रकाशकानि । अयमर्थः—सर्वातीतचिदानन्दघनात्मानुभवरूपाहंभावशालिनी परं ज्योतिरेव मातृमानमेयभावमनुभूय विहरति । तथा च **बृहदारण्यके**—"आत्मैवेदमग्र आसीत् पुरुषविधः सोऽनुवीक्ष्य नान्यदात्मनोऽपश्यत् । सोहमस्मीत्यग्रे व्याहरत । ततोऽहं नामाभवत् । तस्मादप्येतर्ह्यामन्त्रितोऽहमयमित्येवाग्र उक्त्वान्यन्नाम प्रब्रूत" इति । अस्यार्थः—आत्मा परमेश्वर एव । इदं परिदृश्यमानं जगत् । अग्रे प्रथमम् आसीत् । स्वान्तर्गतप्रपञ्चोऽभवदित्यर्थः । तथा स परमात्मा अन्वीक्ष्य स्वात्मसात्कृतप्रपञ्चात्मत्वेनालोक्य अन्यदात्मनो नापश्यत् स्वव्यतिरिक्तं किंचिदपि नाद्रक्ष्यत् । स्वेनैव सर्वेषां कवली-

करणात्। तस्मिन् समये अखण्डसच्चिदानन्दघनात्मानुभवोऽहमिति स्वसाधारणरूपोऽस्मि भवामीति प्रदर्शयन्नग्रे सृष्टेः पूर्वं व्याहरत् प्रादर्शयत्। तत एवाहंनामाभवत्। ब्रह्मण एव स्वस्वरूपप्रदर्शनात् अहमित्येव हि ब्रह्मनामधेयम्। तस्मादिहापि, लोके आमन्त्रितः कस्त्वमिति केनचित्पृष्टः अहमित्येव ब्रह्मस्वरूपमुक्त्वा अन्यन्नामधेयादिकम् पश्चात् ब्रूते। ततश्च सर्वत्र स्वस्वरूपावलोकनद्वारा ब्रह्मण एव ज्ञातृत्वादिभेदः प्रतिपादितोऽभवदित्यर्थः। तथा **चतुःशत्याम्**—

"अतीतं तु परं तेजः स्वसंविदुदयात्मकम्।
स्वेच्छाविश्वमयोल्लेखखचितं विश्वरूपकम्॥
चैतन्यमात्मनो रूपं निसर्गानन्दसुन्दरम्।
मेयमातृप्रमामानप्रसरैः संकुचत्प्रभम्॥"

इति। **प्रत्यभिज्ञायामपि**—

"अखण्डितस्वभावोऽपि विचित्रां मातृकल्पनाम्।
स्वहृन्मण्डलचक्रे यः पृथक् चेत्तं नुमः शिवम्॥"

इति। **धामत्रयम्**; सोमसूर्याग्निमण्डलत्रयम्। **बीजत्रयम्**; वाग्भवादिकम्। **पीठत्रयम्**; कामगिर्यादिकम्; **शक्तित्रयम्**; इच्छादि; एवमादिभेदेन भावितानि महाबिन्दुमयत्वादेतेषु धामादिषु त्रिभेदभिन्नेषु; **क्रमेण**; आनुपूर्व्या, **लिङ्गत्रितयम्**; स्वयंभ्वादि, **मातृकात्रितयम्**; अकथादिभेदभिन्नम्। एवंविधसमस्तवस्तुपूरणात्समष्टिरूपा त्रिपुरा नाम पराशक्तिराविर्भूतेत्याह—**इत्थं त्रितयपुरी या** इति। **इत्थम्**; पूर्वोक्तप्रकारेण त्रितयानि त्रितयसंख्याकानि पुराणि शरीराणि यस्याः सा। अत एव तुरीयपीठा त्रिविधात्मकसर्वप्रपञ्चाविर्भावतिरोभावभूमिरित्यर्थः। तथा **चोक्तम्**—"मातृकां पीठरूपिणीम्" इति। अयमर्थः स्वच्छन्देऽपि विभावितः। **सुबालोपनिषदि च**—"आनन्दमेवास्तमेति तुरीयमेवाप्येति। यस्तुरीयमेव तदेतदमृतमभयमशोकमनन्तं निर्बीजमेवाप्येतीति होवाच" इति। एवंविधतुरीयपीठादिभेदिनी स्वात्मन्येव स्वेच्छया उद्भावितानन्ततत्त्वकदम्बिनी अखण्डसंविदात्मिका। **तथा चोक्तम्**—

"त्रिमूर्तिसर्गाच्च पुरोभवत्वात् त्रयीमयत्वाच्च पुरैव देव्याः ।
लये त्रिलोक्या अपि पूरणाच्च प्रायोऽम्बिकायास्त्रिपुरेति नाम ॥"

इति । "स्वसंवित् त्रिपुरा देवी" इति । "स्वातन्त्र्योल्लासिताशेषतत्त्वप्रोतस्वरूपिणी" "आधैरग्निरवीन्दुबिम्बनिलयैः" इत्यादि च ॥ १३, १४ ॥

इतः परं 'तस्माद्गगनसमीरणदहनोदकभूमिवर्णसंभूतिः' इति प्रथमसृष्टपञ्चभूतनिष्ठगुणवर्णनद्वारा अक्षरसंख्याविशिष्टमहामन्त्रात्मकदेवतास्वरूपं वक्तुमारभते—

शब्दस्पर्शौ रूपं रसगन्धौ चेति भूतसूक्ष्माणि ।
व्यापकमाद्यं व्याप्यं तूत्तरमेवं क्रमेण पञ्चदश ॥ १५ ॥
पञ्चदशाक्षररूपा नित्या चैषा हि भौतिकाभिमता ।
नित्याः शब्दादिगुणप्रभेदभिन्नास्तथानया व्याप्ताः ॥ १६ ॥
नित्यास्तिथ्याकारास्तिथयश्च शिवशक्तिसमरसाकाराः ।
दिवसनिशामय्यस्ताः श्रीवर्णास्तेऽपि तद्द्वयीरूपाः ॥१७॥

शब्दस्पर्शाविति । अस्यार्थः—**शब्द** आकाशगुणः, **स्पर्शो** वायुगुणः, **रूपं** तेजोगुणः, **रसो** वारिगुणः, **गन्धः** पृथिवीगुणः, एते गुणा आकाशमारभ्य पृथिवीपर्यन्तमुत्तरोत्तरमेकैकगुणाधिक्येन पञ्चदशगुणाः संपद्यन्ते । एतेषां गुणानां पञ्चदशभावेन श्रीविद्या पञ्चदशाक्षरी जाता । तत्स्वरूपिणी चेयमाविर्भूतेत्याह—**पञ्चदशाक्षररूपेति** । **भौतिकाभिमता**; भूतसंबन्धेनाभिमता इष्टा । अत एव पञ्चदशाक्षररूपा स्वात्मन आविर्भूतगुणानां पञ्चदशात्मकत्वात् विद्याक्षराणामपि पञ्चदशत्वम् । तद्रूपा तत्स्वरूपिणी नित्या कूटस्था तरङ्गबुद्बुदफेनानामम्बुधिरिव सकलतत्त्वानामाविर्भावभूमिरित्यर्थः । तथा **बृहदारण्यके**—"इदं महद्भूतमनन्तमपारं विज्ञानघन एवैतेभ्यो भूतेभ्यः समुत्थाय तान्येवानुविशति" इति । **मुण्डकोपनिषदि** च—"यस्मिन् भावाः प्रलीयन्ते" इति ॥ **शिवानन्दाश्च**—

"शिवादिक्षितिपर्यन्तं षट्त्रिंशत्तत्त्वसंचयाः ।
यस्योर्मिर्बुद्बुदाभावास्तं वन्दे चिन्महोदधिम् ॥"

इति । कूटस्थाया एव षोडश्याः पञ्चदशावयवात्मकपञ्चदशतिथिनिष्ठितपञ्चदश-देवतामयपञ्चदशाक्षरीरूपतामाह—**नित्यास्तिथ्याकारा** इति। **नित्याः**; कामेश्वरी-प्रभृतिचित्रान्ताः । **तिथ्याकाराः**; तिथ्यभिमानिन्यो देवताः । **तिथयश्च**; प्रति-पत्प्रभृतिपूर्णिमान्ताः । **शिवशक्तिसमरसाकाराः**; प्रकाशविमर्शसंपुटाकाराः । अत एव **दिवसनिशामय्यः**; दिवारात्रिरूपाः। प्रकाशविमर्शयोः दिवारात्रिमयत्वात्। तथा चोक्तं **चिद्विलासे**—"सा निशा सकललोकमोहिनी वासरः स खलु सर्वबोधकः।" इति। तास्तिथयः, **श्रीवर्णाः**; तेऽपि पूर्वोक्तरूपेण पञ्चदशरूपाः श्रीवर्णाः विद्यान्तर्गत-वर्णगणाः । **अपि तद्द्वयीरूपाः**; तादृशप्रकाशविमर्शरूपा इत्यर्थः । इयं च पञ्चदशा-क्षरी ऋग्वेदे **साङ्ख्यायनशाखायामाम्नाता**; यथा—"कामो योनिः कमला" इत्यादि । तस्मिन्नेव वेदेऽन्यत्र—"चत्वार ईं बिभ्रति क्षेमयन्तः" इत्यादावपीयं विद्या विद्योतत इति वर्णयन्ति केचित् । अयमत्र विवेकः— इयमेव प्रकाशविमर्शमयी पराशक्तिः पञ्चभूतात्मिका उत्तरोत्तरगुणवृद्धिद्वारा पञ्चदशसङ्ख्याकमन्त्राक्षरतिथ्यभि-मानिनी देवतास्वरूपिणी जाता । **यथागमः**—

"एक एव प्रकाशाख्यः परः कोऽपि महेश्वरः ।
यस्य शक्तिर्विमर्शाख्या सा नित्या गीयते बुधैः ॥
विमर्शाख्या च सा देवी पाञ्चविध्यं समागता ।
आकाशानिलसप्तार्चिः सलिलावनिभेदतः ॥
एकैकगुणवृद्ध्या तु तिथिसङ्ख्यात्वमागता ।
विमर्शरूपिणी नित्या षोडशी या प्रकीर्तिता ॥
गता सा षोडशैर्भेदैस्त्रिपुरा परमेश्वरी ।
सुन्दर्यादिमहापूर्वं चित्रान्तं च समन्ततः ॥
आगमादेव बोद्धव्यमिति संकेतमात्रतः ।
प्रतिपत्प्रभृतौ देव्याः पौर्णमास्यन्तिकं प्रिये ॥
एकैकं पूजयेद्यस्तु स सौभाग्यमवाप्नुयात् ॥"

इति ।

इति । **सुभगोदयवासनायामपि**—

> "खं वायुर्ज्योतिरब्भूमिशब्दादिगुणभेदतः ।
> दशपञ्चतया व्याप्ता व्यापिकाः पूजयाम्यहम् ॥"

इति ॥ १७ ॥

इतः परं 'विद्यादेवतयोरपि न भेदलेशोऽस्ति वेद्यवेदकयोः' इत्युक्तमेवार्थं द्रढयितुं देवतावद्विद्याया अपि विश्वात्मकत्वात्तदुत्तीर्णत्वं व्यक्तमाह—

अज्व्यञ्जनबिन्दुत्रयसमष्टिभेदैर्विभाविताकारा ।
षट्त्रिंशत्तत्त्वात्मा तत्त्वातीता च केवला विद्या ॥ १८ ॥

अज्व्यञ्जनेति। **अज्व्यञ्जनबिन्दुत्रयसमष्टिभेदैः;** **अचः** स्वराः, **व्यञ्जनानि,** हलः, **बिन्दुत्रयम्** अनुस्वारत्रयम्, एषां **समष्टिः** समुदायभावः, **भेदो**ऽवयवभावः तैः, **विभाविताकारा;** उद्भावितस्वरूपा । अत एव **षट्त्रिंशत्तत्त्वात्मा;** शिवादिक्षित्यन्ततत्त्वविग्रहा; **तत्त्वातीता च;** तत्त्वसंघसमुदायस्थानत्वात्तदुत्तीर्णा च । अत एव **केवला;** स्वव्यतिरिक्तस्याभावादेकाकिनी । एवंभूता **विद्या** श्रीपञ्चदशाक्षरीत्यर्थः । अयमत्र विद्याया अवयवविभागप्रकारः—इह पुण्यानन्दाः हादिविद्यायामत्यन्ताभिमानिनः, अस्या एव विद्याया अवयवसमुदायभावमाश्रित्य तत्त्वात्मकत्वं तदुत्तीर्णत्वं चाचक्षते। अत्र वाग्भवाख्ये प्रथमे खण्डे पञ्च स्वराः, सप्त व्यञ्जनानि, संहत्य द्वादश वर्णाः । कामराजाख्ये द्वितीये खण्डे षट् स्वराः, अष्ट व्यञ्जनानि, संभूय चतुर्दश वर्णाः । शक्त्याख्ये तृतीये खण्डे चत्वारः स्वराः, षड् व्यञ्जनानि, संहत्य दश वर्णाः । सर्वेऽपि संभूय षट्त्रिंशदक्षराणि अवयवरूपाणि ।

केचित्तु—प्रथमखण्डे षट् स्वराः, षड् व्यञ्जतानि। द्वितीयखण्डे सप्त स्वराः, सप्त व्यञ्जनानि । तृतीयखण्डे पञ्च स्वराः, पञ्च व्यञ्जनानीति व्यवहियन्ते । समुदायरूपा विद्या सर्वतत्त्वातिक्रान्तावधिवर्तिनी । ननु कादिविद्यैव उभयात्मिका सर्वत्र प्रसिद्धा श्रूयते । "कामो योनिः कमला" इत्यादौ, तत्कथं हादिविद्यैव उभयात्मिकेत्युच्यते, सत्यम्; कादिविद्या तु "कामो योनिः" इत्याद्यु-

पनिषदि प्रथमतः प्रतिपाद्यते । तथापि हादिविद्यापि तत्रैवोद्धृता । कथम्? "षष्ठं सप्तममथ वह्निसाराथिमस्या मूलत्रिकमादेशयन्तः" इत्यादिना । तस्मात् हादिविद्यापि श्रुतिप्रसिद्धैव । तस्मात्तस्या हादिविद्याया एव उभयात्मकत्वमितीह वर्णितमित्येवावगन्तव्यम् ।

ननु तर्हि कादिविद्याया अपि उभयात्मकत्वाभावे तस्यामुपादेयबुद्धिर्न स्यात् । कुतः? देवतावैजात्यात् । तत्कथं हादेरेवोभयात्मकत्वं प्रतिपाद्यते । अत्रोच्यते—न वयं हादिविद्यैव तादृशी, न कादिरिति वदामः । किंतु हादिरेवाभिप्रेता । न कादिरित्येतावन्मात्रमुक्तम् । अन्यत्र तथा व्याख्यानात् । कादेरपि विद्याया उभयात्मकत्वमस्त्येव । इयानेवानयोर्विद्ययोर्भेदः—हादौ प्रथमे खण्डे षट् स्वराः, षड् व्यञ्जनानि । कादौ प्रथमे खण्डे सप्त स्वराः, पञ्च व्यञ्जनानि । संहत्य विद्याद्वयेऽपि प्रथमखण्डे द्वादशवर्णत्वं समानम् । तस्मादुभयात्मकत्वमुभयोर्विद्ययोरस्त्येव । तदुभयविद्योपासनाप्रकारस्तु गुरुमुखादेवावगन्तव्यः ॥ १८ ॥

देवताया अपि मन्त्रवदुभयात्मकत्वमिति मन्त्रदेवतयोरैक्यमाह—

विद्यापि तादृगात्मा सूक्ष्मा सा त्रिपुरसुन्दरी देवी ।
विद्यावेद्यात्मकयोरत्यन्ताभेदमामनन्त्यार्याः ॥ १९ ॥

विद्यापि तादृगात्मेति । विद्या; चिदानन्दस्वरूपिणी; **तादृगात्मा;** तत्त्वात्मिका विश्वात्मिका, तदुत्तीर्णा च । **सूक्ष्मा;** परिच्छेत्तुमशक्या । **सा;** सर्ववेदान्तेषु प्रसिद्धा । **त्रिपुरसुन्दरी;** त्रिपुरा च सुन्दरी च त्रिधावस्थितसमस्तवस्तुपूरणात् सर्वयोगिभिरुपास्यत्वेन स्पृहणीयत्वाच्च त्रिपुरा; त्रिपुराशब्दनिर्वचनं च पूर्वमेव प्रपञ्चितम् । **देवी;** स्वच्छप्रकाशरूपा विश्वस्य जननादिक्रीडारूपा परा वाक् । **विद्यावेद्यात्मकयोः;** पञ्चदशाक्षरीत्रिपुरसुन्दर्योः, **अत्यन्ताभेदम् आमनन्ति आर्याः;** सार्वकालिकैक्यमामनन्ति सर्वत्र प्रतिपादयन्ति । **आर्याः;** परमेश्वरप्रमुखाः परमयोगिन इत्यर्थः । तथा **चिदम्बररहस्ये**—"अहं पञ्चाक्षरः साक्षात् त्वं तु पञ्चदशाक्षरी ।" इति । **चतुःशत्यां** च—

"यस्य यस्य पदार्थस्य या या शक्तिरुदीरिता ।
सा सा सर्वेश्वरी देवी स सर्वोऽपि महेश्वरः ॥

. . . .

व्याप्ता पञ्चदशार्णैषा विद्याभूतगुणात्मिका ।
पञ्चभिश्च तथा षड्भिश्चतुर्भिरपि चाक्षरैः ॥
स्वरव्यञ्जनभेदेन सप्तत्रिंशत्प्रभेदिनी ।
सप्तत्रिंशत्प्रभेदेन षट्त्रिंशत्तत्त्वरूपिणी ।
तत्त्वातीतस्वरूपा च विद्यैषा भाव्यते सदा ॥"

इति । रहस्योपनिषदि चेयं विद्या सम्यक् प्रतिपाद्यते । यथा "देवा ह वै प्रजापतिमब्रुवन्, केयं तनुः किं रूपा कियद्वर्णा किं करोति किं ददाति केन वा सिध्यति किं करवाम" इति देवैः पृष्टः प्रजापतिः प्रत्युत्तरमाह—नेदृशो लोकातीतोऽचिन्त्यो वाच्यः" इत्यदिना सर्वोत्तमत्वं पञ्चदशाक्षर्याः प्रतिपाद्य, श्रीपञ्चदशाक्षरीमेव देवेभ्य उपदिशति । यथा तदुदाहरिष्यामः—"आदिरादिब्रह्मा, द्वितीया वाणी, तृतीयो मारः, ततो महेन्द्रः, इयं भूवाच्यधर्मसंतानमयमिति" । द्वितीयमुदाहरिष्यामः—"आदिरादिरुद्रः, ततः सुधामयम्, ततः प्रजानामीशः, ततो हंसः, ततो भूमिः ततोऽयमात्मा, अयं भुवो नामार्थसंतानं भोगानन्दमयमिति" । तृतीयमुदाहरिष्यामः—आदौ जीवनेशः, ततो विश्वकृद्धाता, ततो जगन्माता लक्ष्मीः, ततः पराशक्तिः, स्वर्णामेदं नाम चिन्तामणिं भावाभावमयमिति । अत्रायं प्रथमः पाद इति प्रथमखण्डमुपदिशति । द्वितीयखण्डमुदाहरिष्याम इति द्वितीयखण्डमुपदिशति । तृतीयमुदाहहिष्याम इति तृतीयखण्डं चोपदिशति । उपदिश्य सर्वमपि तन्मन्त्रमाहात्म्यमाह—"सानेकधा समभवत् । तदेतन्महामनुरिति सैव शब्दतनुरेषा । सर्ववर्णरूपा परमा त्रिपदा त्रयीभावा त्रिगुणा त्रिवर्गरूपा नित्या निर्मला निरवद्या निष्प्रपञ्चात्मविद्याविभुः । परविद्या इति य एवं वेद विद्वान् भवति । अथाहुर्विद्वांस इति रहो रहस्यमिति । शिवोऽयं शिवोऽयं शिवोयमिति । स एव इमानि भूतानि संसृजति रक्षति संहरति । अन्यथाकरोति अणुर्महत्कृशस्थूलं ह्रस्वदीर्घं व्यासो व्यापकः श्रीभूतेशो वन्द्यो भवति । य एवं वेद सैव सो भवतीति ।" इति । अस्याः श्रुतेरर्थः संप्रदायादेवावगन्तव्य

इति न लिख्यते। तथा **रससारसंग्रहेऽपि** हादिविद्योद्धार उक्तः। तत्र वचनानि कानिचिल्लिख्यन्ते—

"विद्यां तु नवमीं सम्यक् प्रवक्ष्यामि समासतः।
ललिताया महादेव्या मादनेत्यादितः क्रमात् ॥
मादनः प्राणरूपस्तु विकासः शिव उच्यते।
सकारस्त्वपरो ज्ञेयः संकोचः शक्तिरूपतः ॥
संकोचः परमा शक्तिर्विकासः परमः शिवः।
संकोचश्च विकासश्च हंस इत्यक्षरद्वयम् ॥
तयोराधाररूपेण कर्तव्यं बिन्दुमालिनी।
प्राणो बिन्दुरिति प्रोक्तः साहचर्यादपानके ॥
अथोधरेन्द्रमाकाशं ज्वलनं तु तयोरधः।
मायाबिन्दूर्ध्वगा चैव वाग्भवो नाम कीर्तितः ॥"

इति। **श्रीहंसपारमेश्वरेऽपि**—

"मा शक्तिस्तु समाख्याता दनं स्वीकारकृच्छिवः।
सैव मादन इत्युक्तो हकारः शिवसंज्ञकः।
तस्य शक्तिर्यथोर्ध्वत्वे सकारः स विधीयते।
शिवो हकार इत्युक्तः सकारः शक्तिरव्यया।
बिन्दुमालिनिकार्णस्य पर्यायं परमेश्वरम्।
शक्रव्योमानलार्णाश्च मायाबिन्द्वीश्वरादयः।
यथास्थिताश्च तत्तथ्या वाग्भवं सनिलानिलः।
द्वावन्यौ कामशक्त्याख्यौ वर्णौ निष्कलकात्मकौ "

इत्यादिर्द्रष्टव्यम्। **श्रीक्रोधभट्टारकोऽपि**—

"इत्थं त्रीण्यपि मूलवाग्भवमहाश्रीकामराजस्फुर-
च्छक्त्याख्यानि चतुःश्रुतिप्रकटितान्युत्कृष्टकूटानि ते

भूतर्तुश्रुतिसंख्यवर्णविदितान्यारक्तकान्ते शिवे
यो जानाति स एव सर्वजगतां सृष्टिस्थितिध्वंसकः ॥"

इति । अत्र श्रुतिः—

"चत्वारि वाक्परिमितापदानि तानि विदुर्ब्राह्मणा ये मनीषिणः ।
गुहात्रीणि निहिता नेङ्गयन्ति तुरीयं वाचो मनुष्या वदन्ति ॥"

इत्यादिश्रुतिरप्यनुसंधेया ॥ १९ ॥

एवं विद्यादेवतयोरप्यभेदमुक्त्वा चक्रदेवतयोरैक्यं वक्तुं चक्रोत्पत्तिप्रकारमाह—

या सान्तरोहरूपा परा महेशी त्रिभाविता सैव ।
स्पष्टा पश्यन्त्यादित्रिमातृकात्मा च चक्रतां याता ॥ २० ॥

येति । **या सान्तरोहरूपा**; अन्तरमन्तःकरणम् तस्मिन्, ऊहः वितर्कः; इत्थमिति परिच्छेदरहितः, तेन सहितं रूपं यस्याः सा । अयमर्थः—अवाङ्मनसगोचरत्वात् सर्ववेदान्तैरपरिच्छेद्या सर्वकारणभूता शिवादिधरण्यन्ततत्त्वसंक्रातविमर्शभूमिः **महेशी परा** सर्वोत्कृष्टेत्युच्यते । अत्र **यजुःश्रुतिः**—"परास्य शक्तिर्विविधैव श्रूयते" इति । "यतो वाचो निवर्तन्ते, अप्राप्य मनसा सह, आनन्दं ब्रह्मणो विद्वान्" इति । **यथागमश्च**—

"स्वरूपज्योतिरेवान्तः परावागनपायिनी ।
यस्यां दृष्टस्वरूपायामधिकारो निवर्तते ॥"

इति । **लघुभट्टारकश्च**—"सा त्वं काचिदचिन्त्यरूपमहिमा शक्तिः परा गीयसे ।" इति । एवंभूतलक्षणा **सैव** पराशक्तिरेव **त्रिभाविता** त्रिप्रकारत्वेन भाविता सञ्जातभावना । एतदेवाह—**स्पष्टा पश्यन्त्यादित्रिमातृका सेति** । स्पष्टा प्रथमोत्पन्नत्वेन विवक्षिता विषयिणी पश्यन्ती इत्युच्यते । आदिशब्देन मध्यमा वैखरी च ।

सैव वैखरीनामाभिलपनरूपिणी पञ्चदशाक्षरराशिमयी सर्ववैदिकतान्त्रिकशब्दजालात्मिका शक्तिरित्युच्यते । यथोक्तं **सुभगोदयवासनायम्**—

"परा भूजन्म पश्यन्ती वल्लीगुच्छसमुद्भवा ।
मध्यमा सौरभा वैखर्यक्षमाला जयत्यसौ ॥"

इति । **अस्मदुक्तचिदानन्दवासनायामपि**—

"विवक्षाध्यवसायोक्तिरूपा एतास्त्रिमातरः ।
पश्यन्त्यादिमहादेव्या स्वरूपा नात्र संशयः ॥"

इति । एवंरूपा **त्रिमातृका** सैव चक्रतां याता । त्रिखण्डात्मकचक्रैक्यमवाप्तेत्यर्थः ॥ ॥ २० ॥

तदेवाह—

चक्रस्यापि महेश्या न भेदलेशोऽपि भाव्यते विबुधैः ।
अनयोः सूक्ष्माकारा परैव सा स्थूलयोश्च कापि भिदा ॥ २१ ॥

चक्रस्यापीति । **चक्रस्य**; त्रैलोक्यमोहनादिसर्वानन्दमयबैन्दवान्तनवावरणात्मकस्य सुन्दर्यधिष्ठानभूतस्य । **महेश्याः**; तदधिष्ठात्र्याः सुन्दर्याश्च, **भेदलेशः**; ईषद्भेदोऽपि, **बुधैः** माहेश्वरैः न **भाव्यते**; नानुभूयते । कुत? श्रीसुन्दरीस्वरूपत्वात् श्रीचक्रस्य । तथा **चोपनिषत्**—

". . . . . महत्तरा महिमा देवतानाम् ।
नवयोनिर्नवचक्राणि दीधिरे नवैव योगा नवयोगिन्यश्च ॥
नवानां चक्रा अधिनाथाः स्योना नवभद्रा नवमुद्रा महीनम् ।
एका स आसीत् प्रथमा सा नवासीत् . . . . ॥"

इत्यादि । **वामकेश्वरतन्त्रे**—

"तच्छक्तिपञ्चकं सृष्ट्या लयेनाग्निचतुष्टयम् ।
पञ्चशक्तिचतुर्वह्निसंयोगाच्चक्रसंभवः ॥

एतच्चक्रावतारं तु कथयामि वरानने ।
यदा सा परमा शक्तिः स्वेच्छया विश्वरूपिणी ॥

इत्युपक्रम्य ;

चक्रं कामकलारूपं प्रसारपरमार्थतः ॥"

इत्यन्तेन सम्यगभेदः प्रतिपादितः । **क्रोधभट्टारकोऽपि**—"श्रीचक्रं श्रुति-मूलकोशमथितं संसारचक्रात्मकम् ।" इत्यादि । पुनरपि तादृगभेदमेतयोर्व्याचष्टे—**अनयोः सूक्ष्माकारेत्यादिना** । **अनयोः**; सूक्ष्मरूपयोः चक्रदेवतयोः, सूक्ष्मरूपत्वं नामापरिच्छिन्नत्वमेव । तत्र श्रीचक्रस्य सूक्ष्मरूपेणावस्थानं, बिन्द्वात्मना बिन्दोः परिच्छिन्नत्वं, "बैन्दवे परमाकाशे" इत्यादिना प्रपञ्चितमेव । देवताया अपि 'विद्यापि तादृगात्मा' इत्यादिनाभिहितम् । एवं तथा **स्थूलयोः** चक्रदेवतयोश्च । अत्र स्थूलत्वं नाम चक्रस्य त्रिकोणादिचतुरश्रपर्यन्तं विजृम्भणम् । देवताया अपि त्रिपुराम्बिकादित्रिपुराशक्त्यन्तरूपेण मननम् । एवंविधयोश्चक्रदेवतयोः, **भिदा** ; भेद-करणाभावादित्यर्थः । तत्र हेतुमाह—**सा परैव सूक्ष्माकारा** इति । **सा** ; पूर्वोक्त-लक्षणा । **परैव** ; आदिशक्तिरेव । **सूक्ष्माकारा** ; सूक्ष्मभूतः आकारः स्वरूपम् अनयो-रित्यर्थः । तथा चोक्तं **चतुःशत्याम्**—"स्थूलसूक्ष्मविभेदेन त्रैलोक्योत्पत्तिमातृका ।" इति । अत एव हेतोरीषद्भेदोऽपि विद्वद्भिर्नानुभूयते । एवमेव हि विद्याचिन्तनं सर्वत्र । तथा च **श्रुतिः**—"सर्वं खल्विदं ब्रह्म" इति । "सर्वं तं परादाद्योऽन्यत्रात्मनः सर्वं वेद" इति । उत्तरत्र ग्रन्थकरोऽपि वक्ति—'सेयं परा महेशी चक्राकारेण परिणमेत यदा' (श्लोकः ३६) इति देवतारूपत्वं चक्रस्य ॥ २१ ॥

इतः परं परापश्यन्त्यादिशक्तिविकासरूपं नवयोन्यात्मकं श्रीचक्रं वक्तुमादौ बैन्दवं सर्वानन्दमयाख्यं चक्रं पराशक्तिमयमित्याह—

मध्यं चक्रस्य स्यात् परामयं बिन्दुतत्त्वमेवेदम् ।
उच्छूनं तच्च यदा त्रिकोणरूपेण परिणतं स्पष्टम् ॥ २२ ॥

एतत्पश्यन्त्यादित्रितयनिदानं त्रिबीजरूपं च ।
वामा ज्येष्ठा रौद्री चाम्बिकयानुत्तरांशभूताः स्युः ॥ २३ ॥
इच्छाज्ञानक्रियाशान्ताश्चैताश्चोत्तरावयवाः ।
व्यस्ताव्यस्तं तदर्णद्वयमिदमेकादशात्म पश्यन्ती ॥ २४ ॥

मध्यमिति । चक्रस्य; नवयोन्यात्मकस्य, **मध्यं** मध्ये भवम् । **बिन्दुतत्त्वम्;** बिन्दुस्वरूपं पूर्वक्तमेव व्याख्यातम् । इदं स्वसाक्षात्कृतं **परामयमेव;** पराशक्तिस्वरूपमित्यर्थः । **तथा चोक्तम्**—“प्रसृतं विश्वलहरी स्थानं मातृत्रयात्मकम् । बैन्दवं चक्रम्” इति । तत्रैव—

“सूक्ष्मरूपं समस्तार्णावृतं परमलिङ्गकम् ।
बिन्दुरूपं परानन्दकन्दं नित्यपदोदितम् ॥”

इति । **तथा**—“बिन्दुर्विमर्शधर्मा षण्णामेकोऽध्वनां प्राणः” इति **विरूपाक्षपञ्चाशिकायाम्** । एतदेव बिन्दुतत्त्वं यदा विकासभावमयते तदा त्रिकोणचक्रमुदेतीत्याह—**उच्छूनं तच्च यदे**ति । यदा यस्मिन् काले प्राणिनामदृष्टवशादुच्छूनं तच्च बैन्दवमपि उच्छूनं संजातविकासं भवति, तदा **त्रिकोणरूपेण;** अनुत्तरानन्देच्छाशृङ्गाटरूपेण **परिणतम्;** त्रिकोणाकारं भवतीत्यर्थः । तथा चोक्तं **श्रीत्रिशिकाशास्त्रे**—

“अनुत्तरानन्दचितिरिच्छाशक्तौ नियोजिता ।
त्रिकोणमिति तत्प्राहुर्विसर्गानन्दसुन्दरम् ॥
मेयमातृप्रमामानप्रसरैः संकुचत्प्रभम् ।
शृङ्गाटरूपमापन्नमिच्छाज्ञानक्रियात्मकम् ॥”

इति । शृङ्गाटरूपं त्रिकोणमित्यर्थः । **एतत्;** त्रिकोणचक्रम्, **पश्यन्त्यादित्रितयनिदानम्;** पश्यन्तीमध्यमावैखरीप्रमुखशक्तित्रयोत्पत्तिकारणमित्यर्थः । तथा **सुभगोदयवासनायामपि**—

“इच्छादिशक्तित्रितयं पशोः सत्त्वादिसंज्ञकम् ।
महत्त्र्यश्रं भावयामि गुरुवक्त्रादनुत्तरम् ॥”

इति । **प्रत्यभिज्ञायामपि**—

"स्वाङ्गरूपेषु भावेषु सत्त्वज्ञानक्रियेच्छया ।
माया तृतीये ते एव पशोः सत्त्वं रजस्तमः ॥"

इति । इच्छाज्ञानक्रियाशक्तय एव पश्यन्त्यादिशक्तित्रितयतामापन्नाः । तथा **वामकेश्वरे**—

"इच्छाशक्तिस्तथा सेयं पश्यन्ती वपुषा स्थिता ।
ज्ञानशक्तिस्तथा ज्येष्ठा मध्यमा वागुदीरिता ॥
ऋजुरेखामयी विश्वस्थितौ प्रथितविग्रहा ।
तत्संहृतिदशायां तु बैन्दवं रूपमास्थिता ॥
प्रत्यावृत्तिक्रमेणैव शृङ्गाटवपुरुज्ज्वला ।
क्रियाशक्तिस्तु रौद्रीयं वैखरी विश्वविग्रहा ॥"

इति । **श्रीतन्त्रसद्भावेऽपि**—

"या सा तु मातृका लोके परतेजःसमन्विता ।
तया व्याप्तमिदं सर्वमाब्रह्मभुवनान्तरम् ॥"

इत्यारभ्य,

"एकैवेत्थं पराशक्तिः त्रिधा सा तु प्रजायते ।"

इत्यन्तेन पराशक्त्याः पश्यन्त्यादिशक्तिजालनिरूपणं कृतम्; तत्तत्रैवावधार्यम् । इह तु ग्रन्थविस्तरभयान्न लिख्यते । **त्रिबीजरूपं चेति;** त्रिबीजानि, त्रिखण्डात्मकवाग्भवकामराजशक्तिबीजानि ; तेषां बीजानां स्वरूपं यस्य तत् । तथा च **श्रुतिः**—

"तिस्रः पुरस्त्रिपथा विश्वचर्षणा अत्राकथा अक्षराः संनिविष्टाः ।
अधिष्ठायैना अजरा पुराणी महत्तरा महिमा देवतानाम् ॥"

इत्यादिना सर्वमन्त्राविर्भावहेतुभूतत्रिखण्डात्मकमातृकाधिष्ठानकारणदिव्यशृङ्गाटपीठमाह । **वामकेश्वरतन्त्रेऽपि**—

"बीजत्रितययुक्तस्य सकलस्य मनोः पुनः ।
एतानि वाच्यरूपाणि कुलकौलमयानि तु ॥"

इति बीजत्रितयशक्तित्रितयलिङ्गत्रितयमयं त्रिकोणं कामकलाक्षररूपमाह भगवान् परमशिवः । ततः श्रीपराभट्टारिकामयमिदमेव बिन्दुतत्त्वमूर्ध्वाधोमुखनवयोन्यात्मक-श्रीचक्रमभवदित्याह—**वामा** इति । **वामा ज्येष्ठा रौद्री अम्बिका;** चकारात् पराशक्तिश्च । इमाः पञ्चशक्तयः **अनुत्तरांशभूताः;** अनुत्तरांशाः श्रीचक्रान्तर्गताधोमुखानि पञ्चत्रिकोणानि; तत्त्वेन **भूता** जाता इत्यर्थः । **इच्छाज्ञानक्रियाशान्ताः;** इमाः चतस्रः शक्तयः, **उत्तरावयवाः;** ऊर्ध्वमुखत्रिकोणचतुष्टयरूपाः ।

अयं भावः—पराविलसनरूपा एताः वामा ज्येष्ठा रौद्री अम्बिका पराः; तथा इच्छाज्ञानक्रियाशान्ताश्चैता उत्तरावयवाश्चेति; एतच्छक्तिनवकमयं नवत्रिकोणचक्रमिति । **एतच्चतुःशत्याम्**—"आत्मनः स्फुरणं पश्येद्यदा सा परमा कला ।" इत्यारभ्य "वैखरी विश्वविग्रहा" इत्यन्तेन सम्यक् निरूपितम्; तत एव अवधार्यम् । **व्यस्ताव्यस्तं तदर्णद्वयम्;** व्यस्तं व्यष्टिरूपम्, अव्यस्तं समष्टिरूपम्, सर्वोपनिषत्प्रसिद्धम् । **तदर्णद्वयम्;** संदंशन्यायेन अखिलाक्षरात्मकमातृमन्त्रमयप्रकाशविमर्शरूपपूर्णाहंताभावगर्भकामकलाक्षरात्मकबिन्दुतत्त्वमित्यर्थः । अत्रेदं पूर्णाहंतामयं परब्रह्मपत्नीविशिष्टमेव सकलकार्यनिर्वाहकमिति सर्वागमसिद्धम् । तथा **बृहदारण्यके**—"आत्मैवेदमग्र आसीत् पुरुषविधः सोऽन्वीक्ष्य नान्यदात्मनोऽपश्यत्सोऽहमस्मीत्यग्रे व्याहरत् ततोऽहंनामाभवत् तस्मादप्येतर्ह्यामन्त्रितोऽहमयमित्येवाग्र उक्त्वाथान्यन्नाम प्रब्रूते" इत्युपक्रम्य पूर्णाहंतामयं परब्रह्मस्वरूपं दिव्यदंपतीरूपत्वमास्थाय सर्वतत्त्वनिर्मातृत्वेन विद्योतत इति उपरितनवाक्येन समाप्यते । तथा हि; "स वै नैव रेमे तस्मादेकाकी न रमते स द्वितीयमैच्छत् । स हैतावानास यथा स्त्रीपुमांसौ संपरिष्वक्तौ स इममेवात्मानं द्वेधापातयत् । ततः पतिश्च पत्नी चाभवताम्" इत्यादि । तथा **तत्रैवान्यत्र**—"आत्मैवेदमग्र आसीत् । एक एव सोऽकामयत जाया मे स्यादथ प्रजायेय; अथ वित्तं मे स्यात् अथ कर्म कुर्वीयेत्येतावान् वै कामः" इत्यादौ सपत्नीकमेव ब्रह्म प्रतीयते । एवंभूतं तदर्णद्वयं **एकादशात्म** संहत्य विचार्यमाणे एकादशविधं भवतीर्थः । परादिशान्तान्तं शक्तिदशकं व्यष्टिरूपं,

सर्वसमष्टिरूपत्वेन चैकम्, तेन चैकादशात्मकमिदं बिन्दुतत्त्वमेव पश्यन्ती शक्तिकारणम्। "सर्वं खल्विदं ब्रह्म तज्जलानिति शान्त उपासीत" इतिवत् कार्यकारणयोरभेदव्यपदेशः ॥ २२–२४ ॥

इतः परं वसुकोणदशारादिचक्रसृष्टिप्रकारमभिधातुं परमप्रकृतत्रिकोणचक्रक्रमं निगमयति—

एवं कामकलात्मा त्रिबिन्दुतत्त्वस्वरूपवर्णमयी।
सेयं त्रिकोणरूपं याता त्रिगुणस्वरूपिणी माता ॥ २५ ॥

एवमिति। एवम्; पूर्वोक्तप्रकारेण, **कामकलात्मा**; कामः, प्रकाशैकस्वभावः अनुत्तराक्षरात्मा परमशिवः, कला तु, अखिलवर्णान्त्यपरमहंसाक्षरमयी विमर्शविग्रहा। एतदुभयात्मकत्वं नाम स्वाभाविकपरिपूर्णाहंभावशालित्वम्। एतच्च 'बिन्दुरहंकारात्मा' इत्यत्र स्पष्टमभिहितम्। एवंरूपा कामकलात्मा **त्रिबिन्दुतत्त्वस्वरूपवर्णमयी**; त्रिबिन्दवः, पूर्वोक्तरक्तशुक्लमिश्रात्मानः, तेषां स्वभावः तत्त्वम्, तत्स्वरूपा ये वर्णाः वाग्भवादयः तदात्मिका। तथा **रहस्याम्नाये**—

"बिन्दुत्रयात्मकं स्वात्मशृङ्गाटं विद्धि सुन्दरम्।
मिश्रं शुक्लं च रक्तं च पुराणं प्रणवात्मकम् ॥
रेखात्रयावगन्तव्यं संवित्सान्द्रशिवात्मकम्।
रक्तमस्य निराधारमवशिष्टं ततः प्रियम् ॥
तयोर्मिश्रं तु संयोगे निर्वाणं निर्मलं पदम्।"

इति। **चतुःशत्याम्**—

"कूटत्रयात्मिकां देवीं समष्टिव्यष्टिरूपिणीम्।
आद्यां शक्तिं भावयन्तो भावार्थमिति मन्यते ॥"

इति। **सेयं त्रिकोणरूपमापन्ना** चिदानन्दघनपरमार्था सकलाम्नायसारभूता इयं विश्वाहंभावनाशालिभिः महायोगिवर्यैः आत्मसाक्षित्वेनानुभूयमाना, **त्रिगुणा** इच्छाज्ञानक्रियाशक्तिमयी सत्त्वरजस्तमांसि **तत्स्वरूपिणी**। तदवष्टम्भेन हि जगत्सृष्ट्यादि

विधत्ते। गुणाश्च इच्छाज्ञानक्रियाशक्तिमया एव। तथा **प्रत्यभिज्ञायाम्**— "स्वाङ्गरूपेषु भावेषु" इत्यादि। इच्छाज्ञानक्रियामया एव गुणाः सत्त्वरजस्तमांसि इति। अत एव **माता** सर्वजगन्निर्मात्री **एका**; "आत्मा वा इदमेक एवाग्र आसीत्" इति श्रुत्युक्तरीत्या सर्वतत्त्वातीता **परा** शक्तिः। **त्रिकोणरूपम्**; "अनुत्तरानन्देच्छासंघट्टात्त्रिकोणम्" इत्यभियुक्तोक्तरीत्या सर्वसिद्धिप्रदायकातिरहस्यभूतत्रिकोणचक्रं याता तन्मयी जातेत्यर्थः। तथा **वचनम्**—

> "अनुत्तरानन्दचितेरिच्छाशक्तौ नियोजितम्।
> त्रिकोणमिति तत्प्राहुर्विसर्गामोदसुन्दरम्॥"

इति॥ २५॥

इतः परं पराविलसनरूपायाः पश्यन्त्याद्या अपि नवयोनिचक्रात्मना नवात्मकत्वमाह—

एका परा तदन्या वामादिव्यष्टिमातृसृष्ट्यात्मा।
तेन नवात्मा जाता माता सा मध्यमाभिधानाभ्याम्॥२६॥

एका परेति। **तदन्या**; पराविकासभूता पश्यन्ती; **वामादिव्यष्टिमातृसृष्ट्यात्मा**; वामादिशान्तान्तशक्तिनवकमयी यतः **तेन** कारणेन, **सा माता**; पश्यन्ती नाम जननी। **नवात्मा**; वामादिशान्तान्तशक्तिकदम्बकाविर्भावकारणनवयोनिचक्रात्मिका जाता प्रादुर्भूतेत्यर्थः। अत्र वामादिशक्तीनां लक्षणं प्रसङ्गात् किंचिदुच्यते—तत्र वामा नाम स्वान्तःस्थितप्रपञ्चवमनाद्विश्वजनयित्रीत्यभिधीयते। ज्येष्ठा सर्वमङ्गलकारिणी। रौद्री सर्वरोगविद्राविणी। अम्बिका समस्तेष्टप्रदा शक्तिश्च। **तथागमश्च**—

> "वामा विश्वस्य वमनात् ज्येष्ठा शिवमयी यतः।
> द्रावयित्री रुजं रौद्री दोग्ध्री चाखिलकर्मणाम्॥"

इति। अम्बिका च "सा स्फुरत्ता महासत्ता" इति **प्रत्यभिज्ञास्थित्या** सर्वातिशायी परिपूर्णरूपस्वात्मस्फुरणावलोकनचतुरा। तथा **चतुःशत्याम्**—

"आत्मनः स्फुरणं पश्येद्यदा सा परमा कला ।
अम्बिकारूपमापन्ना परा वाक् समुदीरिता ॥"

इति । इच्छाज्ञानक्रियाशक्तयस्तु पश्यन्तीमध्यमावैखरीरूपा इति प्रपञ्चिताः । **चतुः-शत्याम्**—"इच्छाशक्तिस्तथा ज्ञेया पश्यन्ती वपुषा स्थिता ।" इत्यादिना । शान्ता च, "निष्कलं निष्क्रियं शान्तम्" इत्यादिश्रुत्या निरंशा चिन्मयी शक्तिः । तथा व्याचष्टे भगवान**मृतानन्दनाथः**—"निरंशौ नादबिन्दू च" इत्यत्र, "निरंशा शान्ताशक्तिः, शान्ताया निरंशत्वं चिद्रूपत्वात्" इति । **मध्यमाभिधाना-भ्याम्**; मध्यमा परापश्यन्त्योः समरसावस्था, अभिधानाभ्यां नामधेयाभ्याम् ॥ २६ ॥

अनन्तरं मध्यमाया अपि प्रकारान्तरेण नवात्मकत्वं ब्रूते—

द्विविधा हि मध्यमा सा सूक्ष्मा स्थूलाकृतिस्थिता सूक्ष्मा ।
नवनादमयी स्थूला नववर्गात्मा च भूतलिप्याख्या ॥ २७ ॥

द्विविधेति । सा; अन्तर्मुखपरमयोगिभिः दृश्या मध्यमा नाम शक्तिः **द्विविधा**; द्विप्रकारा । स्थूलसूक्ष्मभावात् । तत्र **सूक्ष्मा**; समाधिबलेन अनु-भूयमाना । **स्थूलाकृतिः**; पण्डितपामराभिलपनयोग्यवर्णावल्या स्थिता सर्वदा वर्तमाना । एतदेव व्याचष्टे— **सूक्ष्मा नवनादमयी स्थूला नववर्गात्मा** इति । अयमर्थः—मित्रावरुणसदनात् वायुनिरोधनेन स्वाधिष्ठानादिकमलभेदपुरःसरं द्वादशान्तारविन्दासनस्थपरमशिवाङ्कमुपसर्पन्ती महामातृका कुण्डलिनी बहुविधना-दात्मिका या अनुभूयते, सा समाधिसमधिगतसर्वार्थैः महामाहेश्वरैः स्वात्मत्वेन मन्यते **नवनादमयीति** । अत्र परमहंसोपनिषत् । यथा—"अथ हंसपरमहंसनिर्णयं व्या-ख्यास्यामः । ब्रह्मचारिणे दान्ताय गुरुभक्ताय हंसहंसेति सदायं देहेषु व्याप्तो वर्तते, यथाह्यग्निः काष्ठेषु तिलेषु तैलमिव । तं विदित्वा न मृत्युमेति" इत्यादिना परमहंसं परं ब्रह्म निर्दिश्य, पुनरपि तदुपासनं विशिनष्टि—"गुदमवष्टभ्याधाराद्वायु-मुत्थाप्य स्वाधिष्ठानं त्रिःप्रदक्षिणीकृत्य मणिपूरकं गत्वा अनाहतमतिक्रम्य विशुद्धौ प्राणान्निरुध्य आज्ञामनुधावन् ब्रह्मरन्ध्रं ध्यायन् त्रिमात्रोऽहमित्येव सर्वदा ध्यायन् अथो नादमाधरात् ब्रह्मरन्ध्रपर्यन्तं शुद्धस्फटिकसंकाशं स वै ब्रह्म परमात्मेत्युच्यते" इत्यनेन

मूलाधारात् ब्रह्मरन्ध्रपर्यन्तं व्यापिन्या मूलकुण्डलिन्याः स्वरूपं नादात्मकमिति व्याचष्टे। पुनस्तत्रैव, "यदा हंसो नादे विलीनो भवति, तदा तुर्यातीतमुन्मनाजपोपसंहार इत्यभिधीयते" इत्यादितदुपासनाङ्गजालानि उपन्यस्यन्ते। नादं विभजते— "स च दशविध उपजायते। चिणीति प्रथमः। चिणि चिणीति द्वितीयः। घण्टानादस्तृतीयः। शङ्खनादश्चतुर्थः। पञ्चमस्तन्त्रीनादः। षष्ठस्तालनादः। सप्तमो वेणुनादः। अष्टमो भेरीनादः। नवमो मृदङ्गनादः। दशमो मेघनादः। नवमं परित्यज्य दशममेवाभ्यसेत्। तस्मिन् विलीने मनसि गते संकल्पे विकल्पे च दग्धे पुण्यपापे सदाशिवः शक्त्यात्मा सर्वत्रावस्थितः स्वयंज्योतिः शुद्धो बुद्धो निरञ्जनः शान्तः प्रकाशत इति" इति। **नववर्गात्मा**; अकचटतपयशलात्मिका। **स्थूला**; सर्वव्यवहारविषयिणीत्युच्यते। यथा **श्रीतन्त्रसद्भावे**—

"या सा तु मातृका लोके परतेजःसमन्विता।
तया व्याप्तमिदं सर्वमाब्रह्मभुवनान्तरम्॥
तत्रस्थश्च यथा नादो व्यापितश्च सुरार्चिते।
अवर्णस्थो यथा वर्णस्थितः सर्वगतः प्रिये॥
तथाहं कथयिष्यामि निर्णयार्थं स्फुटं तव।"

इत्यारभ्य—

"या सा शक्तिः परा सूक्ष्मा निराकारेति कीर्तिता।
हृद्बिन्दुं वेष्टयित्वा तु सुषुप्ता भुजगाकृतिः॥
तत्र सुप्तो महायोगी न किंचिन्मन्यते यमी।
चन्द्रार्कानलनक्षत्रैर्भुवनानि चतुर्दश॥
व्याप्तोदरा तु सा देवी विषवन्मूढतां गता।
प्रबुद्धा सा निनादेन परेण ज्ञानरूपिणी॥
मथिता चोदरस्थेन बन्धनादपि वह्निना।
तावद्वै भ्रमयोगेन मन्थनं शक्तिविग्रहे॥
भेदात्तु प्रथमोत्पन्नाद् बिन्दुर्नादत्वमीयते।
समुत्थिता यथा तेन कलासूक्ष्मा तु कुण्डली॥

चतुष्कलमयो बिन्दुः शक्तेश्चोत्तरगः प्रभुः ।
मध्यमन्थनयोगेन ऋजुत्वं जायते प्रिये ॥
ज्येष्ठा शक्तिः स्मृता सा तु बिन्दुद्वयसुमध्यमा ।
बिन्दुनादत्वमायाता रेखयामृतकुण्डली ॥
लाकिनी नाम सा ज्ञेया उभौ बिन्दू यथागतौ ।
त्रिपदा सा समाख्याता रौद्री नाम्ना तु गीयते ॥
रोधिनी सा समुद्दिष्टा मोक्षमार्गनिरोधनात् ।
शशाङ्कशकलाकारा अम्बिका चार्धचन्द्रिका ॥
एकैवेत्थं परा शक्तिः त्रिधा सा तु प्रजायते ।
आभ्यो युक्ता विविक्ताभ्यः संजातो नववर्गकः ॥
नवधा च स्मृता सा तु नववर्गोपलक्षिता ।"

इति । अत्र कश्चित्, 'सूक्ष्मस्थूलाकृतिस्थिरा' इति पाठं कल्पयित्वा सूक्ष्मा स्थिरा स्थूला नववर्गमयीत्याह । एवं च सति नववर्गेति पदानन्वयः संप्रदायनिरोधश्च । स तु स्वबुद्धया संप्रदायमजानान एवमर्थमाह । तस्मादस्मदुक्तार्थस्य तदुक्तार्थस्य चौचित्यमर्थाविशेषज्ञैर्विद्वद्भिरेव ज्ञातव्यमित्यलम् । **भूतलिप्याख्या**; भूताश्च ते लिपयश्च भूतलिपयः । अत्र लिपीनां भूतत्वं नाम चेष्टाविशेषाक्षरविन्यासाभिव्यङ्ग्यत्वम् । तच्च कल्पनामात्रमेव । अक्षराणां तेजोरूपशक्त्यात्मकत्वात् । तथाच **आगमः**—"या सा तु मातृका लोके परतेजःसमन्विता" इति । "सर्वे वर्णात्मका मन्त्रास्ते च शक्त्यात्मकाः प्रिये ।" इत्यादि च । तेषामाख्या अभिधा यस्याः सा । तत्र भ्रान्तिलिप्येति कश्चिद्व्याचष्टे । तत्तु छन्दोभङ्गादनुपपन्नमित्यनादरणीयम् ॥ २७ ॥

सूक्ष्मरूपा हि मध्यमा स्थूलरूपायाः कारणभावमापन्ना एकैवेत्यत आह—

आद्या कारणमन्या कार्यं त्वनयोर्यतस्ततो हेतोः ।
सैवेयं न हि भेदस्तादात्म्यं हेतुहेतुमदभीष्टम् ॥ २८ ॥

आद्येति । **आद्या**; पूर्वोक्ता सूक्ष्मा, **कारणम्**; प्रथमोद्भूतत्वात् । **अन्या**; स्थूला, **कार्यम्**; तज्जन्यत्वात् । **यतः**; तस्मात्कारणात्, **अनयोः**; सूक्ष्मस्थूलयोः, कार्य-

कारणयोर्भावः । **ततो हेतोः** ; तेन कारणेन, **इयम्** ; स्थूला, **सैव** ; सूक्ष्मा शक्तिरेव । **न हि भेदः** ; भेदो नास्त्येव । ननु कथमभेदे कार्यकारणभाव इत्यत्राह—**तादात्म्यं हेतुहेतुमतोर्दिष्टमिति** । **तादात्म्यम्** ; भेदाभेदरूपम् । **हेतुहेतुमत** ; जन्यजनकरूपवत्, **अभीष्टम्** ; मृद्घटवत् । **श्रुतिश्च**—"यथा सोम्यैकेन मृत्पिण्डेन सर्वं मृन्मयं विज्ञातं स्यात्, वाचारम्भणं विकारो नामधेयं मृत्तिकेत्येव सत्यम्" इति । वाचारम्भणमात्रत्वात् एकमेव वस्तु उभयविधं भवतीति सर्ववेदान्तसंमतमित्यर्थः ॥ २८ ॥

अनन्तरं मध्यशृङ्गाटतेजःप्रसरणात्मकवसुकोणादिचक्रनिरूपणद्वारा वैखरीशक्त्याविर्भावमाह—

शषसपवर्गमयं तद्वसुकोणं मध्यकोणविस्तारः ।
नवकोणं मध्यं चेत्यस्मिंश्चिद्दीपदीपिते दशके ॥ २९ ॥

शषसेति । **तद्वसुकोणम्** ; सर्वरोगहराख्यं चक्रम्, **शषसपवर्गमयम्** ; शषसपवर्गात्मकाष्टकोणम्, **मध्यकोणस्य** ; मध्यत्रिकोणस्य, **विस्तारो** विकासो यस्य, तत्तादृशं मध्यकोणसहितं, **नवकोणं मध्यं च** ; बैन्दवाख्यं संहत्य **दशके अस्मिन्** बिन्दुत्रिकोणवसुकोणरूपे, **चिद्दीपदीपिते** ; "बैन्दवासनसंरूढसंवर्तानलचिद्घनम्" इत्युक्तरीत्या बिन्दुचक्राधिरूढायास्तेजोमूर्तेस्त्रिपुरायाः प्रभापटलप्रकाशिते इत्यर्थः ॥ २९ ॥

तच्छायाद्वितयमिदं दशारचक्रद्वयात्मना विततम् ।
तटचकवर्गचतुष्टयविलसनविस्पष्टकोणविस्तारम् ॥ ३० ॥

तच्छायाद्वितयमिदमिति । तस्य, पूर्वोक्तस्य तेजोराशिमयस्य चक्रत्रितयस्य, **छायाद्वितयं** कान्तिद्वितयम् । **दशारचक्रद्वयात्मना** ; अन्तर्दशारबहिर्दशाररूपेण निरवधिकतेजोमण्डलं, तस्य संबन्धि कान्तिद्वितयम् । सर्वरक्षाकरसर्वार्थसाधकाभिधचक्रद्वयात्मना परिणतमित्यर्थः । तथा **चोक्तम्**—"नवत्रिकोणस्फुरितप्रभारूपदशारकम् ।" इति । तच्चक्रद्वयस्वरूपं व्याचष्टे—**तटचकवर्गचतुष्टयविलसनविस्पष्टकोणविस्तारमिति** । तवर्गटवर्गात्मकाक्षरदशकरूपम् अन्तर्दशारम्, चवर्गकवर्गात्मकाक्षरदशकरूपं बहिर्दशारमित्यर्थः ॥ ३० ॥

एतच्चक्रचतुष्कप्रभासमेतं दशारपरिणामः ।
आदिस्वरगणगतचतुर्दशवर्णमयं चतुर्दशारमभूत् ॥ ३१ ॥

एतदिति । **एतच्चक्रचतुष्कप्रभासमेतम्**; एतच्चक्रचतुष्कस्य बिन्दुत्रिकोणवसुकोणान्तर्दशारात्मकस्य चक्रचतुष्कस्य, प्रभा कान्तिः, तया समेतं संयुक्तम् । **दशारपरिणामः**; बहिर्दशारचक्रमिति यावत् । बहिर्दशारचक्रस्य बैन्दवादिचक्रचतुष्टयसंनिधानादिति तात्पर्यम् । तत्र तत्प्रभा व्याप्नोतीत्यर्थः । **तथा चोक्तम्**—"चतुश्चक्रप्रभारूपसंयुक्तपरिणामतः ।" इति । अथवा—एतच्चक्रचतुष्कस्य त्रिकोणवसुकोणदशारद्वयरूपस्य प्रभासमेतं कान्तिसंयुक्तं दशारपरिणामं दशारचक्रभूतं वसुकोणं चक्रमित्यर्थः । तदेवाह—**आदिस्वरगणगतचतुर्दशवर्णमयं चतुर्दशारमिति** । अकारादिचतुर्दशवर्णात्मकचतुर्दशकोणसहितं सर्वसौभाग्यदायकाभिधं चक्रमित्यर्थः ॥ ३१ ॥

एवं बैन्दवादिमनुकोणपर्यन्तचक्रवर्णनद्वारा वैखरीशक्तिराविर्भूतेत्याह—

परया पश्यन्त्यापि च मध्यमया स्थूलवर्णरूपिण्या ।
एताभिरेकपञ्चाशदक्षरात्मिका वैखरी जाता ॥ ३२ ॥

परयेति । परादिशक्तिलक्षणं च पूर्वमेव बहुधा प्रपञ्चितम् । अयमर्थः—आदिक्षान्ताक्षरराशिमयाखिलप्रपञ्चनिर्मात्री सर्वशब्दात्मिका वैखरीति । **तथा चोक्तम्**—"वैखरी विश्वविग्रहा" इति । "वाचा वक्त्रे करणविशदां वैखरीं तां प्रपद्ये" इत्यादि च ॥ ३२ ॥

इतः परं सर्वसंक्षोभणसर्वाशापरिपूरकाभिधचक्रद्वयं वैखरीवर्णात्मकमेवेत्याह—

कादिभिरष्टभिरुपचितमष्टदलाब्जं च वैखरीवर्गैः ।
स्वरगणसमुदितमेतद् द्व्यष्टदलाम्भोरुहं च संचिन्त्यम् ॥ ३३ ॥

कादिभिरिति । **वैखरीवर्गैः**; वैखरीशक्तिस्वरूपैः । **अष्टभिः कादिभिः उपचितम्**; सम्यक् प्रोतम् । **अष्टदलाब्जं च**; सर्वसंक्षोभणचक्रम् । तथा **स्वरगणसमुदितम्**; स्वरगणैः अकारादिषोडशवर्णैः, समुदितं सम्यक् भावितम् । **एतत्**;

परिदृश्यमानम् । **द्वयष्टदलाम्भोरुहम्;** सर्वाशापारिपूरकचक्रम् । **संचिन्त्यम्;** सर्वदा भावनीयमित्यर्थः ॥ ३३ ॥

बिन्दुत्रयमयतेजस्त्रितयविकारश्च तानि वृत्तानि ।
भूबिम्बत्रयमेतत् पश्यन्त्यादित्रिमातृविश्रान्तिः ॥ ३४ ॥

बिन्द्विति । तानि वृत्तानि; मन्वश्रोपरि अष्टदलपद्मोपरि षोडशदलपद्मोपरि च स्थितानि । **बिन्दुत्रयमयतेजस्त्रितयविकारश्च;** बिन्दुत्रयं पूर्वोक्तरक्तशुक्लमिश्रात्मकम्, तन्मयं तत्तेजस्त्रितयं सोमसूर्याग्निरूपम्, तद्विकारश्च, तन्मयानीत्यर्थः । तत्र वृत्तत्रयस्य तेजस्त्रयात्मकत्वकथनेन सोमसूर्यानलात्मत्रिखण्डमयत्वं चक्रस्योक्तम् । **यथागमः**—"त्रिखण्डं मातृकाचक्रं सोमसूर्यानलात्मकम् ।" इति । तथा **सुभगोदये**—

"सोमसूर्यकृशान्वात्मतेजस्त्रितयरूपकम् ।
नेत्रत्रयं भावयामि वृत्तत्रितयमञ्जसा ॥"

इति । तानि वृत्तानि, "वेदाः प्रमाणाम्" इतिवत् द्रष्टव्यम् । **भूबिम्बत्रयम्;** अणिमादिब्राह्म्यादिसर्वसंक्षोभिण्यादिशक्तिकदम्बकावासभूतम् । **पश्यन्त्यादित्रिमातृविश्रान्तिः;** पश्यन्तीमध्यमावैखरीशक्तय एतावत्पर्यन्तं विजृम्भमाणाः त्रिकोणादि भूपुरपर्यन्तं श्रीचक्रात्मना चकासतीत्यर्थः । **एतच्च;** "आत्मनः स्फुरणं पश्येद्यदा सा परमा कला" इत्यारभ्य, "वैखरी विश्वविग्रहा" इत्यन्तेन ग्रन्थजातेन सम्यगुदीरितम् ॥ ३४ ॥

एवं 'मध्यं चक्रस्य स्यात्' इत्युपक्रम्य, 'पश्यन्त्यादित्रिमातृविश्रान्तिः' इत्यन्तं श्रीमहात्रिपुरसुन्दर्याश्चक्रं सम्यङ् निरूप्य, अनन्तरं तदावरणचक्रान्तर्गतशक्तिनिकुरम्बं तन्निकटस्थितश्रीगुरुमण्डलमपि श्रीदेव्यवयवपरिणतिरूपमेवेत्याह—

क्रमणं पदविक्षेपः क्रमोदयस्तेन कथ्यते द्वेधा ।
आवरणं गुरुपङ्क्तिर्द्वयमिदमम्बापदाम्बुजप्रसरः ॥ ३५ ॥

'क्रमणं पदविक्षेपः' इत्यारभ्य, **'अणिमादिभूतयोऽस्याः'** इत्यन्तैः पञ्चदशभिः श्लोकैः। **क्रमणमिति—तत्र क्रमणम्**; पदक्रमः, स च द्विविधः—पदविक्षेपरूपः, क्रमोदयरूपश्च। तत्र पदविक्षेपो नाम सुन्दर्या अनन्तकोटिकिरणात्मकानन्तशक्तिजननसामर्थ्यम्। तथा **चोपनिषत्**—"मरीचयः स्वायंभुवाः। ये शरीराण्यकल्पयन्" इत्यादि। "तमेव भान्तम्" इत्यादि च। **तथा भैरवयामलेऽपि**—

"बैन्दवे जगदुत्पत्तिस्थितिसंहारकारिणी।
सदाशिवेन संपृक्ता तत्त्वातीता महेश्वरी॥
ज्योतीरूपा पराकारा तस्या देहोद्भवाः शिवे।
किरणाश्च सहस्रं च द्विसहस्रं च लक्षकम्॥
कोटिरर्बुदमेतेषां परा संख्या न विद्यते।
तामेवानुप्रविश्यैव भाति सर्वं चराचरम्॥
यस्या देव्या महेशान्या भासा सर्वं विभासते।
तद्भासा रहितं किंचिन्न च यच्च प्रकाशते॥
तस्याश्च शिवशक्तेश्च चिद्रूपायाश्चितिं विना।
आन्ध्यमापद्यते नूनं जगदेतच्चराचरम्॥
तेषामनन्तकोटीनां मयूखानां महेश्वरि।
मध्ये षष्ट्युत्तरं तेऽमी त्रिशतं किरणाः शिवे॥
ब्रह्माण्डं व्यश्नुवानास्ते सोमसूर्यानलात्मना।
अग्नेरष्टोत्तरशतं षोडशोत्तरकं रवेः॥
षट्त्रिंशदुत्तरशतं चन्द्रस्य किरणाः शिवे।
ब्रह्माण्डं भासयन्त्येते पिण्डाण्डमपि पार्वति॥
दिवा सूर्यस्तथा रात्रौ सोमो वह्निश्च संध्ययोः।
प्रकाशयन्तः कालास्ते तस्मात्कालात्मकास्त्रयः॥
षष्ट्युत्तरं च त्रिशतं दिनान्येव तु हायनम्।
हायनात्मा महादेवः प्रजापतिरिति श्रुतिः॥"

इत्यादि। "सर्वपीठनिवासिन्यः सर्वगाश्चिन्मरीचयः।" इत्यादि च। "रश्मिचक्रं

च परितो भक्तिनम्रः प्रपूजयेत ।" इत्यमृतानन्दाः । **क्रमोदयो** नाम दिव्य-सिद्धमानवौघरूपा अनन्तप्रकाशात्मकश्रीगुरुमण्डलात्मकतया प्रसरणम् । तथा **रहस्याम्नाये**—"चरणद्वयचन्द्रार्करश्मयो गुरवः किल ।" इति । एतच्चोत्तरत्र प्रपञ्च्यते । एतदेव क्रमद्वयं विवृणोति--**आवरणमिति** । **आवरणम्;** आवरण-चक्रस्थितशक्तिनिकुरुम्बम्, मञ्चाः क्रोशन्तीतिवत् । **गुरुपङ्क्तिः;** गुरुमण्डलम् । **इदं द्वयम् अम्बापादाम्बुजप्रसरः;** अम्बायास्त्रिपुरायाः पदाम्बुजस्य श्रीपादयुगलस्य, प्रसरणम्, विजृम्भणमिति यावत् । अत्र यजुःश्रुतिः—"ज्योतिष्मद्भ्राजमानं महस्वत्" इत्यादि । तथा **प्रामाणिकवचनम्**—

"अनेककोटिभेदैस्तु गदितं त्रैपुरं महः ।
तत्र मध्ये परा दीप्ता महात्रिपुरसुन्दरी ॥"

इति । **षडन्वयशांभवे** च—

"वरदाभयहस्ताश्च सर्वा वामार्धविग्रहाः ।
तेजोरूपाः परा ध्येयाः केवलं मोक्षकाङ्क्षिभिः ।"

इति ॥ ३५ ॥

तत्प्रसारप्रसरणीं क्रमशो विवृणोति—

सेयं परा महेशी चक्राकारेण परिणमेत यदा ।
तद्देहावयवानां परिणतिरावरणदेवताः सर्वाः ॥ ३६ ॥

सेयमिति । **सेयम्;** अपरिच्छिन्नानन्ततेजोराशिमयी, **परा;** सर्वोत्कृष्टा, **महेशी;** अनन्तकोटियोगिनीबृन्दसमाराधितनित्यनिरवधिकातिशयानन्दमयात्मसाम्राज्य-संपदभिमानशालिनी । अत्र **यजुःश्रुतिः**—"यतो वा" इत्यादि । तथा **चोक्तम्**—

"चतुःषष्टियुताः कोट्यो योगिनीनां महौजसाम् ।
चक्रमेतत् समाश्रित्य संस्थिता वीरवन्दिता ॥"

इति । **ललितोपाख्याने** च—

"वाचामगोचरमगोचरमेव बुद्धेरीदक्तया न कलनीयमनन्यतुल्यम् ।
त्रैलोक्यगर्भपरिपूरितशक्तिचक्रसाम्राज्यसंपदभिमानमभिस्पृशन्ती ॥"

इति । **चक्राकारेण**; "चक्रं नवात्मकमिदं नवधा भिन्नमातृकम्" इति सर्वानन्दमयबैन्दवादित्रैलोक्यमोहनान्तचक्रनवकात्मना, "स्फुरत्तामात्मनः पश्येत्" इति पूर्णानन्दमयात्मावलोकनसमये, **परिणमेत**; आकारान्तरमावहेत । प्रार्थनायां लिङ् । दिङ्मात्रप्रपञ्चप्रादुर्भावस्य प्रार्थनाविषयत्वात् । ब्रह्मणः परिणामश्रुतिरप्येवमभिधीयते । यथा—"सोऽकामयत । बहु स्यां प्रजायेयेति" इति सृष्टिं प्रस्तुत्य, "तत्सृष्ट्वा । तदेवानुप्राविशत् । तदनुप्रविश्य । सच्च त्यच्चाभवत् । निरुक्तं चा निरुक्तं च । निलयनं चानिलयनं च । विज्ञानं चाविज्ञानं च । सत्यं चानृतं च सत्यमभवत् ।" इत्यन्तम् । **स्मृतिश्च**—"अस्यां परिणतायाम्" इत्यादि । **तद्देहावयवानाम्**; तस्याः, त्रिपुरसुन्दर्याः, देहः तेजःपुञ्जात्मकः, तस्य अवयवाः किरणाः, तेषां **परिणतिः**; अवस्थान्तरापत्तिः; इह आवरणदेवताः वशिन्याद्यणिमान्तशक्तिनिकुरुम्बं चिदानन्दसमुद्रात्मकमेव । समुद्रसकाशात्फेनबुद्बुदतरङ्गादिवदनन्तकोटिशक्तय आविर्भावतिरोभावौ भजन्त इत्यर्थः । तथा **चोपनिषत्**—

"यस्मिन् भावाः प्रलीयन्ते लीनाश्च व्यक्ततां ययुः ।
पुनश्चाव्यक्ततां भूयो जायन्ते बुद्बुदा इव ॥"

इति । **चतुःशत्यां** च—

"एवं रूपं परं तेजः श्रीचक्रवपुषा स्थितम् ।
तदीयशक्तिनिकरस्फुरदूर्मिसमाकुलम् ॥"

इति । **सुभगोदयवासनायामपि**—

"चक्रराजे परामृश्य योगिनीः प्रकटादिकाः ।
विमर्शाख्यचिदम्भोधिलहरीस्ता अपि क्रमात् ॥

यस्या उल्लसिता एता योगिन्यश्चिद्घनत्विषः ।
चक्रेश्वरे भजाम्येताश्चक्रं चक्रं समाश्रिताः ॥"

इति ॥ ३६ ॥

वशिन्याद्यावरणशक्तिस्वरूपवर्णनमारभमाणस्तदादौ मूलदेवीस्वरूपमाह—

आसीना बिन्दुमये चक्रे सा त्रिपुरसुन्दरी देवी ।
कामेश्वराङ्कनिलया कलया चन्द्रस्य कल्पितोत्तंसा ॥ ३७ ॥
पाशाङ्कुशेक्षुचापप्रसूनशरपञ्चकाञ्चितस्वकरा ।
बालारुणारुणाङ्गी शशिभानुकृशानुलोचनत्रितया ॥ ३८ ॥

आसीनेत्यादि । बिन्दुमये; सर्वानन्दमयाख्ये परमाकाशे, "बैन्दवे परमाकाशे" इत्युक्तत्वात् । **चक्रे**; आत्मचङ्क्रमणविहरणार्हपीठे । तथा **रहस्योपनिषदि**— "यदेषा चङ्क्रमत्तच्चक्रमभवत्" इति । **आसीना**; उपरिप्रदेशे विराजमाना, **सा**; देशकालाकारानवच्छिन्ना तत्स्वरूपिणी, **त्रिपुरसुन्दरी**; सर्वकारणत्वेन स्पृहणीयस्वभावा, **देवी**; विश्वजनादिसर्वव्यापारविनोदिनी, **कामेश्वराङ्कनिलया**; कामेश्वरस्य श्रीनाथस्य अङ्कं वामोरुतलभागो निलयोऽवस्थानं यस्याः सा । तथा चोक्तं **भैरवयामले**—

"कला विद्या परा शक्तिः श्रीचक्राकाररूपिणी ।
तन्मध्ये बैन्दवं स्थानं तत्रास्ते परमेश्वरी ॥
सदाशिवेन संपृक्ता सर्वतत्त्वातिगा सती ।"

इति । **अन्यत्र च**—

"विश्वाकारप्रथाधारनिजरूपशिवात्मकम् ।
कामेश्वराङ्कपर्यङ्कनिविष्टमतिसुन्दरम् ॥"

इति । **श्रीनाथानन्दश्च**—"आदिश्रीगुरुनाथस्य वामाङ्कोपरि संस्थिताम् ।" इति । **चन्द्रस्य कलया**; विश्वजीविन्याख्यया, **कल्पितोत्तंसा**; कृतभूषणा । अत्र

कल्पितपदेन चन्द्रमण्डलस्य भगवतीलीलोपकरणत्वं लक्ष्यते । तथा **पाशाङ्कुशेक्षुचापप्रसूनशरपञ्चकाञ्चितस्वकरा** इति । पाशः, स्वात्मरूपभेदबन्धनसाधानभूतेच्छाशक्तिस्वरूपः, अङ्कुशः, स्वरूपभेददलनोपायात्मकज्ञानशक्तिमयः, इक्षुचापेषुपञ्चके स्वभिन्नाकारावर्जनसाधनरूपक्रियाशक्तिरूपे, तैः अञ्चिता ; अयमर्थः—इच्छाज्ञान क्रियाशक्तय एव तदाज्ञया पाशादिस्वरूपमापन्नाः तदुपासनमाचरन्तीत्यर्थः । तथा च **चतुःशत्यम्**—

"इच्छाशक्तिमयं पाशमङ्कुशं ज्ञानरूपिणम् ।
क्रियाशक्तिमये बाणधनुषी दधदुज्ज्वला ॥"

इति । **सुभगोदयवासनायामपि**—

"देव्याः संवित्स्वसत्ताया भेदोद्वमनहेतुकाः ।
आयुधाख्याः पराः शक्तीर्बाणाद्याः पूजयाम्यहम् ॥"

इति । **बालारुणारुणाङ्गी** ; उदयादित्यसंकाशा । **शशिभानुकृशानुलोचनत्रितया** ; सोमसूर्याग्निमयत्रिनयना । **तथा चोक्तम्**—

"बालार्कमण्डलाभासां चतुर्बाहुं त्रिलोचनाम् ।
पाशाङ्कुशधरां चापं धारयन्तीं शिवां प्रिये ॥"

इति ॥ ३७, ३८ ॥

एतदेव दिव्यमिथुनं दिव्यसिद्धमानवौघभावेनाविशेषभेदभिन्नगुरुमण्डलस्वरूपमुपास्येत्याह—

तन्मिथुनं गुणभेदादास्ते बिन्दुत्रयात्मके त्र्यश्रे ।
कामेशीमित्रेशप्रमुखद्वन्द्वत्रयात्मना विततम् ॥ ३९ ॥

तन्मिथुनमिति । **तन्मिथुनम्** ; तत्, सर्वातीतत्वेन सर्वोपनिषत्प्रसिद्धं, मिथुनं, कामकामेश्वरीरूपम् । **अयमर्थः**—परमात्मा हि स्वात्मानमेव स्त्रीपुंमयं

कृत्वा मिथुनरूपमापन्नो विहरते। अत्र श्रुतिः—"स एको नैव रेमे तस्मादेकाकी न रमते, स द्वितीयमैच्छत् स हैतावानास यथा स्त्रीपुमांसौ संपरिष्वक्तौ स इममात्मानं द्विधापातयत्। ततः पतिश्च पत्नी चाभवताम्" इत्यारभ्य, "यदिदं किंचिन्मिथुनमापिपीलिकाभ्यस्तत्सर्वं सृजति" इत्यन्तेन मिथुनात्मना विहरणशीलं ब्रह्मेत्याह। तथा रहस्यागमश्च—

"गुरुशिष्यपदे स्थित्वा स्वयमेव सदाशिवः।
प्रश्नोत्तरपदैर्वाक्यैस्तन्त्रं समवतारयत्॥"

इत्यादिप्रकाशविमर्शात्मना मिथुनीभूतः परमशिवादेव सकलं तन्त्रं समभवदित्याह। एवं तन्मिथुनं कामकामेश्वरीरूपं, मित्रेशनाथः कामेश्वरी, श्रीमदुड्डीशनाथो वज्रेश्वरी, षष्ठीशनाथो भगमालिनी; एवमादिमिथुनत्रयात्मना दिव्यसिद्धमानवौघादिक्रमरूपेण विततं मिथुनत्रयं विस्तृतमित्यर्थः।

एतच्च 'आसीनः श्रीपीठे कृतयुगकाले गुरुः शिवो विद्याम्, (श्लोकः ५१) इत्यत्र सम्यक् प्रपञ्चयिष्यामि। रहस्योपनिषदि चायमर्थः सम्यङ्निरूपितः। यथा—"मध्ये चक्रं बिन्दुः बिन्दौ प्रपञ्चो लोकः लोको देहःसनादरूपः अर्थात्मिका शक्तिः चक्रं तनुः बिन्दुः प्राणः मध्ये शक्तिरिति सप्रपञ्चो गुणः गुणो लिङ्गं स्वयंभ्वादिभेदेन त्रिधाभूतं त्रिलिङ्गिनां जयदं कामकामरूपं कैवल्यं उड्याणःपूर्णगिरिजालंधरं यत्पुरुषा देवी सात्त्विका भवति" इति। अत्रेदं व्याख्या स्यात्—यदिदं नीलकण्ठः शमीगर्भायोवाच। "यतो वा इमानि भूतानि जायन्ते येन जातानि जीवन्ति। यत्प्रयन्त्यभिसंविशान्ति पृच्छति यदिदं दृश्यते तदानन्दयोनिः तेनैव जीवति तदेव जीवतीति तदेषाभ्युक्ता" इत्यादिना त्रिपुराचक्रनिरूपणपुरःसरं सकलप्रपञ्चानां त्रिपुराया एव सकाशादुत्पत्तिजीवनलयाः प्रतिपाद्यन्ते। ततश्च सर्वफलप्रदायिनी त्रिपुरैव श्रीदेवीस्वरूपैर्वीरैर्भजनीयेत्युक्तं भवति। तथा रहस्यागमश्च—

"यस्य नो पश्चिमं जन्म यदि वा शंकरः स्वयम्।
तेनैव लभ्यते विद्या श्रीमत्पञ्चदशाक्षरी"

इति॥ ३९॥

इतः परमावरणदेवतास्वरूपभावौ वर्णयति—

वसुकोणनिवासिन्यो यास्ताः संध्यारुणा वशिन्याद्याः ।
पुर्यष्टकमेवेदं चक्रतनोः संविदात्मनो देव्याः ॥ ४० ॥

वसुकोणेति । **वसुकोणनिवासिन्यः** ; सर्वरोगहराख्यचक्रनिवासनशीलाः, **याः**; वशिन्याद्यष्टशक्तयः, **ताः** ; **पूर्णाहंभावदानसमर्थाः** । कथम् ? तत्र रोगहारित्वं नाम पूर्णाहंभावप्रदत्वमेव । "अपूर्णं मन्यतां व्याधिः कार्पण्यैकनिदानभूः" इत्युक्तेः । तथा "सर्वरोगहरा एता विमर्शादिविशेषतः ।" **इत्यभियुक्ततमोक्तेः** । एवंभूतास्ताः **संध्यारुणाः** ; अरुणाकारा भासन्त इत्यर्थः । अत एवेदमष्टकोणचक्रं **संविदात्मनः** सामीप्यात्, ज्ञानमेवात्मा स्वरूपं यस्याः सा तस्याः । "सत्यं ज्ञानमनन्तं ब्रह्म" इति **श्रुतेः**, "स्वसंवित्त्रिपुरादेवी" **इत्यागमश्च** । देव्याः, "बहु स्याम्" इति विहरणस्वभावायाः, **चक्रतनोः**; चक्रात्मिकायाः, **पुर्यष्टकम्**; सूक्ष्मशरीरमित्यर्थः । **तथा चोक्तम्**—

"चितिश्चित्तं च चैतन्यं चेतनाद्वयमेव च ।
जीवः कला शरीरं च सूक्ष्मं पुर्यष्टकं भवेत् ॥

इति । **शिवानन्दाश्च**—

"अष्टारांशप्रवेशोऽयं चिन्निर्याणेषु सादिकम् ।
सूक्ष्मपुर्यष्टकं देव्या मतिरेषा तु गौरवी ॥"

इति ॥ ४० ॥

तद्विषयवृत्तयस्ताः सर्वज्ञादिस्वरूपमापन्नाः ।
अन्तर्दशारनिलया लसन्ति शरदिन्दुसुन्दराकाराः ॥ ४१ ॥

तदिति । **तद्विषयवृत्तयः**; वसुकोणनिकटवासिन्यः । **ताः**; स्वात्मैक्य-रूपरक्षणधारिणीत्वेन प्रसिद्धाः । **सर्वज्ञादिस्वरूपम्**; सर्वज्ञादिशक्तिदशकरूपम्, **आपन्नाः**; प्राप्ताः । **अन्तर्दशारनिलयाः**; सर्वरक्षाकराभिधेयचक्रसमारूढाः निगर्भ-

योगिन्यः । **शरदिन्दुसुन्दराकाराः**; स्वच्छप्रकशधवलाकृतयः । **लसन्ति**; प्रकाशान्ते । तथा **चोक्तम्**—

" अन्तर्दशारगा देव्यो विद्युत्पुञ्जनिभाः शुभाः ।
निगर्भाख्याः पूजनीयाः सर्वरक्षाविधायिनीः ॥ "

इति ॥ ४१ ॥

तद्बाह्यपङ्क्तिकोणेषु योगिन्यः सर्वसिद्धिदाः पूर्वाः ।
देवीधीकर्मेन्द्रियविषयमया विशदवेषभूषाढ्याः ॥ ४२ ॥

तद्बाह्येति । **तद्बाह्यपङ्क्तिकोणेषु**; तस्य, सर्वरक्षाकरचक्रस्य, बाह्यभूतेषु, उपरिस्थितेषु, पङ्क्तिकोणेषु, सर्वार्थसाधके चक्रे तस्य दशकोणात्मकत्वात्, तत्र स्थिताः; **योगिन्यः**; कुलकौलनामधेयाः; **सर्वसिद्धिदाः पूर्वाः**; सर्वसिद्धिप्रदाः-प्रमुखाः शक्तयः । **देवीधीकर्मेन्द्रियविषयमयाः**; देव्याः त्रिपुरायाः, धीकर्मेन्द्रियाणि, श्रोत्रादिज्ञानेन्द्रियाणि, वागदिकर्मेन्द्रियाणि च, तेषां विषयाः, शब्दादयः, अभिलपनादयश्च; तन्मयाः तत्स्वरूपाः । **विशदवेषभूषाढ्याः**; विशदाः, शुभ्राकाराः, वेषाश्च भूषाश्च तैराढ्याः । अयमर्थः—मन्त्रदेवतात्माभेदरूपाः सिद्धिदायिन्यः स्वच्छाकृतयः शुभ्राभरणा भासन्त इति । तथा चोक्तं **चतुःशत्याम्**—

" श्वेतावराभयकराः श्वेताभरणभूषिताः ।
मन्त्राणां स्वप्रभारूपयोगादन्वर्थसंज्ञिकाः ॥
सर्वसिद्धिप्रदाद्यास्तु चक्रे सर्वार्थसाधके । "

इति । **सुभगोदयवासनायां** च—" बाह्यो दशारभागोऽयं बुद्धिकर्माक्षगोचरः । "
इति ॥ ४२ ॥

भुवनारचक्रभवनाः देवीमनुकरणविवरणस्फुरणाः ।
संध्यासवर्णवसनाः संचिन्त्याः संप्रदाययोगिन्यः ॥ ४३ ॥

भुवनारेति । **भुवनारचक्रभवनाः**; भुवनारचक्रं सर्वसौभाग्यदायकचक्रम्,

भवनम् आवासस्थानं यासां ताः । **देवीमनुकरणविवरणस्फुरणाः**; देव्या मनुकरणानि चतुर्दशकरणानि कर्मेन्द्रियाणि पञ्च, ज्ञानेन्द्रियाणि पञ्च, मनोबुद्ध्यहंङ्कारचित्ताख्यानि चत्वारि । **प्रत्यभिज्ञायां** तु—"त्रयोदशविधायाश्च बाह्यान्तःकरणावलिः" इति चित्तव्यतिरेकेण त्रयोदशत्वमुक्तम् । इह तु चित्तेन साकं चतुर्दशत्वमुक्तम् । "चित्तमये श्रीपीठे" इति चित्तस्यापि अभियुक्तैरन्तःकरणत्वेन परिगणनात् । तेषां विवरणं व्याख्यानभूतं स्फुरणं चतुर्दशाररूपं यासां ताः । देवी तु स्वयमेव चतुर्दशकरणात्मकचतुर्दशारचक्रदेवतात्मना स्थिता इत्यर्थः । तथा चोक्तं **शिवानन्दैः**—

"चतुर्दशारसरणीः करणानि चतुर्दश ।
चतुर्दशशिवारण्यं महादेव्याः स्मराम्यहम् ॥"

इति । **संध्यासवर्णवसनाः**; संध्यायाः सवर्णं वसनं सदृशं वस्त्रं यासां ताः । **संप्रदाययोगिन्यः**; आदिशक्तिमयत्वेन सत्संप्रदायदेव्यः सर्वसंक्षोभिणीप्रभृतयः । **संचिन्त्याः**; सम्यग्भावनीयाः । तथा **चतुःशत्याम्**—

"शक्तेः सारमयत्वेन प्रसूतत्वान्महेश्वरी ।
संप्रदायक्रमायाताश्चक्रे सौभाग्यदायके ॥
निरन्तरप्रभारूपसौभाग्यबलरूपतः ।
अन्वर्थसंज्ञका देवी अणिमासदृशाः शुभाः ॥
सर्वसंक्षोभिणीपूर्वा देहैक्यादिविशुद्धिदा ॥"

इति ॥ ४३ ॥

अव्यक्तमहदहंकृतितन्मात्रस्वीकृताङ्गनाकाराः ।
द्विरदच्छदनसरोजे जयन्ति गुप्ततरयोगिनीसंज्ञाः ॥ ४४ ॥

अव्यक्तेति । **अव्यक्तमहदहंकृतितन्मात्रस्वीकृताङ्गनाकाराः**; अव्यक्तं अव्याक्ताख्यं तत्त्वम्, महत् महत्तत्त्वम्, अहंकृतिः अहंकारतत्त्वम्, तन्मात्राः, पृथिव्यादिभूततन्मात्राः पञ्च, संहत्याष्टौ; एतैः स्वीकृतम् अङ्गनानाम् आकारं

स्वरूपं यासां ताः, देव्यात्मिका इत्यर्थः । **गुप्ततरयोगिनीसंज्ञाः;** मूलदेव्या अन्तरङ्गभूतत्वात् । एतासामनङ्गकुसुमादीनां गुप्ततरेति संज्ञा यासां ताः, अनङ्गकुसुमाद्यष्टशक्तयः । वाग्भवाष्टकसर्वसंक्षोभणाह्वये **द्विरदच्छदनसरोजे;** सर्वसंक्षोभणाख्याष्टदलपद्मे, **जयन्ति;** सर्वोत्कर्षेण वर्तन्ते । तथा चोक्तं **शिवेन**—

"कौलिकानुभवाविष्टशीलाः पुर्यष्टकाश्रिताः ।
वाग्भवाष्टकसंबन्धसूक्ष्मवर्गस्वरूपतः ॥
लोके गुप्ततराश्चान्याः सर्वसंक्षोभणाह्वये ।
अनङ्गकुसुमाद्यास्तु रक्तकञ्चुकशोभिताः ॥
वेणीकृतलसत्केशाश्चापबाणधराः शुभाः ॥"

इति । **शिवानन्दाश्च**—

"वसुच्छदनपद्माङ्कदलोऽयं चक्रको विभुः ।
अव्यक्ताद्याः प्रकृतयो भूतानां निश्चिनोम्यहम् ॥"

इति । अनङ्गकुसुमाद्यष्टशक्तयः द्विरदच्छदनसरोजे सर्वसंक्षोभणाख्याष्टदलपद्मे जयन्ति सर्वोत्कर्षेण वर्तन्त इति ॥ ४४ ॥

भूतानीन्द्रियदशकं मनश्च देव्या विकारषोडशकम् ।
कामाकर्षिण्यादिस्वरूपतः षोडशारमध्यास्ते ॥ ४५ ॥

भूतानीति । **भूतानीन्द्रियदशकम्;** भूतानि; पृथिव्यादीनि, **इन्द्रियदशकम्;** ज्ञानकर्मोभयलक्षणं, **मनश्च;** अन्तःकरणप्रधानम्, संहृत्य **विकारषोडशकं देव्या** विकारभूतावस्थान्तरस्वरूपम् । कुतः ?

"विमर्शाख्या च सा देवी पाञ्चविध्यं समागता ।
आकाशानिलसप्तार्चिःसलिलावनिभेदतः ॥"

इत्यादिवचनात् । एवंभूतषोडशकं षोडशारं सर्वाशापरिपूरकनामधेयं चक्रम् । **कामाकर्षिण्यादिस्वरूपतः;** कामाकर्षिण्यादिषोडशशक्त्याकारेण, **अध्यास्ते;** अधितिष्ठति ।

"अधिशीङ्स्थासां कर्म" इति कर्मत्वम्। सर्वाशापरिपूरकचक्रे एताः कामाकर्षिण्यादिगुप्तयोगिन्यः स्वरात्मिका निवसन्तीत्यर्थः। तथा चोक्तं **चतुःशत्याम्**—

"षोडशस्वरसंदोहचमत्कृतिमयीकलाः।
प्राणादिषोडशानां तु तत्त्वानां षोडशात्मिकाः।
बीजभूतस्वरात्मत्वात्तदसौ बीजरूपिकाः।
अन्तरङ्गतया गुप्तयोगिन्यः सुव्यवस्थिताः॥
कामाकर्षणरूपाद्याः सृष्टिः प्राधान्यतः प्रिये।
सर्वाशापूरकाख्ये तु चक्रे वामेन पूजयेत्॥"

इति। **सुभगोदयवासनायाम्**—

"षोडशच्छदपद्मोत्थं भोगभूताक्षमानसम्।
विकारात्मकतापन्नं देव्याः संभावयाम्यहम्॥"

इति॥ ४५॥

मुद्रास्त्रिखण्डया सह संविन्मय्यः समुच्छ्रिताः सर्वाः।
आदिमहीगृहवासा भासा बालार्ककान्तिभिः सदृशाः॥ ४६॥
आधारनवकमस्या नवचक्रत्वेन परिणतं येन।
नवनाथशक्तयोऽपि च मुद्राकारेण परिणतं येन॥ ४७॥

मुद्रा इति। मुद्राः त्रिखण्डया सह; त्रिखण्डमुद्रया साकं, **समुच्छ्रिताः**; सर्वोत्कर्षेण वर्तमानाः, **आदिमहीगृहवासाः**, आदिमचतुरश्रनिलयाः। **भासा**; कान्त्या, **बालार्ककान्तिभिः**; तरुणारुणरुचिभिः, **सदृशाः**; तुल्याः। **संविन्मय्यः**; चिद्घननिष्ठा इत्यर्थः। **तथा चोक्तम्**—"चिद्व्योमचारिणी मुद्रा शिवावस्था तु खेचरी।" इति सर्वसंक्षोभिणीप्रभृतयो दशमुद्रा भयध्वंसिन्यः परमानन्ददायिन्यः परमशक्तय इत्यर्थः। तथा **चोक्तम्**—

"मोचयन्ति ग्रहादिभ्यः पाशौघान् द्रावयन्ति च।
मोचनं द्रावणं यस्मान्मुद्रास्ताः परिकीर्तिताः॥"

इति। एतास्तु मुद्राः चतुरश्रादिबैन्दवान्तनवचक्राधिष्ठाननायिका इति वामकेश्वरे परमशिवेन प्रपञ्चिताः; दिङ्मात्रमुदाह्रियन्ते। तथा हि—

"क्रियाशक्तिस्तु विश्वस्य मोदनाद् द्रावणात्तथा।
मुद्राख्या सा यदा संविदम्बिका त्रिकलामयी॥
त्रिखण्डारूपमापन्ना सदा संनिधिकारिणी।
सर्वस्य चक्रराजस्य व्यापिका परिकीर्तिता॥
योनिप्राचुर्यतः सैषा सर्वसंक्षोभिणी पुनः।
वामाशक्तिप्रधानेयं द्वारचक्रे स्थिता भवेत्॥
क्षुब्धविश्वस्थितिकरी ज्येष्ठाप्राचुर्यमास्थिता।
स्थूलनादकलारूपा सर्वानुग्रहकारिणी॥
सर्वाशापूरकाख्ये तु सैषा स्फुरितविग्रहा।
ज्येष्ठावामासमत्वेन सृष्टेः प्राधान्यमाश्रिता॥
आकर्षिणी तु मुद्रेयं सर्वसंक्षोभिणी स्मृता।
व्योमद्वयान्तरालस्थबिन्दुरूपा महेश्वरि॥
शिवशक्त्यात्मसंश्लेषाद् दिव्यावेशकरी स्मृता।
चतुर्दशारचक्रस्था संविदानन्दविग्रहा॥
बिन्द्वन्तरालविलसत्सूक्ष्मरूपशिखामयी।
ज्येष्ठाशक्तिप्रधाना तु सर्वोन्मादनकारिणी॥
दशारचक्रमास्थाय संस्थिता वीरवन्दिते।
वामाशक्तिप्रधाना तु महाङ्कुशमयी पुनः॥
तद्वद्विश्वं वमन्ती सा द्वितीये तु दशारके।
संस्थिता मोदनपरा मुद्रारूपत्वमाश्रिता॥
बिन्द्वन्तरालविलसत्सूक्ष्मरूपशिखामयी।
धर्माधर्मस्य संघट्टादुत्थिता वित्तिरूपिणी॥
विकल्पोत्थक्रियालोपरूपदोषविघातिनी।
विकल्परूपरोगाणां हारिणी खेचरी परा॥

सर्वरोगहराख्ये तु चक्रे संविन्मयी स्थिता ।
शिवशक्तिसमाश्लेषस्फुरद्व्योमान्तरे पुनः ॥
प्रकाशयन्ती विश्वं सा सूक्ष्मरूपस्थितं सदा ।
संपूर्णस्य प्रकाशस्य लाभभूमिरियं पुनः ।
योनिमुद्रा कलारूपा सर्वानन्दमये स्थिता ॥"

इत्यादि । तत्तु तत एवावधार्यम् । अत्र श्रुतिरपि—"नवानां चक्रा अधिनाथः स्योना नवमुद्रा नवचक्रा महीनाम्" इति । एतदेव विवृणोति—**आधारेत्यादि । आधारनवकम्**; अकुलसहस्रारमूलाधारस्वाधिष्ठानमणिपूरकानाहतविशुद्धिलम्बिकाज्ञाबिन्दुरूपम्, **अस्याः**; उपासकस्वरूपिण्याः संबन्धि । **येन**; हेतुना, **नवचक्रत्वेन**; **परिणतम्**; बैन्दवात्मना परिणतेन कारणेन, **नवनाथशक्तयोऽपि**; पूर्वोक्ता नवमुद्राकारे परिणता जाता इत्यर्थः । एतच्च **स्वच्छन्दसंग्रहे** प्रपञ्चितम्, तत एवावधार्यम् ॥ ४६, ४७ ॥

अस्यास्त्वगादिसप्तकमाकारश्चैवमष्टकं स्पष्टम् ।
ब्राह्म्यादिमातृरूपं मध्यमभूबिम्बमेतदध्यास्ते ॥ ४८ ॥

अस्या इति । **अस्याः**; देव्याः, **त्वगादिसप्तकम्**; त्वगादिसप्तधातवः, **आकारः**; स्वरूपं च, एवंरूपमष्टकम् । **ब्राह्म्यादिमातृरूपम्**; ब्राह्म्याद्यष्टशक्तिस्वरूपमित्यर्थः । **एतत्**; परिदृश्यमानम्, **मध्यमभूबिम्बम्**; मध्यमचतुरश्रम्, **अध्यास्ते**; निवसतीत्यर्थः ॥ ४८ ॥

अणिमादिसिद्धयोऽस्याः स्वीकृतकमनीयकामिनीरूपाः ।
विद्यान्तरफलभूता गुणभावेनान्त्यभूनिकेतनगाः ॥ ४९ ॥

अणिमेति । **अस्याः**; परमेश्वर्याः, **अणिमादिसिद्धयः**; अणिमाद्यष्टशक्तयः, **विद्यान्तरफलभूताः**; विद्यान्तराणां हठयोगादीनां फलीभूताः; **स्वीकृतकमनीयकामिनीरूपाः**; स्वीकृतानि कमनीयानि मनोहराणि कामिनीरूपाणि अङ्गनारूपाणि याभिस्ताः । एवंभूताः, **गुणभावेन**; उपसर्जनभावेन; **अन्त्य-**

भूनिकेतनगाः; सर्वान्त्यचतुरश्रे तिष्ठन्तीत्यर्थः। अयमर्थः—एतादृशपरमात्मोपासनेन साधकः परमेश्वरो भवतीति। तथोक्तमभियुक्तैः—

"तदीयैश्वर्यविप्रुड्भिर्ब्रह्मविष्णुशिवादयः।
ऐश्वर्यवन्तो भासन्ते स एवात्मा सदाशिवः॥"

इति॥ ४९॥

एवं कामकलाविलसनरूपं चक्रक्रमं निगमय्य, एतादृशं चक्रदेवतामन्त्रस्वरूपं परमेश्वरात्मकगुरुक्रमज्ञानभावेन लभ्यत इति परमशिवादिगुरुक्रमं शिष्यानुजिघृक्षया प्रतिपादयितुमुपक्रमते—

परमानन्दानुभवः परमगुरुनिर्विशेषबिन्द्वात्मा।
स पुनः क्रमेण भिन्नः कामेशत्वं ययौ विमर्शांशात्॥ ५०॥

परमानन्द इत्यादि '**गुरुक्रमो विदितः**' इत्यन्तेन श्लोकचतुष्टयेन। तत्र **परमानन्दानुभवः**; परमः सर्वोत्कृष्टः, परिपूर्णाहंभावरूपः, अनुभवः ज्ञानं यस्य सः। "एतस्यैवानन्दस्यान्यानि भूतानि मात्रामुपजीवन्ति" इति **श्रुतेः**। "प्रणमामि महादेवीं परमानन्दरूपिणीम्।" इति **स्मृतेश्च**। **परमगुरुनिर्विशेषबिन्द्वात्मा**; परमगुरुरादिनाथः परमशिवः, तस्मात् आदिनाथात्, निर्विशेषः, अभिन्नः, बिन्दुः, पूर्वोक्तकामकलारूपः स आत्मा स्वरूपं यस्य सः; आदिनाथरूपी परमशिव इत्यर्थः। अयमर्थः—"आनन्दो ब्रह्म, सत्यं ज्ञानमनन्तं ब्रह्म," "चिन्मात्रं सर्वद्रष्टारं सर्वसाक्षिणं सर्वग्राहकं सर्वप्रेमास्पदं सच्चिदानन्दमेकरसमेवायमात्मा सन्मात्रो नित्यः शुद्धो बुद्धः सत्यो मुक्तो निरञ्जनो विभुरद्वय आनन्दः परः" **इत्याद्युपनिषदुक्तरीत्या** चिदानन्दघनपरमार्थप्रकाशविमर्शात्मा परमेश्वर एव परमकारुणिकः स्वयमेव स्वात्मानं कामकलाबिन्दुरूपकामकामेश्वरीरूपदिव्यमिथुनप्रमुखदिव्यसिद्धमानवौघादिक्रमावतीर्णो गुरुमण्डलात्मा सन् कतिचन भक्तिभाजः संरक्षतीति तात्पर्यम्। एतच्च **रहस्योपनिषदि** श्रूयते। यथा—"यदेषा चङ्क्रमत् तच्चक्रमभवत्। यदादौ भिन्ना स बिन्दुरभवत्। स आधारो जातः। सोऽयमात्मा। आत्मैवैषा शक्तिः

सा भावाभावौ सदसत्" इति। तथैवाहुराचार्याः—"एको नानेकः उभयोरुभौ। जायेते उभौ नित्यौ, एकमेवोभौ अविनाभावात्। आधाराधेयभूतानि। ततो गुणा जायन्ते। लिङ्गानि तानि पिण्डानि। स शक्तिरभवत्। तदप्येष श्लोको भवति।

"भावाभावमयो बिन्दुर्भावः षष्ठात्मको भोगः।
भावात्मकं तु तन्मध्यं चारुभावत्रयात्मकम्॥"

इति। तदेषाभ्युक्ता। मध्ये चक्रं शिवे बिन्दौ प्रपञ्चो लोकः। लोको देहः स नादरूपः स शब्दरूपः। अर्थात्मिका शक्तिः। चक्रं तनुः बिन्दुः प्राणः मध्ये शक्तिः" इत्यादिना चक्रदेवतास्वरूपनिरूपणपुरःसरं कामकामेश्वरीस्वरूपमेव निरूपितम्। "तदेषाभ्युक्ता परो वा एष आनन्दः। स भोगयोनिः कामरूपा देवता। स आनन्दयोनिः आनन्दो ब्रह्म"। "ब्रह्मैव सन् ब्रह्माप्येति" "ब्रह्म वेद ब्रह्मैव भवति" "ब्रह्मविदाप्नोति परम्" "ब्रह्म ब्रह्मैवैकानेकप्रपञ्चः स्यात्" इत्यादिना च वाक्येन कामेश्वरीमभिधायान्तेऽपि "तत्सर्वं त्रिपुरा लोकमाता पायाद्देवी सर्वदा सर्वरूपा" इति सर्वोत्तरत्वं सर्वात्मकत्वं च कामेश्वर्याः प्रतिपाद्यन्त इति सर्वरक्षक एव परमशिव इति। अथवा परमगुरुरिति छेदः। परमगुरुरादिनाथः, निर्विशेषः निष्प्रपञ्चो बिन्दुः सच्चिदानन्दलक्षणः, आत्मा स्वरूपं यस्य स इति।

"बैन्दवे परमाकाशे सच्चिदानन्दलक्षणे।
निष्प्रपञ्चे निराभासे निर्विकल्पे निरामये॥"

इत्यमृतानन्दवचनात्। रहस्याम्नायेऽपि—

"अनुप्रविश्य तां शक्तिं वामाद्यैः पिण्डितो भवान्।
समस्तबीजगर्भाढ्यः सूक्ष्मबिन्दुत्वमेति सः।"

इति। विरूपाक्षपञ्चाशिकायामपि—

"बिन्दुर्विमर्शधर्मा षण्णामेकोऽध्वनां प्राणः।"

इति । **तथा**—

"सांख्यादयोऽपि हंसाः सदा प्रणवसंस्थितान् ।
नादोपरि महादेवं पश्यन्ति ज्ञानचक्षुषा ॥"

इत्यादिना भगवान् **वसिष्ठोऽपि** बिन्दुनादात्मकं परमेश्वरमाह । एवंविधबिन्द्वात्मा परमेश्वर एव कामकामेश्वरीप्रमुखगुरुमण्डलात्माभूदित्याह—**स पुनः क्रमेण भिन्न** इति । **सः**; पूर्वोक्तः परमात्मा, **क्रमेण**; वक्ष्यमाणदिव्यसिद्धरूपेण, **भिन्नः**; द्वैरूप्यं प्रापितः । **विमर्शांशात्**; विमर्शः पूर्वोक्तलक्षणः स्वात्मशक्तिः कामकलारूपा, तदंशः तदर्धभागः । तस्माद्धेतोः **कामेशत्वम्**; श्रीकामराजभावं, **ययौ**; प्राप । **अयमर्थः**—परमात्मा स्वयमेव स्वात्मानं विभज्य कामकामेश्वरीरूपः गुरुशिष्यभावमापन्नः सकलतन्त्रं प्रवर्तयामासेति । तथा **बृहदारण्यके**—"स इममेवात्मानं द्विधापातयत् ततः पतिश्च पत्नी चाभवताम् ।" इति; "आत्मैवेदमग्र आसीत् एक एव सोऽकामयत जाया मे स्यात् अथ प्रजायेय" इत्येकस्यैव ब्रह्मणो मिथुनरूपत्वं वक्ति । मिथुनीभूतस्य कामेश्वरत्वमपि श्रुतिरेवाह । यथा तत्रैव—"काम एव यस्यायतनं हृदयं लोको मनो ज्योतिर्यो वै तं पुरुषं विद्यात् सर्वस्यात्मनः परायणं स वै वेदिता स्यात् । याज्ञवल्क्य वेद वा अहं तं पुरुषं सर्वस्यात्मनः परायणं यमात्थ य एवायं काममयः पुरुषः स एष वदैव शाकल्य तस्य का देवतेति स्त्रिय इति होवाच" इति कामेश्वरस्य विहरणयोग्यां स्त्रियं कामेश्वरीं प्रत्यक्षं ब्रूते । **रहस्यागमश्च**—

"गुरुशिष्यपदे स्थित्वा स्वयमेव सदाशिवः ।
लोकसंरक्षणार्थाय तन्त्रं समवतारयत् ॥"

इति ॥ ५० ॥

एतदेव विशदयति—

आसीनः श्रीपीठे कृतयुगकाले गुरुः शिवो विद्याम् ।
तस्यै ददौ स्वशक्त्यै कामेश्वर्यै विमर्शरूपिण्यै ॥ ५१ ॥

आसीन इति । **श्रीपीठे**; मध्यत्र्यश्रान्तर्गतोड्याणपीठे, **आसीनः**; नित्यसंनिहितः, **गुरुः**; ज्ञानोपदेष्टा । तथा च **शिवसूत्रम्**—"गुरुरुपायः" इति[1] ।

"गुशब्दस्त्वन्धकारः स्याद्रुशब्दस्तन्निवर्तकः ।
अन्धकारनिरोधित्वाद्गुरुरित्यभिधीयते ॥"

इति । **शिवः**; सर्वप्रवर्तकः परमात्मा, **कृतयुगकाले**; कृतयुगादौ; **तस्यै**; सर्वभूतानां निरवधिकानन्ददायिन्यै; **स्वशक्त्यै** । **रहस्योपनिषदि**—"ब्रह्मा विष्णुश्च रुद्रश्च वाणी लक्ष्मीः भवानीति ताः संप्रदायकाः क्रमात् । सर्वलोकप्रसूत्वेन सैव त्रिपुरा सैवानन्दं ददातीति ।" इति। **अन्यत्रापि**—

"परोऽपि शक्तिरहितः शक्तः कर्तुं न किंचन ।
शक्तश्च परमेशानि शक्त्या युक्तो भवेद्यदि"

इत्याद्यागमानुसंधानेन स्वस्वरूपसत्तासंप्रदायिन्यै; **विमर्शरूपिण्यै**; हकारोऽन्त्यः कलारूपो विमर्शाख्यः प्रकीर्तितः" इति **संकेतपद्धत्युक्तरीत्या** अनुत्तरानन्दविश्रान्तिस्थानभूतशक्तिपररूपिण्यै; **कामेश्वर्यै**; "सा कामा सर्वकामा काम एव लोका एव पुराणी तस्मात् त्रिपुरा" इत्युपनिषदुक्तरीत्या, "सर्वदा सर्वप्रकारेण सर्वाभीष्टप्रदायिन्यै स्वात्मभूतायै विद्यान्तरे तन्महामनुरिति सैव शब्दा तनुः अस्य सवर्णरूपा परमा त्रिपदाभिधाभावा त्रिगुणा त्रिवर्गरूपा नित्या निर्मला निष्प्रपञ्चा आत्मविद्या विभुर्वरविद्या य एवं वेद विद्वान् भवति । अथाहुर्विद्वांस इति । रहो रहस्यमिति । शिवोऽयमिति । स एवेमानि भूतानि सृजति रक्षति

[1] "सम्यग्ज्ञानक्रियाप्राणमन्त्रमुद्रायथास्थितिम् ।
गृणात्युपदिशत्यर्थं तद्वीर्यं चेत्यतो गुरुः ॥
स एव मन्त्रमुद्राणां वीर्यव्याप्तिप्रकाशनात् ।
उपायः कथ्यते साक्षादुपेयं परमं प्रति ॥
यद्वा गुरुः परा शक्तिरीश्वरानुग्रहात्मिका ।
अवकाशप्रदत्वेन सैव यायादुपायताम् ॥"

इति वरदराजः ।

संहरति । अन्यथा वा करोति । सैव सो भवति" इति रहस्योपनिषत्प्रतिपाद्यामात्मैक्यदायिनीमत्यन्तमात्मविद्यां ददौ उपदिदेश ।

अयमत्र संप्रदायः—यद्यपि, "समप्रधानौ समसत्त्वौ समोजौ तयोः शक्तिरजरा विश्वयोनिः । आदिशक्तिररुणा विश्वजन्या ।" इति सांख्यानशाखायामुभयोः कामकामेश्वर्योः समप्रधानमुक्तम् । तथापि विश्वयोनिर्विश्वजन्या इति सर्वकारणरूपिण्या एतयैव कामेश्वर्या रहस्यतन्त्रं सर्वोपनिषत्सारभूतं प्रवर्तयितुकामः परमशिवः प्रपञ्चसृष्ट्यनन्तरम् आदियुगे—

"महामध्यं च चक्रस्य महानन्दात्मकं पुनः ।
अनुत्तरविमर्शैकसारं संविन्मयं भजे ॥"

इत्युक्तप्रकारेण प्रकाशानन्दसारमयमोड्याणपीठमास्थाय स्वयमपि श्रीविद्याक्रममुपदिदेश । सा पराभट्टारिका त्रेतायुगद्वापरयुगकलियुगेषु वक्ष्यमाणदेशिकस्वरूपिणी ह्यतिरहस्यं शांभवतन्त्रं प्रवर्तयामासेति । अयमिह विवरणक्रमः—इह श्रीविद्यारत्नावगमने साधनद्वयमस्ति । कामराजसंतानं, लोपामुद्रासंतानं चेति । कामराजसंतानक्रमस्तु सकलविद्यानुसंध्यविच्छिन्न इति प्राचीनगुरवोऽप्याचक्षते । लोपामुद्रासंतानक्रमस्तु विच्छिन्नतया प्रवर्तत इति वर्णयन्ति । तत्क्रमप्रकारस्तु लिख्यते—तत्र दिव्यक्रमो यथा; कृतयुगादौ परमशिव एव ओड्याणपीठात्मकमध्यबिन्दुनिवासी श्रीचर्यानन्दनाथनामा सन् स्वात्मशक्त्याख्यश्रीमहात्रिपुरसुन्दरीविमृष्टतनुः प्रथमो गुरुः । तथा चोक्तम्—

"त्र्यश्राग्रोड्याणपीठस्था कामराजशरीरिणी ।
अस्वराकारतां प्राप्य त्र्यश्रसंकेतमध्यगात् ॥"

इति । मध्यत्र्यश्राग्रकोणकामरूपपीठवाग्भवाधिष्ठातृकामेश्वरीरूपविमृष्टरूपः श्रीमदूर्ध्वदेवनाथस्त्रेतायुगगुरुः । तथा चोक्तम्—"त्र्यश्राग्रकोणगा या सा कामेशी कामपीठगा ।" इति । मध्यत्र्यश्रदक्षिणकोणस्थितजालंधरपीठस्थितकामराजाभिधेयवज्रेश्वरीमिलितस्वरूपः श्रीषष्ठनाथदेवो द्वापरगुरुः । तथा चोक्तम्—

"त्र्यश्रदक्षिणकोणस्था वज्रेशी जालपीठगा।" इति। मध्यत्र्यश्रोत्तरकोणगतपूर्णगिरिपीठस्थितशक्तिबीजाभिधेयभगमालिनीविमृष्टदेहः श्रीमित्रदेवनाथः कलियुगगुरुः। तथा चोक्तम्—"त्र्यश्रस्योत्तरकोणस्था भगेशी पूर्णपीठगा।" इति। मित्रेशदेवः कलियुगादौ भगवतीं लोपामुद्राम्, अगस्त्यं च महातपःपुञ्जमिथुनमनुगृहीतवान्। एतत्सप्तकं दिव्यौघसंज्ञकं गुरूपदेशादवगन्तव्यम्। इह तु प्रसङ्गादेतावदुक्तम्। प्रकृतमनुरामः ॥ ५१ ॥

एतदेवाह—

सेयाय मित्रसंज्ञां स्थानेशान् ज्येष्ठमध्यबालाख्यान्।
चित्प्राणविषयभूतान् त्रेतायुगादिकारणत्रिगुरून् ॥ ५२ ॥
बीजत्रितयाधिपतीन् परीक्ष्य विद्यां प्रकाशयामास।
एतैरोघत्रितयं तमनुगृहीतं गुरुक्रमो विदितः ॥ ५३ ॥

सेयायेति। सा; पूर्वोक्ता परमशिवप्राणनायिका मित्रनाथसंज्ञा, भीमो भीमसेन इतिवत् मित्रशब्दो मित्रदेवनाथपर्यन्तं धावति। स च मित्रदेवनाथः कलियुगगुरुः, तत्संज्ञां तन्नामधेयम्। इयाय प्राप। एतच्चोपलक्षणम्—त्रेतायुगद्वापरयुगगुरुनामधेयधारणस्य त्रेतायुगादियुगत्रयगुरुस्वरूपिणी भूत्वा संप्रदायं प्रवर्तयेदित्यर्थः। एतदेव विवृणेति—**स्थानेशेत्यादिना**। **स्थानेशः**; स्थानानां मध्यत्र्यश्राग्रकोणदक्षिणकोणोत्तरकोणानां कामेश्वरीवज्रेश्वरीभगमालिनीनिलयानाम्। ईशा, अधिष्ठात्री, अत एव ज्येष्ठः श्रीमदूर्ध्वदेवनाथः, मध्यः श्रीषष्ठदेवनाथः, बालः श्रीमित्रदेवनाथः, तेषामाख्या नामधेयं यस्याः सा; तत्स्वरूपत्वादेतेषामिति भावः। **चित्प्राणविषयभूताः**; चित्प्राणः परमशिवः, चित्स्वरूपत्वात् प्राणरूपत्वाच्च। तथा **माण्डूक्योपनिषदि**—"नान्तः प्रज्ञं न बहिः प्रज्ञं नोभयतः प्रज्ञं न प्रज्ञानघनं न प्रज्ञं नाप्रज्ञम्। अदृष्टमव्यवहार्यमग्राह्यमलक्षणमचिन्त्यमव्यपदेश्यमेकात्मप्रत्ययसारं प्रपञ्चोपशमं शान्तं शिवमद्वैतं चतुर्थं मन्यन्ते। स आत्मा स विज्ञेयः।" इति चिन्मय एव श्रूयते। तथा प्राणमयत्वेनापि श्रूयते। तथा **छान्दोग्ये**—"यथा वा अरा नाभौ

समर्पिताः एवमस्मिन् प्राणे सर्वं समर्पितम् प्राणः प्राणेन याति प्राणः प्राणं ददाति प्राणाय ददाति प्राणो ह पिता प्राणो माता प्राणो भ्राता प्राणः स्वसा प्राण आचार्यः ।" इति । एतादृशचित्प्राणस्वरूपस्य परमशिवस्य विषयभूता भोग्यभूता । कुतः ? "एष देवोऽनया देव्या नित्यं क्रीडारसोत्सुकः ।" इत्यभिनवगुप्तपादोक्तिः । अथवा **स्थानेशान**; ज्येष्ठमध्यबालाख्यान् । **चित्प्राणविषयभूतानिति** गुरुविशेषणं वा । तथापि स एवार्थः । एवंविधा सा पराभट्टारिका । **त्रेतायुगादिकारणत्रिगुरून्**; पूर्वोक्तश्रीमदूर्ध्वदेवनाथादीन् । **बीजत्रितयाधिपतीन्**; बीजत्रितयं वाग्भवादिकम्; तस्याधिपतीन् वाच्यभूतान् । एतच्च पूर्वमेवोक्तम् । एतान् त्रिविधदेशिकान्, **परीक्ष्य**; शोधयित्वा, **विद्यां**;

"पञ्चभूतमयं विश्वं तन्मयी सा सदानघे ।
तन्मयी मूलविद्या च तथा च कथयामि ते ॥"

इति परमशिवाननारविन्दनिःसृताखिलकारणभूतामादिविद्याम्, **प्रकाशयामास**; प्रवर्तयामासेत्यर्थः ।

अत्र किंचिद्वदामः—इह 'परीक्ष्य विद्यां प्रकाशयामास' इत्यनेन श्रीसदाशिवात्मा देशिकोत्तमः सत्संप्रदायसिद्धमिदं मार्गं बहुकालमात्मोपासनमाचरते ।

"दान्तायोपसन्नाय शिष्यायोपदिदेश च ।
दीक्षापूर्वं महेशानि विद्यामुपदिशेद् गुरुः" ॥

इत्यादिना । दीक्षा च, "शिवसायुज्यदायिनी" इति ।

"ददाति शिवतादात्म्यं क्षिणोति च मलत्रयम् ।
अतो दीक्षेति सा प्रोक्ता दीक्षा शब्दार्थवेदिभिः ।"

इति स्मृतेः । "दीयते परशिवैक्यभावना क्षीयते सकलपापसंचयः ।" इत्यभियुक्तोक्तेश्च । सा च त्रिविधा, आणवशाक्तशांभवभेदात्;

"त्रिविधा सा भवेद्दीक्षा प्रथमा आणवी परा ।
शाक्तेयी शांभवी चेति सद्यो मुक्तिप्रदायिनी ।"

इति **स्मरणात्** । तत्र **आणवदीक्षा**; विधिविशेषविहितद्रव्याणि निर्वर्त्य परदेवतातर्पणध्यानासक्तरूपिणीत्युक्तेः । **शाक्तेयी तु**; यथोपनतशक्तिसिद्धार्थसाध्या; **शांभवी च**—

"सिद्धे शक्तिं समालोक्य तया केवलया शिशौ ।
निरुपायं कृता दीक्षा शाक्तेयी परिकीर्तिता ॥"

इति ।

"अभिसंधिं विनाचार्यशिष्ययोरुभयोरपि ।
देशिकानुग्रहेणैव शिवताव्यक्तिकारिणी ।
सेयं हि शांभवी दीक्षा शिवावेशनकारिणी ॥"

इति च । एवंविधदीक्षाभावे न कुत्राप्यधिकारी । तथा **श्रीमालिनीविजयकारः** प्राह—

"न चाधिकारिता दीक्षां विना योगोऽस्ति शांकरे ।
. . . . . .
न च योगाधिकारित्वं शांभवीमेकमेव वा ।"

इत्यभिसंधिरहिताचार्यकृपामात्रसाध्या यथेयं भवेत् । "अपि मन्त्राधिकारित्वमुक्तं च शिवदीक्षया ।" इति । शिष्यस्य वित्ताभावेऽप्याचार्यः शिष्ययोग्यतामवधार्य स्वधनेन वा दीक्षां कुर्यात् । स्वस्याप्यभावे लघूपायेन वा कुर्यात् । **यथा**—

"स्वधनेन दरिद्रस्य कुर्याद्दीक्षां स्वयं गुरुः ।
अपि दूर्वाम्बुभिर्यद्वा दीक्षया मोचयेच्छिशुम् ।"

इति सर्वात्मना दीक्षितस्य ब्रह्मविद्यायामधिकारो नान्यस्येति स्थितिः । दीक्षा च

परदेवतासंतर्पणसाध्येत्युक्तम् । संतर्पणं च द्रवद्रव्यविशेषसाध्ययुगविशेषतर्पणं तृप्तिमयदम् । "दैवतस्यामृतेन तु" इत्युक्तत्वात् । अत एव "तमेतं वेदानुवचनेन ब्राह्मणा विविदिषन्ति यज्ञेन दानेन तपसानाशकेन" इति यज्ञस्यापि ब्रह्मविषयत्वात् । श्रूयते स च यज्ञश्च पूजा सा च त्रिधा मता । परा, अपरा, परापरा चेति । तथा च परमशिवः परमेश्वरीं प्रत्याह—

"तव नित्योदिता पूजा त्रिभिर्भेदैर्व्यवस्थिता ।
परा चाप्यपरा गौरि तृतीया च परापरा ॥
प्रथमाद्वैतभावस्था सर्वप्रचरगोचरा ।
द्वितीया चक्रपूजा च सदा निष्पाद्यते मया ॥
एवं ज्ञानमये देवि तृतीया तु परापरा ।
उत्तमा सा परा ज्ञेया विधानं शृणु सांप्रतम् ॥
महापद्मवनान्तस्थां कारणानन्दविग्रहाम् ।
तदङ्गोपाश्रयां देवीं वाग्भवे गुरुपादुकाम् ॥
आप्यायितजगद्रूपां परमामृतवर्षिणीम् ।
संचिन्त्य परमाद्वैतभावनामदघूर्णितः ॥
दहरान्तरसंसर्पन्नादालोकनतत्परः ।
विकल्परूपसंजल्पविमुखोऽन्तर्मुखः सदा ॥
चित्कल्लोल्लासललितसंकोचस्त्वतिसुन्दरः ।
इन्द्रियप्रीणनैर्द्रव्यैर्विहितस्वात्मपूजनः ॥
न्यासं निर्वर्तयेद्देहे षोढान्यासपुरःसरम् ॥"

इत्यादिपरापूजा । अत्र स्वरूपमध्यं—

"द्वितीया चक्रपूजा च सदा निष्पाद्यते मया ।"

इति परमशिवः स्वयमेव बाह्यवर्ती वरिवस्यां करोमीति चक्रपूजां प्रशंसयामास । सोऽपि बाह्ययोगः पञ्चविधः—"केवलो यामलो मिश्रश्चक्रयुग्वीरसंकरः" इति स्मृतेः । एतल्लक्षणमाम्ना यादेवावगन्तव्यम् । ततश्च संतर्पणपूर्वकमेवाभिषेचनादिकर्म कर्तव्यम् ।

तच्च संतर्पणद्रव्यं निष्पाद्यमित्युक्तम्। द्रवद्रव्यं च हेतुभूतनिदानकारणप्रथमादिशब्दाभिधेयं परमामृतरूपं मधु। तेनैव परदेवतायागस्य साध्यत्वात्। सोमेनाग्निष्टोमयागवत्।

न च "अग्नीषोमीयं पशुमालभेत" "सोमग्रहान् गृह्णति" इत्यादिविधिसद्भावाद्युक्तम्। इतरेषां यागानां सोमसाध्यत्वमुक्तम्। इह तु "ब्राह्मणो न सुरां पिबेत्", "न मांसमश्नीयात्" इत्यादिना निषेधादिदं दर्शनमनुपपन्नमिति वाच्यम्। न वयं निषेधविधिमुल्लंघ्य स्वातन्त्र्येणैव निदानात्परदेवतातर्पणं कर्तुमुचितमिति ब्रूमः। किंतु इदमेव शांभवदर्शनमौपनिषदसंप्रदायादागतमिति निश्चित्य ह्येवमवोचाम। तर्हि निषेधस्य का गतिरिति चेदुच्यते—अदीक्षितपुरुषविषयोऽयं निषेधविधिः। दीक्षितस्यानेनैव हेतुना देवतायागः कर्तव्य इति मुख्यविधिसद्भावात्। तथाच ऋग्वेदाम्भोधिमध्योद्धृतसांख्यायनशाखायाम् आदिसुन्दरीवरिवस्याद्वारा देवतासाम्राज्यसाधनतानिदानस्य श्रूयते—

"इमां विज्ञाय सुरया मदन्ती परिस्रुता तर्पयन्तः स्वपीठम्।
नाकस्य पृष्ठे महतो वसन्ति परं धाम त्रैपुरं चाविशन्ति।"

इति। अत्र परिस्रुतं द्रव्यमित्यर्थः। तथा निघण्ट्वादिप्रसिद्धिः। अत एव वाजपेयादिप्रसिद्धक्रतुष्वपि परमेश्वर्या मन्त्रनायिकाया विहितत्वादेव निषिद्धस्यापि द्रव्यस्य स्वीकारो दरीदृश्यते। कुत्र वा परमेश्वरीविधिः श्रूयते। ललितेपाख्याने च—

"परितुष्टास्मि मद्याब्धे त्वया साह्यमनुष्ठितम्।
देवकार्यमिदं किंच त्वया निर्विघ्नितं कृतम्॥
इतः परं मत्प्रसादाद्वाजपेयादिके मखे।
सोमपानवदत्यन्तमुपयोज्यो भविष्यसि॥
यागेषु मन्त्रपूतं त्वां पास्यन्त्यखिलदेवताः।
यागेन मन्त्रपूतेन पीतेन भवता जनाः॥
सिद्धिमृद्धिं बलं स्वर्गमपवर्गं च बिभ्रतु।

महेश्वरी महादेवो बलदेवश्च भार्गवः ।
दत्तात्रेयो विधिर्विष्णुस्त्वां पास्यन्ति महाजनाः ॥"

इति । परमशिवोऽपि **पूजासंकेतके**—"प्रधानादिवरीवस्यां निर्वर्त्य" इत्याह । **यथा वा**—

"महापद्मवनान्तस्थां कारणानन्दविग्रहाम् ।
मदङ्कोपाश्रितां देवीमिच्छाकामफलप्रदाम् ॥
भवतीं त्वन्मयैरेव नैवेद्यादिभिरर्चयेत् ।"

इत्यादित उक्त्वा, अन्ते नैवेद्यद्रव्यं स्पष्टमाचष्टे । यथा वा—

"अर्चनापिशितैर्गन्धैर्धूपैराराध्य देवताम् ।
चक्रपूजां विधायेत्थं कुलदीपं निवेदयेत् ।
कौलिकाचारसंयुक्तैर्वीरैस्तु सह पूजयेत् ॥"

इति । अन्यच्च रहस्यागमे परमेश्वरः मादिपदार्थपञ्चकस्य देवतायागमाह—"मादिपञ्चकमीशानि देवताप्रीतिकारकम् ।" इति । ननु शिव एव स्वतन्त्र-प्रवर्तकः इति । तदुक्तं महामायाशाम्बराद्यनेकतन्त्रानुष्ठानप्रसङ्गः प्राप्नोतीति चेत्तदुक्त्वा विशेषादिति चेन्न । तेनैव तत्तदधिकारिभेदेनुष्ठेयानीमानि तन्त्राणि । इह तु शांभवदर्शनं मुमुक्षूणामेवोपास्यमिति प्रपञ्चितत्वात् । **यथा**—

"मोहशास्त्राणि सर्वाणि मयैव कथितानि वै ।
मुक्त्यन्तरं तु गत्वैव मोहनाय दुरात्मनाम् ।"

इत्युक्त्वा ;

"मथित्वा ज्ञानमन्थेन वेदागममहार्णवम् ।
सारज्ञेन मया देवि कुलधर्मः समुद्धृतः ॥
मेरुसर्षपयोर्यद्वत्सूर्यखद्योतयोरिव ।
तथान्यसमयस्याम्ब कुलस्य महदन्तरम् ॥"

इत्यादि कुलदर्शनस्वरूपमभिधाय तत्तन्निष्ठस्यैव मोक्षो नान्यसमयनिष्ठस्य इत्याह— "एतज्ज्ञात्वा वरारोहे सद्यः खेचरतां व्रजेत् ।" इति ॥ ५२, ५३ ॥

स्वकृतकामकलाविलासाख्यं ग्रन्थमुपसंहरति—

उदितः पुण्यानन्दादिति कामकलाङ्गनाविलासोऽयम् ।
परशिवभुजङ्गभावाकर्षणहर्षाय कल्पते नित्यम् ॥ ५४ ॥

उदित इति । पुण्यानन्दात्; पुण्यानन्दाख्यात् स्वस्मात्, उदितः; उत्पन्नः । अयं कामकलाङ्गनाविलासः, कामेश्वराविनाभूता विमर्शशक्तिः कामकला, सैवाङ्गना सुन्दरी, तस्या विलासः चक्रावरणदेवतादिरूपः, तद् विलासः दयितेक्षणे सति तत्कालोचितविकारः । परशिवभुजङ्गभावाकर्षितचित्ताय; परशिवः प्रकाशैकस्वभावः, स एव भुजङ्गः रसिकः विटः, तस्य भावो रागः, तेन आकर्षितं चित्तं तस्मै । भावाकर्षणहर्षायेति पाठान्तरे—तस्या अवलोकनेन भावस्याकर्षणमुदयः, तेन यो हर्षः । विलासेक्षणेन समुत्पन्नान्तरो विकारविशेषो भावः । तेनोपार्जितो विलासो भावजननद्वारा हर्षहेतुर्भवतीत्यर्थः । लोकेऽपि प्रियतमविलासदर्शने रसिकनायकस्य शृङ्गारभावोदयपूर्वको हर्ष उत्पद्यते । तद्वत्परशिवस्यात्मशक्तीक्षणाभिमुखस्य चिच्छक्तिभूतकामकलाविलासः पदविक्षेपादिरूपनिरवधिकानन्दप्रदो भवति । आर्यारूपेण स्वमुखारविन्दनिःसृतो ग्रन्थरूपः कामकलाविलासः परशिवप्रीतिं नित्यं हर्षाय कल्पते उत्पादयतीत्यर्थः । कामकलाविलासानुभवतः पुण्यानन्दमहात्मा एवं वदतीति प्रतीयते । इतिशब्दः, स्तवस्य परिसमाप्तिद्योतक इत्यवगन्तव्यम् ॥ ५४ ॥

स्वगुरून् नमस्करोति—

चिन्तान्तरङ्गतरलस्तृष्णासलिलः प्रपञ्चवाराशिः ।
यदनुग्रहेण तीर्णस्तस्मै श्रीनाथनाविकाय नमः ॥ ५५ ॥

॥ इति श्रीपुण्यानन्दविरचितः कामकलाविलासः समाप्तः ॥

चिन्तातरङ्गेति। प्रपञ्चः संसार एव वाराशिः वारिधिः। श्रीनाथ एव नाविकः पोतः तस्मै। "अधिगतमध्ययनमननुभावितं चार्थतः स्वरस्य चन्दनभारवत्केवलं परिश्रमकरं भवति" इति निरुक्तकारादिवचनेनार्थज्ञानहीनस्याध्ययनस्य निष्फलत्वश्रवणात्।

"ज्ञातव्यः सर्ववेदार्थो वेदानां कर्मसिद्धये।
पाठमात्रमधीता च पङ्के गौरिव सीदति॥
वेदस्याध्ययनं सर्वं धर्मशास्त्रस्य चैव हि।
अजानतोऽर्थं तत्सर्वं तुषाणां खण्डनं यथा॥"

इत्यादिश्रुतिसिद्धकामकलास्वरूपं परिपूर्णं प्रपञ्चितमिति शिवम्॥ ५५॥

॥ इति श्रीनटनानन्दविरचिता कामकलाव्याख्या चिद्वल्ली समाप्ता॥

॥ शुभमस्तु॥

श्रीगणेशाय नमः

श्रीमहेशनाथकृता

श्रीनाथनवरत्नमालिका

श्रीभासुरानन्दनाथविरचितया

मञ्जूषाख्यया व्याख्यया संवलिता

श्रीनाथादित्रितयं नत्वा गम्भीररायसूरिसुतः ।
नाथनवरत्नमालागूढार्थव्यावृतिं तनुते ॥

इह खलु निखिलोपासनाः गुरुप्रसादलभ्याः, "गुरुमूलाः क्रियाः सर्वाः" इति वचनात् । तत्प्रसादश्च तत्स्वरूपोपास्तिमन्तरा दुर्लभः । तद्रूपं तु त्रिविधम्—स्थूलं, सूक्ष्मं, परं चेति । तेषु आद्यं, "सहस्रदलपङ्कजे सकलशीतरश्मिप्रभम्" इत्यादिना करणचरणाद्यवयववैशिष्ट्येनोक्तं प्रसिद्धम् । द्वितीयं तु गुरुपादुकामन्त्ररूपम् । तृतीयं वासनात्मकम् । तच्च रहस्यत्वात् संकेतभाषयोपासकानुजिघृक्षया विवृणोति—

हंसः सोऽहं मन्त्रमयैः श्वासनिकायै-
र्या गायत्री जन्तुषु सर्वेषु पिनद्धा ।
तद्रूपः सन्नाविरभूद्वासनया य-
स्तं सन्मार्गे मत्तमयूरं गुरुमीडे ॥ १ ॥

हंस इति । प्राथमिकसृष्टौ यद्बिन्दुत्रयं प्रादुरभूत् । तत्र बिन्दुः पुमान्; विसर्गः प्रकृतिः; ताभ्यां क्रमेण स्वस्य विशिष्टौ हकारसकारावुत्पन्नौ । सोऽहं हंसः, स त्वजपानामको मन्त्रः । तस्यैव वैपरीत्यकथनेन सोऽहमिति परमात्ममन्त्रः; परमात्मनि योगे तु, "पराप्रासादमन्त्रः" इत्यादिशारदायां चरमपटलेऽन्यत्र चोक्तम् । तदिदं परस्पर-

भिन्नमन्त्रपञ्चकमुच्छ्वासनिश्वासरूपम्। "उच्छ्वासे चैव निःश्वासे हंस इत्यक्षरद्वयम्।" इति वचनात्। स च मन्त्रः सर्वैः प्राणिभिः अहोरात्रसंमिते काले षट्शताधिकैकविंशतिसहस्र(२१६००)मावर्त्यते। सोऽयमनायासेन जपः। तथात्वेन ज्ञानमात्रेण मोक्षप्रदत्वात्सर्वमन्त्रोत्तमः। तदुक्तम्—

"हंसः पदं परेशानि प्रत्यहं जपते नरः।
मोहान्धो यो न जानाति मोक्षस्तस्य न विद्यते॥
श्रीगुरोः कृपया देवि ज्ञायते जप्यते ततः।
तस्माच्छ्वासैश्च निःश्वासैस्तदा बन्धक्षयो भवेत्॥
अजपा नाम गायत्री योगिनां मोक्षदायिनी।
तस्या विज्ञानमात्रेण नरः पापैः प्रमुच्यते॥
अनया सदृशी विद्या चानया सदृशो जपः।
अनया सदृशं पुण्यं न भूतं न भविष्यति॥"

इति च तदुपासनेतिकर्तव्यता शारदायां चतुर्दशे पटले, अन्यत्र च विस्तृतेति नेहोच्यते। गुरुदेवतामन्त्राणामैक्यं च, ते सर्वे श्वासाः नाथरूपा एव।

अक्षरार्थस्तु—हंस इत्यजपामन्त्रादिरूपश्वाससमूहाभिन्ना या गायत्री सर्वप्राणिष्वाच्छन्ना वर्तते, तदभिन्नः सन् वासनात्मकरूपेण यः प्रादुर्भूतः, तं गुरुं नौमीति। स एव च गुरुः, सतां मार्गः, मुक्तिपुरगमनोपायः; "गुरुरुपायः" इति शिवसूत्रात्। आनन्दमन्त्रो हि मयूरः स्वपिञ्च्छावयवान् प्रसार्य नृत्यकाले यथा विचित्ररूपो दृश्यते, तेन तथा कालान्तरे, अतः तस्य तद्रूपमाच्छन्नम्। एवं गुरोरपि वक्ष्यमाणं विचित्ररूपमाच्छन्नमस्तीति गौण्या मत्तमयूरपदेन गुरुः स्तूयते।

अस्मिन् स्तोत्रे दशापि श्लोकाः मत्तमयूराभिधवृत्तरूपाः। तल्लक्षणं चोक्तं पिङ्गलमुनिना—"मत्तमयूरं म्तौ य्सौ ग्समुद्र(४) नवकौ" इति। मतयसगणाः गुरुश्च, प्रतिपदं चतुर्भिर्नवभिश्च यतिरिति तदर्थः। प्रकृतेऽप्युक्तैरेव पदैः सूच्यार्थकथनादिह मुद्रालंकारः। तल्लक्षणं चोक्तं चन्द्रालोके—

"सूच्यार्थसूचकं मुद्रा प्रकृतार्थपदैः पदैः।
नितम्बगुर्वी तरुणी दृग्युग्मविपुलालसा॥"

इति। संकेतरीत्या अनुक्तश्वाससंख्याया अपि पदद्वयेन सूचनात् स एवालंकारः। तत्प्रकारस्तु—

"क-ट-प-य-वर्गभवैरिह पिण्डान्त्यैरक्षरैरङ्का ।
नञ्शून्यं विज्ञेयं तथा स्वरे केवले कथिते ॥"

इति श्लोकरीत्या मकार: पञ्चसंख्याङ्के; तकार: षष्ठाङ्के; पुनर्मकार: पञ्चाङ्के, यकाररेफ-गकारा: एकद्वित्र्यङ्केषु संकेतिता: । तथा, "अङ्कानां वामतो गति:" इत्युक्तरीत्या लेखने कृते सति, म ५, त ६, म ५, यू १, र २, पदेन एकविंशतिसहस्राणि पञ्चशतानि पञ्चषष्टिश्च कथितानि भवन्ति । सन्; विद्यमानो मार्ग: (३५) यस्मिन्निति व्युत्पत्या मार्गशब्दोक्तपञ्चत्रिंशत्संख्यया अस्या मेलनेन षट्शताधिकैकविंशतिसहस्रसंख्यानिष्पत्ति-(२१६००) रिति । एवमग्रेऽपि संकेतोऽवगन्तव्य: ॥ १ ॥

तन्त्रराजे हि सप्तविंशे पटले श्वासानां वासनाद्वयमुक्तम्;

"संख्याभिर्वासनाव्याप्तिं श्वासानां शृणु सुन्दरि ।
यया विदितया मन्त्री सदा दर्शनवान्भवेत् ॥"

इत्यादिना । तयो: प्रथमां वासनामुद्यदित्यादिभि: चतुर्भि: श्लोकै: प्रदर्शयति—

उद्यद्भास्वन्मण्डलकालाद्दिननित्या-
विद्यारूप: प्राप षडथीनरभावम् ।
यस्तीर्थातमा मण्डलपूर्णाक्षिरवर्ष्मा
तं सन्मार्गं मत्तमयूरं गुरुमीडे ॥ २ ॥

उद्यदिति । सूर्यमण्डलोदयकालमारभ्य प्रथमत: श्वासा एकैकदिनविद्यारूपा: । अ आ इ ई इत्यारभ्य क्ष: क्षायै इत्यन्ता मन्त्रा: षट्त्रिंशदधिकसप्तदशोत्तरविंशतिसहस्रसंख्याका (५७६×३६=२०७३६) । षट्त्रिंशद्वर्णा अपि षोडशस्वरसंयोगेनोक्ता: ३६×१६=(५७६) प्रतिदिनमेवं षट्त्रिंशद्दिनपर्यन्तं जप्तास्तावन्त एव भवन्ति । यतस्तन्त्रे प्रसिद्ध: एता एव स्त्रीदैवत्यतया विद्या इत्युच्यन्ते । "स्त्रीदैवत्या स्मृता विद्या पुंदैवत्यास्तु मन्त्रका:" इति कोशात् । गुरुनाथस्तु तावद्रूप: । ते च विद्याया अर्था योगिनी-हृदयव्याख्यायामस्माभि: प्रपञ्चिता: ।

षडथीनरपदेन दिननित्याविद्यानां संख्योक्ता: (२०७३६) । एवमुत्तरत्र सर्वत्रापि संख्यासंकेताक्षरपदानां श्रीगुरो: श्लेषेण द्व्यर्थता अवसेया । तत्परत: षट्सप्तत्युत्तरपञ्चशतं (५७६) श्वासा: पूर्णमण्डलाक्षररूपा: । अकार एक:, ककारादिक्षकारान्ता: पञ्चत्रि-

शद्वयञ्जनानि चेत्येवं षट्त्रिंशदक्षराणां प्रत्येकमकारादिषोडशस्वरसंयोगे सत्युक्तसंख्यानि (५७६) अक्षराणि भवन्ति। तानि पूर्णमण्डलपदेन दिनार्णवपदेन च तन्त्रे व्यवह्रियन्ते। तदभिन्नं वर्ष्मा, शरीरं यस्य सः, तीर्थात्मा (५७६) गुरुरूपा एव, "तीर्थमृषिजुष्टजले गुरौ" इत्यमरः ॥ २ ॥

तीर्थात्मापदं चोक्तसंख्यां (५७६) व्यनक्ति—

तत्पश्चात्यप्राणसमूहनवनाथा
य: षट्त्रिंशत्तत्त्वमय: षोडश नित्या: ।
एवं रीत्या वासितसंध्यात्रयमूर्ति-
स्तं सन्मार्गं मत्तमयूरं गुरुमीडे ॥ ३ ॥

तदिति। पूर्णमण्डलात् परे नव (९) श्वासा: प्रकाशादिसुभगान्ता नाथनवकरूपा:। तत: परे शिवादिक्षित्यन्ततत्त्वरूपा: षट्त्रिंशत् (३६)। तदुत्तरं त्रिपुरसुन्दरीकामेश्वर्यादिचित्रान्तरूपास्तु नित्या: षोडश (१६)। एत एव क्रमेण संध्यात्रये उपास्यन्ते। तेन तद्वासनारूपा गुरुरेवेत्यर्थ: ॥ ३ ॥

श्वासै: षष्ट्या षष्टिघटीदेवतरूपो (६०)
मेषप्रष्ठद्वादशराशि (१२) प्रतिमान: ।
अर्काद्यात्मा यो नवसंख्याग्रहमूर्ति-
स्तं सन्मर्गं मत्तमयूरं गुरुमीडे ॥ ४ ॥

श्वासैरिति। तदनन्तरं विसर्गरहितानां पञ्चाशन्मातृकाणां दशाक्षरैरेकैको वर्ग इत्येवं पञ्च वर्गा: ; अ (६०), ए (६०), च (६०), त (६०), य (६०) मान:। तेषु प्रथमवर्गस्य आदावन्ते च जपे सति, षष्टिर्वर्णा अहोरात्रघटिका रूपा भवन्तीति तन्त्रे स्पष्टम्। नित्यश्वासानन्तरं षष्टि: श्वासा: तद्देवतात्मान: (६०); ततो द्वादश मेषादिराशिरूपा:। प्रष्टशब्दोऽग्रेसरवाची सन् प्रभृतिपर:, "प्रष्टोऽग्रगामिनि" इति निपातनात्। (१२) तदुत्तरं नव श्वासा: (९) अर्कादिनवग्रहरूपा: ; तत्स्वरूपो गुरुरित्यर्थ: ॥४॥

पञ्चात्मा भूतनिकायो गतमायो य:
पञ्चाशद्वर्ण (५०) वपुश्चक्रगताभि: ।
शक्त्यालीभि: सङ्गतिमानेकनवत्या
तं सन्मार्गं मत्तमयूरं गुरुमीडे ॥ ५ ॥

पश्चात्मेति। ग्रहात्मकश्वासानन्तरं पञ्च श्वासाः आकाशादिपञ्चभूतरूपाः (५)। तदुत्तरं पञ्चशच्छ्वासाः मातृकारूपाः (५०) तासामेकपञ्चाशतो (५१) मध्येऽपि सर्गस्वरत्यागात्तच्छेषेणाह—**गतमाय इति।** मायाशब्दोऽपि सर्गस्वरवाचकः, तद्रहित इत्यर्थः। तदनन्तरमेकनवतिश्वासाः चक्रश्चिदावरणशक्तिसमूहपराः। तासामेकनवतित्वं (९१) मूल एव नवमश्लोके विशदीकरिष्यते। ततश्च पूर्वोक्तदिननित्याविद्या (२०७३६) पूर्णमण्डला (५७६) नवनाथ (९) तत्त्व (३६) नित्या (१६) घटिका (६०) राशि (१२) नवग्रह-(९) भूत (५) मातृका (५०) वर्णशक्ति (९१) संख्यानामेकीकरणे श्वाससंख्या-पूर्तिः (२१६००) संपद्यते। तदुक्तं तन्त्रराजे—

"नित्यातत्त्वाप्तिविद्यानां संख्याः स्युः पूर्वमेकशः।
ततो दिनार्णाः संध्याश्च ततश्च घटिकार्णकाः॥
राशयो द्वादश ततो ग्रहभूतानि पञ्च वै।
मातृकाश्चापि पञ्चाशच्छ्रीचक्रस्थाश्च शक्तयः॥
सैका नवतयः प्रोक्ता देवी सर्वात्मना स्थिता।"

इति। नित्याः षोडश (१६) स्वराः, तत्त्वाक्षराणि (३६) पूर्वोक्तानि, तेषामाप्तिः परस्परसंयोगविशेषरूपः प्रस्तरः तत्संवर्धितानां दिननित्याविद्यानामित्यर्थः। शिष्टं स्पष्टम्॥ ५॥

एतावता प्रबन्धेन श्वासानामवयवशो विभागेन वासना उपदिश्येदानीं संपूर्णस्यैव श्वाससमूहस्यैकैका वासना उपदिशति--

यद्वा पञ्चाशल्लिपिपीडैकरदाना—
मावृत्त्यासीद्यः फलवान् देशिकवर्यः।
ज्ञानोत्तुङ्गो(३६००)ऽरलकसहषट्कवृते-
स्तं सन्मार्गे मत्तमयूरं गुरुमीडे॥ ६॥

यद्वेति। उक्तानां वक्ष्यमाणानां च वासनानामन्यतमानुसंधाने विकल्पद्योतनार्थो वाकारः। इमाश्च वासना मूलेऽनुक्ता अपि पूज्यपादमुखादवगन्तव्या इति तु मनोरमाकारः।

"**अथ षोडश नित्यानां कालेन प्राणतोच्यते।**
मातृकाभूतनाथाद्यैः श्रीचक्रेण च शक्तिभिः॥"

इति पटलारम्भप्रतिज्ञाश्लोके सूचिता इति तु निधिकारः। कालेन प्राणतः श्वासात्मककालभेदः। अत्राद्यपदेन ग्रहतत्त्वनित्याघटिकाराशयो गृह्यन्ते। श्रीचक्रशब्देन तदन्तर्गतत्रैलोक्यमोहनादिनवचक्राणि। शक्तिशब्देन श्रीचक्रस्थाः षण्णवतीः शक्तय उच्यन्ते। वस्तुतस्तु—मातृकापदेन गणेशग्रहनक्षत्रयोगिनीराशिपीठानां लघुषोढान्यासदेवतारूपाणां ग्रहाणां, तैः सह मातृकाभेदस्तु तन्त्रराज एव 'गणेशग्रहनक्षत्र-' इत्यादिद्वादशश्लोकीस्तवने कथनात्। गुरुदेव्याः तैः सहाभेदस्तु योगिनीहृदये कौलिकार्यप्रकरणे वर्णनात्; नित्याहृदये, "संप्रदायोक्तं स्फुटोपायेन भावयेत्" इति वचनेन योगिनीहृदयोक्तभावनासापेक्षतया स्वतन्त्रे स्वीकारात्। तस्मादाद्यपदेननित्यातत्त्वादेरेव ग्रहणम्; लिपयः, अकाराद्या वर्णाः; पीठाः, कामरूपादयः; एकरदाः, विघ्नेश्वरादयो गणेशाः; एते त्रयोऽपि गतप्रायाः सन्तः पञ्चाशदेव श्वाससंख्या, पिण्डस्य (२१६००) पञ्चाशता विभागे द्वात्रिंशदुत्तरचतुःशती (४३२) लब्धा। तेन तावद्वारमावृत्ता लिप्यादयो देवश्वासा इति वासनात्रयमावृत्तिश्च दण्डकलितन्यायेन स्वस्वस्थानविवृद्ध्या वेति तु गुरुमुखादेव निर्णेयम्। फलवानिति पदेन लब्धसंख्योक्तिः (४३२)। डाकिन्यादियोगिनीषट्कात्मकतया श्वासवासनामाह—ज्ञानेति। ज्ञकारनकारौ शून्यपरौ, तकारगकारौ षट्त्र्यङ्कपरे। तेन त्रिसहस्राणि षट्शतानीति ज्ञानोत्तुङ्ग (३६००) पदेन सूचितानीत्यर्थः। षड्भिः श्वाससंख्याविभागे तावत एव लाभात् 'डरलकसह' इत्यनेन नामैकदेशेन नामग्रहणमिति न्यायेन डाकिन्यादय उच्यन्ते। याकिन्या सह सप्तसंख्या तु नाशङ्कनीया। "शाक्तैः षड्भिर्यथाक्षरैः" इत्यादिना योगिनीहृदये षण्णामेव ग्रहणम्। "याकिन्याः षट्समष्टिरूपत्वेन व्यष्टितो भेदाभावात् सप्तानां ग्रहणम्" इत्यमृतानन्दव्याख्या तु सेतुबन्ध एवास्माभिर्निरस्ता।

यत्तु योगिनीपदस्य वशिन्याद्यष्टकपरत्वेन काश्मीराणां व्याख्यानम्; तत्पक्षोऽपि न दोषः। अष्टभिः श्वासानां विभागोऽपि सप्तदशोत्तरसहस्रद्वयस्य लाभेन श्वाससंख्याया निःशेषत्वसंभवात्। अत्रावृत्तेः पञ्चमाष्टमाक्षरयोः गुरुत्वस्यावश्यकत्वेऽपि तयोः स्थाने द्विद्विलघुनिवेशौ, "लौ सः" इति सूत्रेण लघुद्वयस्य गुरुकार्यकारित्वविधानबलात्स्वीकृतः। तत्सूत्रस्य मात्राच्छन्दोविषयकत्वेऽपि वर्णच्छन्दसोऽपि कतिपयवृत्तेषु तदङ्गीकारो ज्ञापकसिद्ध इति तु छन्दोभास्करादौ प्रपञ्चितमस्माभिः। प्रयोगेऽपि; "वन्दे रामं मरकतवर्णं मुनिवन्द्यम्" इत्यादिः ॥ ६ ॥

नेत्रोद्गाढो(४३२०)देशिकराड्भूत(५)समूहै-

रेनो वारी यो नवनाथग्रहचक्रैः।

नक्षत्रस्यावृत्तिभिरानन्दशरीर-

स्तं सन्मार्गं मत्तमयूरं गुरुमीडे ॥ ७ ॥

नेत्रेनि। नेत्रांशे उद्गाढो दृढ इत्यनेन दूरदर्शित्वादिकं गुरोरुक्तम्। पञ्चभूतसंख्यायाः श्वासविभागे सति चत्वारि सहस्राणि त्रीणि शतानि विंशतिश्च (४३२०) लभ्यन्त इति तावद्वारं मारुताः श्वासाः गुरुरूपा एवेत्यर्थः। नेत्रोद्गाढपदेन तत्संख्या दर्शिता। नाथादिनवकरूपवासनात्रयमाह—एनो वारीति। पापहा महागुरुः चतुःशताधिकसहस्र-द्वयव्यावृत्त्या नाथादिद्वय इत्यर्थः। द्वयं वारा वृत्यादि (२४००) नाथादिरूप इत्यर्थः। नवनाथा नवग्रहाः नवचक्राणि चेति वासनात्रयम्। अष्टशतावृत्त्यागुरुर्नक्षत्ररूपो-ऽभूदि त्याह—नक्षत्रस्येति। जातावेकवचनम्। आनन्द (८००) शब्देनोक्तसंख्या प्रदर्शिता ॥ ७ ॥

नित्यावृत्तावीशलयः सन्नचलोऽभू-

न्नाड्यावृत्तौ राशिषु नानाजपरूपः।

अभ्यस्यद्भिस्तत्त्वगणैरुन्नतमूर्ति-

स्तं सन्मार्गं मत्तमयूरं गुरुमीडे ॥ ८ ॥

नित्येति। षोडशनित्याभिः (१६) श्वासानां (२१६००) विभागे सहस्रोत्तरसार्ध-त्रिशती (१३५०) लब्धा। ईशे, परमशिवे, लयो यस्य स गुरुः; तत्संख्याकनित्या-वृत्तिरूपः। "दशध्यानसमो लयः" इति लक्षितसमाधिविशेषो लय इत्युच्यते। षष्टिनाडीदेवतासंख्यया विभागे तु अचलो भवेत्, षष्ट्युत्तरशतत्रयसंख्यो (३६०) जातः। राशिषु; राशिव्यावर्तमानेषु, नानाजपात्मा; अष्टशत्यधिकसहस्र (१८००) जपरूपः। षट्त्रिंशत्तत्वगणाभ्यासेन उन्नतस्वरूपः (६००) षट्शतसंख्य इत्यर्थः ॥ ८ ॥

धृत्युर्वीशाष्टेन्द्रदिगाशाहियुगत्रि-

प्रोक्ताभिः पुंहेतिभिरम्बाभिरभिन्नः।

आवृत्त्यैवं षण्णवतेर्यः शिखरात्मा

तं सन्मार्गं मत्तमयूरं गुरुमीडे ॥ ९ ॥

धृतीति। धृतयोऽष्टादश (१८) देवताः, भूपुरस्थाः अणिमादयो दश (१०); ब्राह्मयाद्या अष्टौ (८) कादिमते तृतीयरेखाया अकथनेन तत्रत्यमुद्रादेवतादशकस्या-

भावात् । उर्वीशा: षोडश (१६) कामाकर्षिण्याद्या: षोडशदलपद्मस्था:, अष्टौ (८) अनङ्ग: कुसुमादयोऽष्टदलपद्मस्था: । इन्द्रा: चतुर्दश (१४) सर्वसंक्षोभिण्यादयो मन्वश्रगता: । दिशो दश (१०) बहिर्दशारगा: सर्वसिद्धिप्रदादय: । आशा अपि दश (१०) अन्तर्दशारगा- सर्वज्ञाद्या: । अहयोऽष्टौ (८) वशिन्याद्या अष्टकोणस्था: । अम्बायुधदेवताश्चतस्र: (४) ; त्रिकोणगतकामेश्वर्यादिदेवतास्तिस्र: (३) एता: संहत्यैकनवति (९१) संख्याकत्वेन पञ्चमश्लोके प्रोक्ता: तावतीनामेव ग्रहणे श्वाससंख्याया एकनवत्या विभागे नि:शेषताया असंभवात् विभाजकाङ्के पञ्चानां मेलनेन षण्णवतित्वमापादयितुमाह—पुंहेतिभिरिति । कामेश्वर्यायुधदेवताभि: चतसृभिरित्यर्थ: । इमा: पञ्चनवतिभि: (९५) अम्बाभिरभिन्नस्था: प्रधानांशेष्वित्येकशेषाभिप्रायेण अम्बाभिरित्युक्तम् । एवंप्रकारेण षण्णवतेर्देवतानामावृत्त्या शिखरात्मा सर्वोत्तमस्वरूपो गुरु: सपादशतद्वयावृत्तिमानासीदित्यर्थ: ।

ननु च "चक्रेण शक्तिभि:" इत्यत्र शक्तिसामान्यवाचकस्यापि पदस्यैकानवतय: प्रोक्ता: । "श्रीचक्रस्थास्तु शक्तय:" इत्यनेनोपसंहारादेकनवतिदेवता: सिद्ध्यन्तीति न पुंहेत्यादि ग्रहणे मानं पश्याम: । न च तया संख्यया श्वाससंख्याविभागे निरवशेषता- संभवादेव पञ्चानामङ्कानां योग इति वाच्यम् । कस्यापि कतिपयान्यूनतादिकल्पनेनापि संभवात् । धृत्यादिनवसंख्याभि: प्रत्येकं १८, १६, ८, १४, १०, १०, ८, ४, ३ विभजनेऽपि तत्संभवाद्वा इन्द्रसंख्यया विभागे द्वादशनामान्येतेषां राशिवासनाकल्पना- संभवात् ।

न चैवं वासनासांकर्ये यथावस्थितैकनवतिविभागशेषस्यापि वासनान्तरकल्पनयै- वोपपत्तौ प्रतिचित्रदेवतासंख्यानां प्रातिस्विकं विभजकत्वकल्पना न स्यादिति वाच्यम् । एकनवत्या विभागे त्रयस्त्रिंशतावशेषेण तस्योक्तमातृकादिभिन्नत्वेन स्वेच्छया देवतान्तर- कल्पनायामव्यवस्थापत्तिरिति चेत्, मैवम् । इह संप्रदायस्यैव शरणत्वात् । अत एव मनोरमायां शक्तिभिरिति पदमेकनवतिषण्णवतिपरत्वेन द्वेधा व्याख्यायैकत्र वचनमन्यत्र गुरुमुखागम एवोत्तरग्रन्थे प्रमाणमुपन्यस्तम् । इदं तु सुवचम्—श्रीचक्रेणेति चकारात् नवचक्रसंख्यामेकनवतौ संमेल्योभयसमुच्चयरूपयांशसंख्यया निरवशेषेण विभागो विधी- यत इति ।

न चैकनवत्या विभाजकत्वायोगात् तदाधारचक्रनवकमेलनस्य न्यायसिद्धत्वेन मन्वश्रेऽपि तदाधारचक्रमात्रस्य मेलनेन तावन्मात्रांशे पञ्चदशसंख्याया विभाजकत्व- कल्पने निरवशेषतासंभवात् धृत्यादिभि: पार्थक्येन विभाग: सिद्ध इति वाच्यम् ।

महात्रिपुरसुन्दर्या एकनवत्यनन्तर्गतत्वात् तदाधारचक्रस्य तत्र मेलने उपपत्त्यभावेन नवचक्रसंख्यामेलनस्य वाचनिकत्वाङ्गीकारेणैव निर्वाहादिति दिक् ॥ ९ ॥

महेशनाथकृतस्य नाथनवरत्नमालिकानाम्नः स्तवस्योपसंहारपूर्वकं पाठपराणां गुरुभक्तानां श्रीविद्योपासकानां सद्यः परशिवभावप्राप्तिः फलतीत्याह—

इत्यग्रभाद्भास्कररायो नवरत्नै-
र्मालाममग्र्यां नाथरहस्यं गमयन्तीम् ।
येषामेषा कण्ठगता ते जगदम्बा
विद्याभ्यासादत्र जनुष्येव महेशः ॥ १० ॥

इति श्रीमहेशनाथकृता नाथनवरत्नमाला समाप्ता ।

इतीति । मालास्तोत्रयो रूपकानुगुण्याय प्रबन्धरचनमालारचनोभयवाचिग्रथिधातुः प्रयुक्तः । नाथरहस्यं परं रूपम् । अत्र जनुष्येव ; अस्मिन्नेव जन्मनि, महेशः ; परमशिवरूपः । उक्तं च तन्त्रराजे ; "एवंविधां भावनां यो भावयेत्स महेश्वरः" इति सर्वं शिवम् ॥ १० ॥

इति श्रीमन्नाथनवरत्नमालाभिधास्तुतेः ।
मञ्जूषा भासुरानन्दनाथेनाकारि गुप्तये ॥

इति श्रीमत्पदवाक्यप्रमाणपारावारपारीणधुरीणनिखिलतन्त्रस्वतन्त्रश्रीमद्गम्भीरराजभारतीदीक्षितसूनुना भासुरानन्दनाथदीक्षाभिधानेन भास्कररायेण विरचिता श्रीनाथनवरत्नमालाव्याख्या मञ्जूषा समाप्ता ।

APPENDIX 1

Index of Half Verses

श्रीकामकलाविलासश्लोकार्धानुक्रमणिका

APPENDIX 2

Index of Works Quoted

चिद्वल्ल्यां स्मृता ग्रन्थाः

APPENDIX 3

Index of Authors Quoted

चिद्वल्ल्यां स्मृता ग्रन्थकर्तारः

APPENDIX 4

Index of Citations

चिद्वल्ल्यामुद्राहृतप्रमाणवाक्यानामनुक्रमः

र

Abbreviations used in the Appendix IV

अज० प्र० सि०	अजडप्रमातृसिद्धिः	कैवल्य०	कैवल्योपनिषत्
अथर्व०	अथर्वशिर:	कौषी०	कौषीतक्युपनिषत्
अभि०	अभियुक्ता:	गी० नि०	गीतानिष्यन्द:
अभि०गु०	अभिनवगुप्तपादा:	चतु०	चतु:शती
अमृत०	अमृतान्द:	चिद० र०	चिदम्बररहस्यम्
अरु० उ०	अरुणोपनिषत्	चिदा०	चिदानन्दवासना
आज्ञा०	आज्ञावतार:	चिद्वि०	चिद्विलास:
ईश०	ईशावास्यम्	चूलि०	चूलिको गनिषत्
उप०	उपनिषत्	छान्दो०	छान्दोग्यम्
ऋ० सं०	ऋक्संहिता	तैत्ति० ब्रा०	तैत्तिरीयब्राह्मणम्
ऐत०	ऐतरेयम्	तैत्ति० उ०	तैत्तिरीयोपनिषत्
ऐत० उ०	ऐतरेयोपनिषत्	त्रिपु० उ०	त्रिपुरोपनिषत्
कठ०	कठोपनिषत्	नि० हृ०	नित्याहृदयम्
कात्या० वा०	कात्यायनवार्तिकम्	निरु०	निरुक्तकार:
कुला०	कुलार्णवतन्त्रम्	नृ० ता०	नृसिंहतापिनी

पर० हं०	परमहंसोपनिषत्	लघु०	लघुभट्टारकः
परमा० गु०	परमानन्दगुरुः	ललि०	ललितोपाख्यानम्
परमा० यो०	परमानन्दयोगी	वाक्य०	वाक्यपदीयम्
परा० प०	परापञ्चाशिका	वाम०	वामकेश्वरतन्त्रम्
परा० प्रा०	पराप्रावेशिका	विज्ञा० भ०	विज्ञानभट्टारकः
परा० वा०	परावासना	शंकर०	शंकरानन्दः
पाणि० सू०	पाणिनिसूत्रम्	शक्ति०	शक्तिमहिम्नस्तवः
पू० सं०	पूजासंकेतः	शिव० सू०	शिवसूत्रम्
प्रत्यक्ष०	प्रत्यक्षोपनिषत	शिव० वृ०	शिवसूत्रवृत्तिः
प्रत्य० का०	प्रत्यभिज्ञाकरिका	शिवा०	शिवानन्दः
प्रत्य० हृ०	प्रत्यभिज्ञाहृदयम्	श्रीतन्त्र०	श्रीतन्त्रसद्भावः
प्रामा०	प्रामाणिकवचनम्	श्रीनाथ०	श्रीनाथानन्दः
बृह०	बृहदारण्यकम्	श्वेत०	श्वेताश्वतरम्
ब्रह्म०	ब्रह्मोपनिषत्	षड० म०	षडन्वयमहारत्नम्
भैर० या०	भैरवयामलम्	षड० शा०	षडन्वयशांभवम्
महा० ना०	महानारायणोपनिषत्	संके०	संकेतपद्धतिः
माण्डू०	माण्डूक्योपनिषत्	सच्चि०	सच्चिदानन्दवासना
मालि०	मालिनीविजयः	सु० उ०	सुबालोपनिषत्
मुण्ड०	मुण्डकोपनिषत्	सुभ०	सुभगोदयः
यजु०	यजुःश्रुतिः	सुभ० वा०	सुभगोदयवासना
योगि० हृ०	योगिनीहृदयम्	सौभ० सु०	सौभाग्यसुभगोदयम्
योगि० हृ० व्या०	योगिनीहृदयव्याख्या	सौभा० हृ०	सौभाग्यहृदयम्
रस० सा०	रससारसंग्रहः	स्पन्द०	स्पन्दकारिका
रह० आग०	रहस्यागमः	स्वच्छ०	स्वच्छन्दतन्त्रम्
रह० आम्ना०	रहस्याम्नायः	हंस०	हंसपारमेश्वरम्
रह० उ०	रहस्योपनिषत्	अम्बा०	अम्बास्तवः

APPENDIX 5

मञ्जूषासहिताया नाथनवरत्नमालिकाया वाक्यानुक्रमः

मञ्जूषायां स्मृता ग्रन्थाः

अमरकोशः, ८४
कादिमतम्, ८७
कुला० कुलार्णवतन्त्रम्, ८१
चन्द्रा० चन्द्रालोकम्, ८२
छन्दो० छन्दोभास्करम्, ८७
तन्त्र० तन्त्रराजम्, ८३, ८५, ८६, ८९
नित्या० नित्याहृदयम्, ८६
पाणि० पाणिनिसूत्रम्, ८४
पिङ्गल० पिङ्गलसूत्रम्, ८२
योगि० योगिनीहृदयम्, ८६
शारदा० शारदातिलकम्, ८१, ८२
शिव० शिवसूत्रम्, ८२

मञ्जूषायां स्मृता ग्रन्थकर्तारः

अमृतानन्दः, ८६
काश्मीराः, ८६
निधिकारः, ८६
पिङ्गलमुनिः, ८२
मनोरमाकारः, ८५

मञ्जूषायां प्रमाणत्वेनोद्धृतानां वाक्यानामनुक्रमः

अङ्कानां वामतो गतिः, ८३
अजपा नाम गायत्री, ८२, शारदा० १४
अथषोडशनित्यानां, ८६, तन्त्र० २७-१
अनया सदृशं पुण्यं, ८२, शारदा० १४
अनया सदृशी विद्या ,, ,, ,,
अभ्यस्यन्निस्तत्त्वगणैः, ८७
अर्काद्यात्मा यो नव०, ८४
आवृत्त्यैवं षडावर्तैः, ८८
इत्यप्रज्ञाज्ञास्कररायः, ८९
उच्छ्वासे चैव निःश्वासे, ८१
उद्यद्भास्वन्मण्डल०, ८३
एवं रीत्या वासित०, ८३
एवंविधां भावनां यः, ८९, तन्त्र० २७-३२
क-ट-प-य-वर्गभवैः, ८२
गणेशग्रहनक्षत्र०, ८६, तन्त्र० २-८८
गुरुमूलाः क्रियाः सर्वाः, ८१, कुला० १२-१४
गुरुरुपायः, ८२, शिव० २-६
चक्रेण च शक्तिभिः, ८८, तन्त्र० २७-१
ज्ञानोत्तुङ्गे उरकल०, ८६
ततो दिनानां संख्याश्च, ८५, तन्त्र० २७-३०
तत्पश्चात्यप्राणसमूहैः, ८३
तद्रूपः सन्नाविरभूत्, ८१
तस्माच्छ्वासैव निःश्वासैः, ८२, शारदा० १४
तस्या विज्ञानमात्रेण, ८२ ,, १४
तीर्थमृषिजुष्टजले गुरौ, ८३, अमर० ३-३-८६
दशध्यानसमो लयः, ८७
धृत्युर्वीशाष्टेन्द्रं, ८८
नक्षत्रस्यावृत्तिभिः, ८७
नञ् शून्यं विज्ञेयं, ८२
नितम्बगुर्वी तरुणी, ८२, चन्द्रा० १३९
नित्यातत्त्वाप्तिविधानां, ८५, तन्त्र० २७-३०
नित्यावृत्तावीशलयः, ८७
नेत्रोद्गलो देशिकषड्, ८७
प्रज्ञात्मा भूतनिकायैः, ८५
पराप्रासादमन्त्रः, ८१, शारदा०
प्रष्ठोऽग्रगामिनि, ८५, पाणि० ८-३-९२
मत्तमयूरं मृतौ, ८२, पिङ्गल०
मातृकाभूतनाथाद्यैः, ८६, तन्त्र० २७-१
मातृकाश्चापि पञ्चाशत्, ८५, तन्त्र० २७-३१
मोहान्धो यो न जानाति, ८२, शारदा० १४
यद्वा पञ्चाशल्लिपि० ८५

Addenda and Corregenda

PAGE	LINE	
४	५	संकल्पात्मा
,,	२३	तथा बृहदारण्यके
६	५	एष देव:
,,	१७	"पुरुषो वेद", "आचार्यस्तु . . . . तारयति"
१०	१५	तत्त्वातीतं
११	२०	य ईशे
१२	३	समालिख्य
१३	१६	भोगयोनि:
१६	१२	देशकालाविशोषिणी
१७	१४	वेदैरनेके०
,,	२०	गीतानिष्यन्दे
२०	६	समस्तबीजगर्भाढ्य:
२४	१५	तत्त्वातीतं
२६	४	इहापि, "विद्या०
,,	११	"तदा प्रकाश०
,,	१४	यस्यैषा
३४	२१	तान्येवानुविनश्यति
३८	११	"नेदृशो
,,	१३	आदिरादिर्ब्रह्मा
,,	२४	शिवोऽयमिति
४०	४	गुहा त्रीणि
४१	१५	कुत: ?
४३	८	तत्रैव
४७	४	अनुत्तरानन्देच्छितेरिच्छासंघ-ट्टत्रिकोणगम्
५०	४	बिन्दुर्नादत्व०
५५	२३	वीरवन्दिते
५६	,,	विमर्शाख्याश्चिदा०
५९	१४	बिन्दौ
६१	१६	श्वेता वरा०
६२	१८	देहाक्षादि०
६३	१०	शिवान०
६४	३	कृतिमयी:
,,	७	सृष्टे:
६५	१९	दशारचक्र०
६९	२	स्यु: . . . . संस्थिता:
७४	६	सिद्धौ०
७७	९	अलिना
,,	१७	पञ्चशास्त्राणि
,,	१८	मूर्त्यन्तरं
८८	११	चक्रेण च
९४	३	मुदाहृत०
९८	१८	मुपास्यमि०

By the same Author

THE GREAT LIBERATION

(MAHANIRVANATANTRA)

Sanskrit Text, English Translation and Commentary

CONTENTS

"It seems as if the World-Mother has again willed it and has again desired to manifest Her Power so that Arthur Avalon is studying the Tantras and has published so beautiful a version of the Mahānirvaṇa"—*Sahitya.*

3rd Edition (1953) Cloth Bound—Over 1,000 Pages. Price Rs. 30/-